DATE DUE

OXFORD READINGS IN PHILOSOPHY

CONDITIONALS

Also published in this series

Other volumes are in preparation

CONDITIONALS

edited by

FRANK JACKSON

OXFORD UNIVERSITY PRESS
1991

reet, Oxford OX2 6DP
'oronto
dras Karachi
g Kong Tokyo
Cape Town
and
and associated companies in
Berlin Ibadan

Oxford is a trade mark of Oxford University Press

Published in the United States
by Oxford University Press, New York

Introduction and selection © *Oxford University Press, 1991*

British Library Cataloguing in Publication Data
Data available

Library of Congress Cataloging in Publication Data
Conditionals/edited by Frank Jackson.
p.   cm.—(Oxford readings in philosophy)
Includes bibliographical references and index.
1. Conditionals (Logic)   2. Languages—Philosophy.   3. Language
and logic.   I. Jackson, Frank, 1943–   II. Series.
BC199.C56C65 1991   160—dc20   90–26225
ISBN 0–19–875096–X
ISBN 0–19–875095–1 *(Pbk.)*

Set by Litho Link Limited, Welshpool
Printed in Great Britain
by Biddles Ltd, Guildford & King's Lynn

CONTENTS

INTRODUCTION

FRANK JACKSON

HERE are some conditionals. 'If Bush continues to perform well, he will win a second term'; 'if today is Tuesday, then I am in Frankfurt'; 'if I forgot to put water in the radiator, then that noise means trouble': 'if the stock-market crash had not occurred, inflation would have become rampant'. Despite the ease with which we understand them, the frequency with which we assert or deny them, and the importance we attach to them, there is no theory of conditionals which has won general acceptance. Instead, there are a number of competing theories. This collection aims to introduce the reader to some of the most interesting current theorizing about conditionals. The Selected Bibliography at the end of the volume contains suggestions for further reading, both on the topics covered in the collection and on related topics.

What is a theory of conditionals? Some seek to answer this question by offering an account of the truth conditions of a conditional: an account of the conditions under which 'if A then B' is true, and of the conditions under which it is false. Others seek to answer this question by offering an account of the acceptance or justified assertability conditions of a conditional: an account of the conditions under which 'if A then B' is acceptable, or acceptable to a certain degree. The two approaches are often seen as opposed, but it is not compulsory to view the situation in this way. Indeed, the ideal would be plausible accounts of the truth conditions and of the acceptance conditions of conditionals, combined with a story which explains each in terms of the other. This ideal, in one form or another, is attempted by Robert Stalnaker (Essay VII in this collection), David Lewis (Essay IV), and Frank Jackson (Essay VI), whereas Dorothy Edgington (Essay IX) argues that considerations deriving from the acceptance conditions of conditionals show that conditionals do not have truth conditions.

The oldest and simplest account of a conditional's truth conditions is: 'if A then B' is true if and only if A is false or B is true, or, equivalently, if and only if it is not the case that A is true and B is false. The term 'material conditional' is sometimes used for a statement which *by definition* has these truth conditions, and the material conditional with antecedent A and consequent B is often written 'A ⊃ B'. So this account is often characterized as holding that 'if A then B' is a material conditional equivalent to 'A ⊃ B'. It is also often referred to as the truth-functional account, as it makes the truth value of 'if A then B' a function of the truth values of A and B. One way to motivate the material account is to observe that instead of saying 'if it rains, then the match will be cancelled', one could have said, to much the same effect, 'either it will not rain, or it will and the match will be cancelled'; and the latter is true if and only if either 'it will rain' is false or 'the match will be cancelled' is true; that is if and only if 'A ⊃ B' is true. Other arguments for the material or truth-functional account are outlined early on in Edgington (Essay IX), but as a preliminary to rejecting it and arguing for her no-truth-conditions view.

The oldest and simplest objection to the material account is that it makes it too easy for a conditional to be true, for it makes the falsity of a conditional's antecedent logically sufficient for the conditional to be true, and also makes the truth of its consequent logically sufficient for the conditional to be true. Consider the conditional 'if Jones lives in London, then he lives in Scotland.' It is plausible that we can say straight off that this conditional is false without waiting to find out whether or not Jones lives in London, or whether or not he lives in Scotland. But, on the proffered truth conditions, it seems that we should wait: for should it turn out that he does not live in London, then the conditional will be true rather than false, and should it turn out that he lives in Scotland, then the conditional will be true rather than false.

The only reply to this objection that is at all plausible is to argue that all we can say straight off about 'if Jones lives in London, then he lives in Scotland' is that it is highly unassertable, and that this is compatible with the conditional turning out to be true by virtue of having a false antecedent or by virtue of having a true consequent. The immediately evident property of the conditional is high unassertability, not falsity. To make this reply more than a whistling-in-the-wind, it needs to be set in a theory of assertability, a theory of the pragmatics of conversational and written exchanges. Some ingredients for such a theory are laid out by H. P. Grice (Essay VIII) in his account of conversational and conventional implicature. See also the essays by Lewis (Essay IV) and Jackson (Essay VI) where these ideas and associated ones, in one form or another, are deployed in defence of the material theory of the conditional. There are also remarks on assertability in Stalnaker (Essay VII), though there the intent is not to bolster the material account but instead to undermine the material account by explaining away the intuitive appeal of a certain argument for it.

The truth-functional or material account has certain consequences regarding which inference patterns involving conditionals are valid (in the classical sense of being necessarily truth-preserving). Notoriously, it makes the inferences 'not-A, therefore, if A then B', and 'B, therefore, if A and then B' valid. These two results are often used to nail home the objection that the material account makes it too easy for a conditional to be true, see Edgington (Essay IX). However, the material account also makes valid more initially attractive patterns, such as: 'if A then B, therefore, if not-B then not-A' (Contraposition); 'if A then B, if B then C, therefore, if A then C' (Hypothetical Syllogism); and 'if A then B, therefore, if A and C, then B' (Strengthening the Antecedent). And there are putative counter-examples to these patterns. An instance for the case of Contraposition is: 'if he has made a mistake, then it is not a big mistake, therefore, if he has made a big mistake, he has not make a mistake.' A defender of the material account must reply that although this inference is, contrary to one's immediate intuitive response, necessarily truth-preserving, it dramatically fails to preserve assertability, and it is this fact which gives intuitive appeal to the claim that the inference takes us from truth to falsity. Clearly, as was the case for the reply to the earlier objection to the material theory, this reply must be set within a theory of assertability for conditionals. This is attempted in Jackson (Essay VI).

The major alternative to the account which holds that a conditional's truth conditions are those of the material conditional is due to Lewis and Stalnaker. It is framed in terms of possible worlds. A possible world is a way things might be, one of which is the way things actually are, the actual world. The leading idea behind the possible-worlds approach to giving the truth conditions of a conditional turns on the plausibility of a certain model of the thought processes we go through when we contemplate a conditional. Take, for instance, what happens when I consider what to do. I typically consider a range of possibilities corresponding to the various actions available to me: serving to the forehand, serving to the backhand, serving into the body, and so on. And I frame my deliberations in conditional terms. That is to say, I ask myself what will be likely to happen *if* I serve to the forehand, *if* I serve to the backhand, and so on. Putting these two points together, we get the idea that when I ask myself what will happen if I serve to the forehand, what I am doing is asking myself how things are in the possible situation where I serve to the forehand. Extending this idea to conditionals in general, we get the view that a conditional is about how things are in certain possible situations where the antecedent is true. One way (but far from the only way) of fleshing out this idea is to give roughly the following account of a conditional's truth conditions: 'if A then B' is true at the actual world if and only if, of the possible-worlds where A is true, those closest or most similar to the actual world are possible worlds where B is true. This account avoids the consequences of the material account that any conditional with a false antecedent is true, and that any conditional with a true consequent is true. Neither the falsity of a conditional's antecedent (that is, its falsity at the actual world), nor the truth of a conditional's consequent (that is, its truth at the actual world), is, in and of itself, enough to ensure that the closest possible worlds where the antecedent is true are ones where the consequent is true. Perhaps the easiest way to see this is to note that another way of putting our rough illustration of the possible-worlds accounts is: 'if A then B' is true at the actual world if and only if, of the possible worlds where A is true, those closest to the actual world are possible worlds where 'A $\supset$ B' is true. This is because A and 'A $\supset$ B' are true together if and only if A and B are true together.

Hence, the truth of 'A ⊃ B' at the actual world is not enough for the truth of 'if A then B' on the possible-worlds account. Stalnaker (Essay II) and Lewis (Essay III) defend and discuss their versions of the possible-worlds account. (How can Lewis in Essay III defend the possible-worlds account while defending the material account in Essay IV? By distinguishing the kinds of conditionals to which the distinct accounts are directed, see below.)

A notable feature of the possible-worlds account is that it can handle the putative counter-examples to Contraposition, Strengthening the Antecedent, and Hypothetical Syllogism in the most natural way, namely by allowing them to be genuine ones. On the possible-worlds approach, it is perfectly possible for 'if A then B' to be true when 'if not-B then not-A' is false, for 'if A then B and if B then C' to be true when 'if A then C' is false, and for 'if A then B' to be true when 'if A and C, then B' is false. See Stalnaker (Essay II).

An obvious question to ask about the possible-worlds approach is what makes certain possible worlds where the antecedent is true the *closest* ones to the actual world, and more generally how the theory understands the similarity relation among possible worlds that features in it. This question is treated in both Stalnaker (Essay II) and, in detail, in Lewis (Essay III).

Between the venerable material account and the recent possible-worlds account comes a theory commonly called the metalinguistic theory. A typical version runs roughly and schematically as follows: 'if A then B' is true and only if there is a statement X, meeting condition ϕ, such that 'A and X' logically entails B. The major issue for this approach is how to specify ϕ. This approach is represented in our collection by Nelson Goodman (Essay I). With the benefit of hindsight, we can see the metalinguistic approach as a natural precursor of the possible-worlds approach. 'A and X' entails B if and only if every possible world where 'A and X' is true is one where B is true. This in turn is true if and only if, for every world where A is true, any world where X is true is a world where B is true. So the problem of specifying the condition ϕ that X must meet parallels the problem in the possible-worlds of approach of deciding which worlds where

A is true should be counted as closest, that is, as the worlds that need to be worlds where B is true in order for 'if A then B' to be true.

The most widely discussed account of a conditional's acceptance or (justified-assertion) conditions identifies the acceptability of 'if A then B' with the conditional probability of B given A. For instance, how reasonable it is to assert that if Bush does well in his first term, then he will be re-elected is given by how probable it is that Bush will be re-elected given he does well in his first term. An attractive feature of this account is that it explains why we count someone who asserts that if A then B as disagreeing with someone who asserts that if A then not B. For, as the conditional probability of B given A is one minus the conditional probability of not B given A, the account implies that 'if A then B' is highly assertable if and only if 'if A then not-B' is lowly assertable. The account is detailed and defended by Dorothy Edgington (Essay IX) drawing on work by Ernest Adams (see, for example, *The Logic of Conditionals* in Selected Bibliography). She defends it as a preliminary to arguing for her view that denies truth conditions to conditionals. The alternative strategy of seeking to explain this account of a conditional's acceptance or assertion conditions in terms of an account of its truth conditions (in fact, in terms of the material or truth-functional account of its truth conditions) is pursued in Lewis (Essay IV) and Jackson (Essay VI). A major theme in these three essays is the argument given by Lewis (Essays IV and V) to the conclusion that the simplest explanation of this account of a conditional's acceptance conditions cannot be right. The simplest explanation would, of course, be that the truth conditions of 'if A then B' are such as to ensure that the probability of 'if A then B' is one and the same as the probability of B given A.

Thus far we have spoken simply of conditionals. They come, however, in many shapes and sizes, and many writers have urged that, in particular, there is an important distinction between indicative conditionals and subjunctive conditionals. A typical subjunctive conditional (also often called a counterfactual conditional) is 'if Oswald had not killed Kennedy, then someone else would have.' A typical indicative conditional is 'if Oswald did not kill Kennedy, then someone else did.' As this pair (due to Adams, see 'Subjunctive and Indicative Conditionals' in Selected Bibliography) famously illustrates, the switch in mood can make a great difference to our intuitive responses. Many doubt that if Oswald had not killed Kennedy, then someone else would have; everyone agrees that if Oswald did not kill Kennedy, then someone else did. How should we respond to this and similar examples?

One response is to offer different truth conditions for indicative and subjunctive conditionals. Thus Lewis gives possible-world truth conditions for subjunctive conditionals (Essay III), and material truth conditions for indicative conditionals (Essay IV); see also Jackson (Essay VI). Indeed, the distinction between indicative and subjunctive conditionals is central to the defence of a material account of certain conditionals. It is hard to take seriously the material account applied to 'if it had rained, the match would have been cancelled.' Surely the mere fact that it did not rain is not sufficient to make that true. Accordingly, the material account has to be restricted to indicative conditionals, and another story—the possible-worlds one or whatever—has to be on hand for subjunctive conditionals. A different response to our example pair is to attempt to give essentially the same account, typically a possible-worlds one, of both types of conditionals, and to locate the intuitive difference in terms of pragmatics rather than semantics or truth conditions. This is Stalnaker's approach (Essay VII). A third response is to attack the whole idea that there is a viable distinction between indicative and subjunctive conditionals, and to urge that the needed distinctions are to be found elsewhere. This is the approach of V. H. Dudman (Essay X), who sets his discussion in the context of an argument for a radical rethinking of the conceptual apparatus philosophers and logicians have traditionally brought to bear on the topic of conditionals.

I

THE PROBLEM OF
COUNTERFACTUAL CONDITIONALS*

NELSON GOODMAN

1. THE PROBLEM IN GENERAL

THE analysis of counterfactual conditionals is no fussy little grammatical exercise. Indeed, if we lack the means for interpreting counterfactual conditionals, we can hardly claim to have any adequate philosophy of science. A satisfactory definition of scientific law, a satisfactory theory of confirmation or of disposition terms (and this includes not only predicates ending in 'ible' and 'able' but almost every objective predicate, such as 'is red'), would solve a large part of the problem of counterfactuals. Conversely, a solution to the problem of counterfactuals would give us the answer to critical questions about law, confirmation, and the meaning of potentiality.

I am not at all contending that the problem of counterfactuals is logically or psychologically the first of these related problems. It makes little difference where we start if we can go ahead. If the study of counterfactuals has up to now failed this pragmatic test, the alternative approaches are little better off.

What, then, is the *problem* about counterfactual conditionals? Let us confine ourselves to those in which antecedent and consequent are inalterably false—as, for example, when I say of a

Nelson Goodman, 'The Problem of Counterfactual Conditionals' from Chapter I, *Fact, Fiction, and Forecast* (Cambridge, Mass., 1984). First published in *The Journal of Philosophy*, 44 (1947): 113–28. Used with permission.

* My indebtedness in several matters to the work of C. I. Lewis has seemed too obvious to call for detailed mention.

piece of butter that was eaten yesterday, and that had never been heated,

> If that piece of butter had been heated to 150°F, it would have melted.

Considered as truth-functional compounds, all counterfactuals are of course true, since their antecedents are false. Hence

> If that piece of butter had been heated to 150°F, it would not have melted

would also hold. Obviously something different is intended, and the problem is to define the circumstances under which a given counterfactual holds while the opposing conditional with the contradictory consequent fails to hold. And this criterion of truth must be set up in the face of the fact that a counterfactual by its nature can never be subjected to any direct empirical test by realizing its antecedent.

In one sense the name 'problem of counterfactuals' is misleading, because the problem is independent of the form in which a given statement happens to be expressed. The problem of counterfactuals is equally a problem of factual conditionals, for any counterfactual can be transposed into a conditional with a true antecedent and consequent, for example

> Since that butter did not melt, it wasn't heated to 150° F.

The possibility of such transformation is of no great importance except to clarify the nature of our problem. That 'since' occurs in the contrapositive shows that what is in question is a certain kind of connection between the two component sentences; and the truth of statements of this kind—whether they have the form of counterfactual or factual conditionals or some other form—depends not upon the truth or falsity of the components but upon whether the intended connection obtains. Recognizing the possibility of transformation serves mainly to focus attention on the central problem and to discourage speculation as to the nature of counterfacts. Although I shall begin my study by considering counterfactuals as such, it must be borne in mind that a general solution would explain the kind of connection involved irrespective of any assumption as to the truth or falsity of the components.

The effect of transposition upon conditionals of another kind, which I call 'semifactuals', is worth noticing briefly. Should we assert

> Even if the match had been scratched, it still would not have lighted,

we would uncompromisingly reject as an equally good expression of our meaning the contrapositive,

> Even if the match lighted, it still wasn't scratched.

Our original intention was to affirm not that the non-lighting could be inferred from the scratching, but simply that the lighting could not be inferred from the scratching. Ordinarily a semifactual conditional has the force of denying what is affirmed by the opposite, fully counterfactual conditional. The sentence

> Even had that match been scratched, it still wouldn't have lighted

is normally meant as the direct negation of

> Had the match been scratched, it would have lighted.

That is to say, in practice full counterfactuals affirm, while semifactuals deny, that a certain connection obtains between antecedent and consequent.[1] Thus it is clear why a semifactual generally has not the same meaning as its contrapositive.

There are various special kinds of counterfactuals that present special problems. An example is the case of 'counteridenticals', illustrated by the statements

> If I were Julius Caesar, I wouldn't be alive in the twentieth century,

and

> If Julius Caesar were I, he would be alive in the twentieth century.

---

[1] The practical import of a semi-factual is thus different from its literal import. Literally a semifactual and the corresponding counterfactual are not contradictories but contraries, and both may be false (cf. n. 8, below). The presence of the auxiliary terms 'even' and 'still', or either of them, is perhaps the idiomatic indication that a not quite literal meaning is intended.

Here, although the antecedent in the two cases is a statement of the same identity, we attach two different consequents which, on the very assumption of that identity, are incompatible. Another special class of counterfactuals is that of the 'countercomparatives', with antecedents such as

If I had more money, . . .

The trouble with these is that when we try to translate the counterfactual into a statement about a relation between two tenseless, non-modal sentences, we get as an antecedent something like

If 'I have more money than I have' were true, . . . ,

which wrongly represents the original antecedent as self contradictory. Again there are the 'counterlegals', conditionals with antecedents that either deny general laws directly, as in

If triangles were squares, . . . ,

or else make a supposition of particular fact that is not merely false but impossible, as in

If this cube of sugar were also spherical, ...

Counterfactuals of all these kinds offer interesting but not insurmountable special difficulties.[2] In order to concentrate upon the major problems concerning counterfactuals in general, I shall usually choose my examples in such a way as to avoid these more special complications.

As I see it, there are two major problems, though they are not independent and may even be regarded as aspects of a single problem. A counterfactual is true if a certain connection obtains between the antecedent and the consequent. But as is obvious

---

[2] Of the special kinds of counterfactuals mentioned, I shall have something to say later about counteridenticals and counterlegals. As for countercomparatives, the following procedure is appropriate: Given 'If I had arrived one minute later, I would have missed the train', first expand this to '($\exists t$). t is a time. I arrived at t. If I had arrived one minute later than t, I would have missed the train.' The counterfactual conditional constituting the final clause of this conjunction can then be treated, within the quantified whole, in the usual way. Translation into 'If "I arrive one minute later than t" were true, then "I miss the train" would have been true' does not give us a self-contradictory component.

from examples already given, the consequent seldom follows from the antecedent by logic alone. (1) In the first place, the assertion that a connection holds is made on the presumption that certain circumstances not stated in the antecedent obtain. When we say

If that match had been scratched, it would have lighted,

we mean that conditions are such, i.e. the match is well made, is dry enough, oxygen enough is present, etc., that 'That match lights' can be inferred from 'That match is scratched'. Thus the connection we affirm may be regarded as joining the consequent with the conjunction of the antecedent and other statements that truly describe relevant conditions. Notice especially that our assertion of the counterfactuals is *not* conditioned upon these circumstances obtaining. We do not assert that the counterfactual is true *if* the circumstances obtain; rather, in asserting the counterfactual we commit ourselves to the actual truth of the statements describing the requisite relevant conditions. The first major problem is to define relevant conditions: to specify what sentences are meant to be taken in conjunction with an antecedent as a basis for inferring the consequent. (2) But even after the particular relevant conditions are specified, the connection obtaining will not ordinarily be a logical one. The principle that permits inference of

That match lights

from

That match is scratched. That match is dry enough. Enough oxygen is present. Etc.

is not a law of logic but what we call a natural or physical or causal law. The second major problem concerns the definition of such laws.

2. THE PROBLEM OF RELEVANT CONDITIONS

It might seem natural to propose that the consequent follows by law from the antecedent and a description of the actual state-of-affairs of the world, that we need hardly define relevant conditions because it will do no harm to include irrelevant ones. But if we say that the consequent follows by law from the antecedent and *all* true statements, we encounter an immediate difficulty: among true sentences is the negate of the antecedent, so that from the antecedent and all true sentences everything follows. Certainly this gives us no way of distinguishing true from false counterfactuals.

We are plainly no better off if we say that the consequent must follow from *some* set of true statements conjoined with the antecedent; for given any counterfactual antecedent A, there will always be a set S, namely the set consisting of *not-A*, such that from $A \cdot S$ any consequent follows. (Hereafter I shall regularly use the following symbols: 'A' for the antecedent, 'C' for the consequent; 'S' for the set of statements of the relevant conditions or, indifferently, for the conjunction of these statements.)

Perhaps then we must exclude statements logically incompatible with the antecedent. But this is insufficient; for a parallel difficulty arises with respect to true statements which are not logically but are otherwise incompatible with the antecedent. For example, take

If that radiator had frozen, it would have broken.

Among true sentences may well be (S)

That radiator never reached a temperature below 33°F,

Now we have as true generalizations both

All radiators that freeze but never reach below 33°F break,

and also

All radiators that freeze but never reach below 33°F fail to break;

for there are no such radiators. Thus from the antecedent of the counterfactual and the given S, we can infer any consequent.

The natural proposal to remedy this difficulty is to rule that counterfactuals cannot depend upon empty laws; that the connection can be established only by a principle of the form 'All x's are y's' when there are some x's. But this is ineffectual. For if empty principles are excluded, the following non-empty principles may be used in the case given with the same result:

Everything that is either a radiator that freezes but does not reach below 33°F, or that is a soap bubble, breaks

Everything that is either a radiator that freezes but does not reach below 33°F, or is powder, does not break.

By these principles we can infer any consequent from the A and S in question.

The only course left open to us seems to be to define relevant conditions as the set of all true statements each of which is both logically and non-logically compatible with A where non-logical incompatibility means violation of a non-logical law.[3] But another difficulty immediately appears. In a counterfactual beginning

If Jones were in Carolina, . . .

the antecedent is entirely compatible with

Jones is not in South Carolina

and with

Jones is not in North Carolina

and with

North Carolina plus South Carolina is identical with Carolina;

but all these taken together with the antecedent make a set that is self-incompatible, so that again any consequent would be forthcoming.

Clearly it will not help to require only that for *some* set S of true sentences, A·S be self-compatible and lead by law to the consequent; for this would make a true counterfactual of

If Jones were in Carolina, he would be in South Carolina,

and also of

If Jones were in Carolina, he would be in North Carolina,

which cannot both be true.

It seems that we must elaborate our criterion still further, to characterize a counterfactual as true if and only if there is some set

[3] This of course raises very serious questions, which I shall come to presently, about the nature of non-logical law.

S of true statements such that $A \cdot S$ is self-compatible and leads by law to the consequent, while there is no such set S' such that $A \cdot S'$ is self-compatible and leads by law to the negate of the consequent.[4] Unfortunately even this is not enough. For among true sentences will be the negate of the consequent: $-C$. Is $-C$ compatible with A or not? If not, then A alone without any additional conditions must lead by law to C. But if $-C$ is compatible with A (as in most cases), then if we take $-C$ as our S, the conjunction $A \cdot S$ will give us $-C$. Thus the criterion we have set up will seldom be satisfied; for since $-C$ will normally be compatible with A, as the need for introducing the relevant conditions testifies, there will normally be an S (namely $-C$) such that $A \cdot S$ is self-compatible and leads by law to $-C$.

Part of our trouble lies in taking too narrow a view of our problem. We have been trying to lay down conditions under which an A that is known to be false leads to a C that is known to be false; but it is equally important to make sure that our criterion does not establish a similar connection between our A and the (true) negate of C. Because our S together with A was to be so chosen as to give us C, it seemed gratuitous to specify that S must be compatible with C; and because $-C$ is true by supposition, S would necessarily be compatible with it. But we are testing whether our criterion not only admits the true counterfactual we are concerned with but also excludes the opposing conditional. Accordingly, our criterion must be modified by specifying that S be compatible with both C and $-C$.[5] In other words S by itself must not decide between C and $-C$, but S together with A must lead to C but not to $-C$. We need not know whether C is true or false.

Our rule thus reads that a counterfactual is true if and only if there is some set S of true sentences such that S is compatible with

[4] Note that the requirement that $A \cdot S$ be self-compatible can be fulfilled only if the antecedent is self-compatible; hence the conditions I have called 'counterlegals' will all be false. This is convenient for our present purpose of investigating counterfactuals that are not counterlegals. If it later appears desirable to regard all or some counterlegals as true, special provisions may be introduced.

[5] It is natural to enquire whether for similar reasons we should stipulate that S must be compatible with both A and $-A$, but this is unnecessary. For if S is incompatible with $-A$, then A follows from S; therefore if S is compatible with both C and $-C$, then $A \cdot S$ cannot lead by law to one but not the other. Hence no sentence incompatible with $-A$ can satisfy the other requirements for a suitable S.

C and with $-C$, and such that $A \cdot S$ is self-compatible and leads by law to C; while there is no set S' compatible with C and with $-C$ and such that $A \cdot S'$ is self-compatible and leads by law to $-C$.[6] As thus stated, the rule involves a certain redundancy; but simplification is not in point here, for the criterion is still inadequate.

The requirements that $A \cdot S$ be self-compatible is not strong enough; for S might comprise true sentences that although *compatible with A*, were such that *they would not be true if A were true*. For this reason, many statements that we would regard as definitely false would be true according to the stated criterion. As an example, consider the familiar case where for a given match m, we would affirm

(i) If match m had been scratched, it would have lighted,

but deny

(ii) If match m had been scratched, it would have been dry.[7]

According to our tentative criterion, statement (ii) would be quite as true as statement (i). For in the case of (ii), we may take as an element in our S the true sentence

Match m did not light,

which is presumably compatible with A (otherwise nothing would be required along with A to reach the opposite as the consequent of the true counterfactual statement (i)). As our total $A \cdot S$ we may have

Match m is scratched. It does not light. It is well made, Oxygen enough is present . . . etc.;

[6] Since this essay was first published, W. T. Parry has pointed out that no counterfactual satisfies this formula; for one can always take $-(A \cdot -C)$ as S, and take $-(A \cdot C)$ as S'. Thus we must add the requirement that neither S nor S' follows by law from $-A$. Of course this does not alleviate the further difficulties explained in the following paragraphs of the text above. (See Parry's 'Reexamination of the Problem of Counterfactual Conditionals', *Journal of Philosophy*, 54 (1957): 85–94, and my 'Parry on Counterfactuals', ibid. 442–5.)

[7] Of course, some sentences similar to (ii), referring to other matches under special conditions may be true; but the objection to the proposed criterion is that it would commit us to many such statements that are patently false. I am indebted to Morton G. White for a suggestion concerning the exposition of this point.

and from this, by means of a legitimate general law, we can infer

> It was not dry.

And there would seem to be no suitable set of sentences S' such that $A \cdot S'$ leads by law to the negate of this consequent. Hence the unwanted counterfactual is established in accord with our rule. The trouble is caused by including in our S a true statement which though compatible with A would not be true if A were. Accordingly we must exclude such statements from the set of relevant conditions; S, in addition to satisfying the other requirements already laid down, must be not merely compatible with A but 'jointly tenable' or *contenable* with A. A is contenable with S, and the conjunction $A \cdot S$ self-cotenable, if it is not the case that S would not be true if A were.[8]

Parenthetically it may be noted that the relative fixity of conditions is often unclear, so that the speaker or writer has to make explicit additional provisos or give subtle verbal clues as to his meaning. For example, each of the following two counterfactuals would normally be accepted:

> If New York City were in Georgia, then New York City would be in the South.

> If Georgia included New York City, then Georgia would not be entirely in the South.

Yet the antecedents are logically indistinguishable. What happens is that the direction of expression becomes important, because in the former case the meaning is

> If New York City were in Georgia and the boundaries of Georgia remained unchanged, then . . . ,

while in the latter case the meaning is

---

[8] The double negative cannot be eliminated here; for '. . . if S would be true if A were' actually constitutes a stronger requirement. As we noted earlier (n. 1, above), if two conditionals having the same counterfactual antecedent are such that the consequent of one is the negate of the consequent of the other, the conditionals are contraries and both may be false. This will be the case e.g. if every otherwise suitable set of relevant conditions that in conjunction with the antecedent leads by law either to a given consequent or its negate leads also to the other.

If Georgia included New York City, and the boundaries of New York City remained unchanged, then . . . .

Without some such cue to the meaning as is covertly given by the word-order, we should be quite uncertain which of the two consequents in question could be truly attached. The same kind of explanation accounts for the paradoxical pairs of counteridenticals mentioned earlier.

Returning now to the proposed rule, I shall neither offer further corrections of detail nor discuss whether the requirement that S be contenable with A makes superfluous some other provisions of the criterion; for such matters become rather unimportant besides the really serious difficulty that now confronts us. In order to determine the truth of a given counterfactual it seems that we have to determine among other things, whether there is a suitable S that is cotenable with A and meets certain further requirements. But in order to determine whether or not a given S is cotenable with A, we have to determine whether or not the counterfactual 'If A were true, then S would not be true' is itself true. But this means determining whether or not there is a suitable S_1, cotenable with A, that leads to $-S$ and so on. Thus we find ourselves involved in an infinite regressus or a circle; for cotenability is defined in terms of counterfactuals, yet the meaning of counterfactuals is defined in terms of cotenability. In other words to establish any counterfactual, it seems that we first have to determine the truth of another. If so, we can never explain a counterfactual except in terms of others, so that the problem of counterfactuals must remain unsolved.

Though unwilling to accept this conclusion, I do not at present see any way of meeting the difficulty. One naturally thinks of revising the whole treatment of counterfactuals in such a way as to admit those that depend on no conditions other than the antecedent, and then use these counterfactuals as the criteria for the cotenability of relevant conditions with antecedents of other counterfactuals, and so on. But this idea seems initially rather unpromising in view of the formidable difficulties of accounting by such a step-by-step method for even so simple a counterfactual as

If the match had been scratched, it would have lighted.

3. THE PROBLEM OF LAW

Even more serious is the second of the problems mentioned earlier: the nature of the general statements that enable us to infer the consequent upon the basis of the antecedent and the statement of relevant conditions. The distinction between these connecting principles and relevant conditions is imprecise and arbitrary; the 'connecting principles' might be conjoined to the condition-statements, and the relation of the antecedent conjunction $(A \cdot S)$ to the consequent thus made a matter of logic. But the same problems would arise as to the kind of principle that is capable of sustaining a counterfactual; and it is convenient to consider the connecting principles separately.

In order to infer the consequent of a counterfactual from the antecedent A and a suitable statement of relevant conditions S, we make use of a general statement, namely the generalization[9] of the conditional having $A \cdot S$ for antecedent and C for consequence. For example, in the case of

If the match had been scratched, it would have lighted

the connecting principle is

Every match that is scratched, well made, dry enough, in enough oxygen, etc., lights.

But notice that *not* every counterfactual is actually sustained by the principle thus arrived at, *even* if that principle is *true*. Suppose, for example, that all I had in my right pocket on VE day was a group of silver coins. Now we would not under normal circumstances affirm of a given penny P

If P had been in my pocket on VE day, P would have been silver,[10]

---

[9] The sense of 'generalization' intended here is that explained by C. G. Hempel in 'A Purely Syntactical Definition of Confirmation', *Journal of Symbolic Logic*, 8 (1943): 122–43. See also my *Fact, Fiction, and Forecast* (Cambridge, Mass., 1984): ch. 3.

[10] The antecedent in this example is intended to mean 'If P, while remaining distinct from the things that were in fact in my pocket on VE day, had also been in my pocket then', and *not* the quite different, counteridentical 'If P had been

even though from

> *P* was in my pocket on VE day

we can infer the consequent by means of the general statement

> Everything in my pocket on VE day was silver.

On the contrary, we would assert that if P had been in my pocket, then this general statement would not be true. The general statement will *not* permit us to infer the given consequent from the counterfactual assumption that *P* was in my pocket, because the general statement will not itself withstand that counterfactual assumption. Though the supposed connecting principle is indeed general, true, and perhaps even fully confirmed by observation of all cases, it is incapable of sustaining a counterfactual because it remains a description of accidental fact, not a law. The truth of a counterfactual conditional thus seems to depend on whether the general sentence required for the inference is a law or not. If so, our problem is to distinguish accurately between causal laws and casual facts.[11]

The problem illustrated by the example of the coins is closely related to that which led us earlier to require the cotenability of the antecedent and the relevant conditions, in order to avoid resting a counterfactual on any statement that would not be true if the antecedent were true. For decision as to the cotenability of two sentences depends partly upon decisions as to whether certain general statements are laws, and we are now concerned directly with the latter problem. Is there some way of so distinguishing laws from non-laws, among true universal statements of the kind in question, that laws will be the principles that will sustain counterfactual conditionals?

identical with one of the things that were in my pocket on VE day'. While the antecedents of most counterfactuals (as, again, our familar one about the match) are—literally speaking—open to both sorts of interpretation, ordinary usage normally calls for some explicit indication when the counteridentical meaning is intended.

[11] The importance of distinguishing laws from non-laws is too often overlooked. If a clear distinction can be defined, it may serve not only the purposes explained in the present essay but also many of those for which the increasingly dubious distinction between analytic and synthetic statements is ordinarily supposed to be needed.

Any attempt to draw the distinction by reference to a notion of causative force can be dismissed at once as unscientific. And it is clear that no purely syntactical criterion can be adequate, for even the most special descriptions of particular facts can be cast in a form having any desired degree of syntactical universality. 'Book *B* is small' becomes 'Everything that is *Q* is small' if '*Q*' stands for some predicate that applies uniquely to *B*. What then does distinguish a law like

All butter melts at 150°F

from a true and general non-law like

All the coins in my pocket are silver?

Primarily, I would like to suggest, the fact that the first is accepted as true while many cases of it remain to be determined, the further, unexamined cases being predicted to conform with it. The second sentence, on the contrary, is accepted as a description of contingent fact *after* the determination of all cases, no prediction of any of its instances being based upon it. This proposal raises innumerable problems, some of which I shall consider presently; but the idea behind it is just that the principle we use to decide counterfactual cases is a principle we are willing to commit ourselves to in deciding unrealized cases that are still subject to direct observation.

As a first approximation then we might say that a law is a true sentence used for making predictions. That laws are used predictively is of course a simple truism, and I am not proposing it as a novelty. I want only to emphasize the Humean idea that rather than a sentence being used for prediction because it is a law, it is called a law because it is used for prediction; and that rather than the law being used for prediction because it describes a causal connection, the meaning of the causal connection is to be interpreted in terms of predictively used laws.

By the determination of all instances, I mean simply the examination or testing by others means of all things that satisfy the antecedent, to decide whether all satisfy the consequent also. There are difficult questions about the meaning of 'instance', many of which Professor Hempel has investigated. Most of these are avoided in our present study by the fact that we are concerned with a very narrow class of sentences: those arrived at by generalizing conditionals of a certain kind. Remaining problems about the meaning of 'instance' I shall have to ignore here. As for 'determination', I do not mean final discovery of truth, but only enough examination to reach a decision as to whether a given statement or its negate is to be admitted as evidence for the hypothesis in question.

Our criterion excludes vacuous principles as laws. The generalizations needed for sustaining counterfactual conditionals cannot be vacuous, for they must be supported by evidence.[12] The limited scope of our present problem makes it unimportant that our criterion, if applied generally to all statements, would classify as laws many statements, for example true singular predictions, that we would not normally call laws.

For convenience, I shall use the term 'lawlike' for sentences that, whether they are true or not, satisfy the other requirements in the definition of law. A law is thus a sentence that is both lawlike and true, but a sentence may be true without being lawlike, as I have illustrated, or lawlike without being true, as we are always learning to our dismay.

Now if we were to leave our definition as it stands, lawlikeness would be a rather accidental and ephemeral property. Only statements that happen actually to have been used for prediction would be lawlike. And a true sentence that had been used predictively would cease to be a law when it became fully tested, i.e. when none of its instances remained undetermined. The definition, then, must be restated in some such way as this: A general statement is lawlike if and only if it is acceptable prior to the determination of all instances. This is immediately objectionable because 'acceptable' itself is plainly a dispositional term; but I propose to use it only tentatively, with the idea of eliminating it eventually by means of a non-dispositional

---

[12] Had it been sufficient in the preceding section to require only that $A \cdot S$ be self-*compatible*, this requirement might now be eliminated in favour of the stipulation that the generalization of the conditional having $A \cdot S$ as antecedent and C as consequent should be non-vacuous; but this stipulation would not guarantee the self-*cotenability* of $A \cdot S$.

definition. Before trying to accomplish that, however, we must face another difficulty in our tentative criterion of lawlikeness.

Suppose that the appropriate generalization fails to sustain a given counterfactual because that generalization, while true, is unlawlike, as is

Everything in my pocket is silver.

All we would need to do to get a law would be to broaden the antecedent strategically. Consider, for example, the sentence

Everything that is in my pocket or is a dime is silver.

Since we have not examined all dimes, this is a predictive statement and—since presumably true—would be a law. Now if we consider our original counterfactual and choose our S so that $A \cdot S$ is

P is in my pocket. P is in my pocket or is a dime,

then the pseudo-law just constructed can be used to infer from this the sentence 'P is silver'. Thus the untrue counterfactual is established. If one prefers to avoid an alternation as a condition-statement, the same result can be obtained by using a new predicate such as 'dimo' to mean 'is in my pocket or is a dime'.[13]

The change called for, I think, will make the definition of lawlikeness read as follows: A sentence is lawlike if its acceptance does not depend upon the determination of any given instance.[14] Naturally this does not mean that acceptance is to be independent of all determination of instances, but only that there is no particular instance on the determination of which acceptance depends. This criterion excludes from the class of laws a statement like

That book is black and oranges are spherical

[13] Apart from the special class of connecting principles we are concerned with, note that under the stated criterion of lawlikeness, any statement could be expanded into a lawlike one; for example: given 'This book is black' we could use the predictive sentence 'This book is black and all oranges are spherical' to argue that the blackness of the book is the consequence of a law.

[14] So stated, the definition counts vacuous principles as laws. If we read instead 'given class of instances', vacuous principles will be non-laws since their acceptance depends upon examination of the null class of instances. For my present purposes the one formulation is as good as the other.

on the ground that acceptance requires knowing whether the book is black; it excludes

Everything that is in my pocket or is a dime is silver

on the ground that acceptance demands examination of all things in my pocket. Moreover, it excludes a statement like

All the marbles in this bag except Number 19 are red, and Number 19 is black

on the ground that acceptance would depend on examination of or knowledge gained otherwise concerning marble Number 19. In fact the principle involved in the proposed criterion is a rather powerful one and seems to exclude most of the troublesome cases.

We must still, however, replace the notion of the acceptability of a sentence, or of its acceptance *depending* or *not depending* on some given knowledge, by a positive definition of such dependence. It is clear that to say that the acceptance of a given statement depends upon a certain kind and amount of evidence is to say that given such evidence, acceptance of the statement is in accord with certain general standards for the acceptance of statements that are not fully tested. So one turns naturally to theories of induction and confirmation to learn the distinguishing factors or circumstances that determine whether or not a sentence is acceptable without complete evidence. But publications on confirmation not only have failed to make clear the distinction between confirmable and non-confirmable statements, but show little recognition that such a problem exists.[15] Yet obviously in the case of some sentences like

Everything in my pocket is silver

or

No twentieth-century president of the United States will be between 6 feet 1 inch and 6 feet 1½ inches tall,

not even the testing with positive results of all but a single instance

[15] The points discussed in this and the following paragraph have been dealt with a little more fully in my 'A Query on Confirmation', *Journal of Philosophy*, 43 (1946): 383–5.

is likely to lead us to accept the sentence and predict that the one remaining instance will conform to it; while for other sentences such as

All dimes are silver

or

All butter melts at 150°F.

or

All flowers of plants descended from this seed will be yellow,

positive determination of even a few instances may lead us to accept the sentence with confidence and make predictions in accordance with it.

There is some hope that cases like these can be dealt with by a sufficiently careful and intricate elaboration of current confirmation theories; but inattention to the problem of distinguishing between confirmable and non-confirmable sentences has left most confirmation theories open to more damaging counter-examples of an elementary kind.

Suppose we designate the 26 marbles in a bag by the letters of the alphabet, using these merely as proper names having no ordinal significance. Suppose further that we are told that all the marbles except d are red, but we are not told what colour d is. By the usual kind of confirmation theory this give strong confirmation for the statement

$$R a. \, Rb. \, Rc. \, Rd \ldots. \, Rz$$

because 25 of the 26 cases are known to be favourable while none is known to be unfavourable. But unfortunately the same argument would show that the very same evidence would equally confirm

$$R a. \, Rb. \, Rc. \, Re. \ldots. \, Rz - Rd,$$

for again we have 25 favourable and no unfavourable cases. Thus 'Rd' and '$-$Rd' are equally and strongly confirmed by the same evidence. If I am required to use a single predicate instead of both 'R' and '$-$R' in the second case, I will use 'P' to mean:

is in the bag and either is not *d* and is red, or is *d* and is not red.

Then the evidence will be 25 positive cases for

All the marbles are P

from which it follows that *d* is P, and thus *d* is not red. The problem of what statements are confirmable merely becomes the equivalent problem of what predicates are projectible from known to unknown cases.

So far, I have discovered no way of meeting these difficulties. Yet as we have seen, some solution is urgently wanted for our present purpose; for only where willingness to accept a statement involves predictions of instances that may be tested does acceptance endow that statement with the authority to govern counterfactual cases, which cannot be directly tested.

In conclusion, then, some problems about counterfactuals depend upon the definition of cotenability, which in turn seems to depend upon the prior solution of those problems. Other problems require an adequate definition of law. The tentative criterion of law here proposed is reasonably satisfactory in excluding unwanted kinds of statements and, in effect, reduces one aspect of our problem to the question how to define the circumstances under which a statement is acceptable independently of the determination of any given instance. But this question I do not know how to answer.

II

A THEORY OF CONDITIONALS*

ROBERT STALNAKER

1. INTRODUCTION

A CONDITIONAL sentence expresses a proposition which is a function of two other propositions, yet not one which is a *truth* function of those propositions. I may know the truth values of 'Willie Mays played in the American League' and 'Willie Mays hit four hundred' without knowing whether or not Mays would have hit four hundred if he had played in the American League. This fact has tended to puzzle, displease, or delight philosophers, and many have felt that it is a fact that calls for some comment or explanation. It has given rise to a number of philosophical problems; I shall discuss three of these.

My principal concern will be with what has been called the *logical problem of conditionals*, a problem that frequently is ignored or dismissed by writers on conditionals and counterfactuals. This is the task of describing the formal properties of the *conditional function*: a function, usually represented in English by the words 'if . . . then', taking ordered pairs of propositions into propositions. I shall explain informally and

Robert Stalnaker, 'A Theory of Conditionals' from *Studies in Logical Theory*, *American Philosophical Quarterly*, Monograph: 2 (Blackwell, 1968), pp. 98–112. Reprinted in E. Sosa, *Causation and Conditionals* (OUP, 1975). Used by permission.

* I want to express appreciation to my colleague, Professor R. H. Thomason, for his collaboration in the formal development of the theory expounded in this essay, and for his helpful comments on its exposition and defence. The preparation of this essay was supported in part by a National Science Foundation grant, GS–1567.

defend a solution, presented more rigorously elsewhere, to this problem.[1]

The second issue—the one that has dominated recent discussions of contrary-to-fact conditionals—is the *pragmatic problem of counterfactuals*. This problem derives from the belief, which I share with most philosophers writing about this topic, that the formal properties of the conditional function, together with all of the *facts*, may not be sufficient for determining the truth value of a counterfactual; that is, different truth valuations of conditional statements may be consistent with a single valuation of all non-conditional statements. The task set by the problem is to find and defend criteria for choosing among these different valuations.

This problem is different from the first issue because these criteria are pragmatic, and not semantic. The distinction between semantic and pragmatic criteria, however, depends on the construction of a semantic theory. The semantic theory that I shall defend will thus help to clarify the second problem by charting the boundary between the semantic and pragmatic components of the concept. The question of this boundary line is precisely what Rescher, for example, avoids by couching his whole discussion in terms of conditions for belief, or justified belief, rather than truth conditions. Conditions for justified belief are pragmatic for any concept.[2]

The third issue is an epistemological problem that has bothered empiricist philosophers. It is based on the fact that many counterfactuals seem to be synthetic, and contingent, statements about unrealized possibilities. But contingent statements must be capable of confirmation by empirical evidence, and the investigator can gather evidence only in the actual world. How are conditionals which are both empirical and contrary-to-fact possible at all? How do we learn about possible worlds, and where are the

[1] R. C. Stalnaker and R. H. Thomason, 'A Semantic Analysis of Conditional Logic', *Theoria*, 36 (1976): 23–42. In this paper, the formal system, C2, is proved sound and semantically complete with respect to the interpretation sketched in the present paper. That is, it is shown that a formula is a consequence of a class of formulas if and only if it is derivable from the class in the formal system, C2.

[2] N. Rescher, *Hypothetical Reasoning* (Amsterdam, 1964).

facts (or counterfacts) which make counterfactuals true? Such questions have led philosophers to try to analyse the conditional in non-conditional terms[3] — to show that conditionals merely appear to be about unrealized possibilities. My approach however, will be to accept the appearance as reality, and to argue that one can sometimes have evidence about nonactual situations.

In Sects. 2 and 3 of this paper, I shall present and defend a theory of conditionals which has two parts: a formal system with a primitive conditional connective, and a semantical apparatus which provides general truth conditions for statements involving that connective. In Sects. 4, 5, and 6, I shall discuss in a general way the relation of the theory to the three problems outlined above.

2. THE INTERPRETATION

Eventually, I want to defend a hypothesis about the truth conditions for statements having conditional form, but I shall begin by asking a more practical question: how does one evaluate a conditional statement? How does one decide whether or not he believes it to be true? An answer to this question will not be a set of truth conditions, but it will serve as a heuristic aid in the search for such a set.

To make the question more concrete, consider the following situation: you are faced with a true–false political opinion survey. The statement is, 'If the Chinese enter the Vietnam conflict, the United States will use nuclear weapons.' How do you deliberate in choosing your response? What considerations of a logical sort are relevant? I shall first discuss two familiar answers to this question, and then defend a third answer which avoids some of the weaknesses of the first two.

The first answer is based on the simplest account of the

[3] Cf. R. Chisholm, 'The Contrary-to-fact Conditional', *Mind*, 55 (1946): 289–307, repr. in *Readings in Philosophical Analysis*, ed. H. Feigl and W. Sellars (New York, 1949): 482–97. The problem is sometimes posed (as it is here) as the task of analysing the *subjunctive* conditional into an indicative statement, but I think it is a mistake to base very much on the distinction of mood. As far as I can tell, the mood tends to indicate something about the attitude of the speaker, but in no way affects the propositional content of the statement.

conditional, the truth-functional analysis. According to this account, you should reason as follows in responding to the true–false quiz: you ask yourself, first, will the Chinese enter the conflict? and second, will the United States use nuclear weapons? If the answer to the first question is no, *or* if the answer to the second is yes, then you should place your *X* in the 'true' box. But this account is unacceptable since the following piece of reasoning is an obvious *non sequitur*: 'I firmly believe that the Chinese will stay out of the conflict; *therefore* I believe that the statement is true.' The falsity of the antecedent is never sufficient reason to affirm a conditional, even an indicative conditional.

A second answer is suggested by the shortcomings of the truth-functional account. The material implication analysis fails, critics have said, because it leaves out the idea of *connection* which is implicit in an if-then statement. According to this line of thought, a conditional is to be understood as a statement which affirms that some sort of logical or causal connection holds between the antecedent and the consequent. In responding to the true–false quiz, then you should look, not at the truth values of the two clauses, but at the relation between the proposition expressed by them. If the 'connection' holds, you check the 'true' box. If not, you answer 'false'.

If the second hypothesis were accepted, then we would face the task of clarifying the idea of 'connection', but there are counter-examples even with this notion left as obscure as it is. Consider the following case: you firmly believe that the use of nuclear weapons by the United States in this war is inevitable because of the arrogance of power, the bellicosity of our president, rising pressure from congressional hawks, or other *domestic* causes. You have no opinion about future Chinese actions, but you do not think they will make much difference one way or another to nuclear escalation. Clearly, you believe the opinion survey statement to be true even though you believe the antecedent and consequent to be logically and causally independent of each other. It seems that the presence of a 'connection' is not a necessary condition for the truth of an if-then statement.

The third answer that I shall consider is based on a suggestion made some time ago by F. P. Ramsey.[4] Consider first the case where you have no opinion about the statement, 'The Chinese will enter the Vietnam war.' According to the suggestion, your deliberation about the survey statement should consist of a simple thought-experiment: add the antecedent (hypothetically) to your stock of knowledge (or beliefs), and then consider whether or not the consequent is true. Your belief about the conditional should be the same as your hypothetical belief, under this condition, about the consequent.

What happens to the idea of connection on this hypothesis? It is sometimes relevant to the evaluation of a conditional, and sometimes not. If you believe that a causal or logical connection exists, then you will add the consequent to your stock of beliefs along with the antecedent, since the rational man accepts the consequences of his beliefs. On the other hand, if you already believe the consequent (and if you also believe it to be causally independent of the antecedent), then it will remain a part of your stock of beliefs when you add the antecedent, since the rational man does not change his beliefs without reason. In either case, you will affirm the conditional. Thus this answer accounts for the relevance of 'connection' when it is relevant without making it a necessary condition of the truth of a conditional.

Ramsey's suggestion covers only the situation in which you have no opinion about the truth value of the antecedent. Can it be generalized? We can of course extend it without problem to the case where you believe or know the antecedent to be true; in this case, no changes need be made in your stock of beliefs. If you already believe that the Chinese will enter the Vietnam conflict, then your belief about the conditional will be just the same as your belief about the statement that the US will use the bomb.

What about the case in which you know or believe the antecedent to be false? In this situation, you cannot simply add it to your stock of beliefs without introducing a contradiction. You must make adjustments by deleting or changing those beliefs

---

[4] F. P. Ramsey, 'General Propositions and Causality' in Ramsey, *Foundations of Mathematics and other Logical Essays* (New York, 1950): 237–57. The suggestion is made on 248. Chisholm, in 'The Contrary-to-Fact Conditional', 489 quotes the suggestion and discusses the limitations of the 'connection' thesis which it brings out, but he develops it somewhat differently.

which conflict with the antecedent. Here, the familiar difficulties begin, of course, because there will be more than one way to make the required adjustments.[5] These difficulties point to the pragmatic problem of counterfactuals, but if we set them aside for a moment, we shall see a rough but general answer to the question we are asking. This is how to evaluate a conditional:

> First, add the antecedent (hypothetically) to your stock of beliefs; second, make whatever adjustments are required to maintain consistency (without modifying the hypothetical belief in the antecedent); finally, consider whether or not the consequent is then true.

It is not particularly important that our answer is approximate—that it skirts the problem of adjustments—since we are using it only as a way of finding truth conditions. It is crucial, however, that the answer not be restricted to some particular context of belief if it is to be helpful in finding a definition of the conditional function. If the conditional is to be understood as a function of the propositions expressed by its component clauses, then its truth value should not in general be dependent on the attitudes which anyone has toward those propositions.

Now that we have found an answer to the question, 'How do we decide whether or not we believe a conditional statement?' the problem is to make the transition from belief conditions to truth conditions; that is, to find a set of truth conditions for statements having conditional form which explains why we use the method we do use to evaluate them. The concept of a *possible world* is just what we need to make this transition, since a possible world is the ontological analogue of a stock of hypothetical beliefs. The following set of truth conditions, using this notion, is a first approximation to the account that I shall propose:

> Consider a possible world in which A is true, and which otherwise differs minimally from the actual world. '*If A, then*

[5] Rescher, *Hypothetical Reasoning*, 11–16, contains a very clear statement and discussion of this problem, which he calls the problem of the ambiguity of belief-contravening hypotheses. He argues that the resolution of this ambiguity depends on pragmatic considerations. Cf. also Goodman's problem of relevant conditions in N. Goodman, *Fact, Fiction, and Forecast* (Cambridge, Mass., 1984): 17–24. (Essay I in this volume.)

B' is true (false) just in case B is true (false) in that possible world.

An analysis in terms of possible worlds also has the advantage of providing a ready-made apparatus on which to build a formal semantical theory. In making this account of the conditional precise, we use the semantical systems for modal logics developed by Saul Kripke.[6] Following Kripke, we first define a *model structure*. Let M be an ordered triple (K,R,λ). K is to be understood intuitively as the set of all possible worlds; R is the relation of relative possibility which defines the structure. If α and β are possible worlds (members of K), than $\alpha R\beta$ reads 'β is possible with respect to α'. This means that, where α is the actual world, β is a possible world. R is a reflexive relation; that is, every world is possible with respect to itself. If your modal intuitions so incline you, you may add that R must be transitive, or transitive and symmetrical.[7] The only element that is not a part of the standard modal semantics is λ, a member of K which is to be understood as the *absurd world*—the world in which contradictions and all their consequences are true. It is an isolated element under R; that is, no other world is possible with respect to it, and it is not possible with respect to any other world. The purpose of λ is to allow for an interpretation of 'If A, then B' in the case where A is impossible; for this situation one needs an impossible world.

In addition to a model structure, our semantical apparatus includes a *selection function*, f, which takes a proposition and a possible world as arguments and a possible world as its value. The *s*-function selects, for each antecedent A, a particular possible world in which A is true. The *assertion* which the conditional makes, then, is that the consequent is true in the world selected. A conditional is true in the actual world when its consequent is true in the selected world.

[6] S. Kripke, 'Semantical Analysis of Modal Logics, I', *Zeitschrift für mathematische Logik und Grundlagen der Mathematik*, 9 (1963): 67–96.

[7] The different restrictions on the relation R provide interpretations for the different modal systems. The system we build on is von Wright's M. If we add the transitivity requirement, then the underlying modal logic of our system is Lewis's S4, and if we add both the transitivity and symmetry requirements, then the modal logic is S5. Cf. Kripke, 'Semantical Analysis'.

Now we can state the semantical rule for the conditional more formally (using the corner, $>$, as the conditional connective):

$A>B$ is true in α if B is true in $f(A, \alpha)$;
$A>B$ is false in α if B is false in $f(A, \alpha)$.

The interpretation shows conditional logic to be an extension of modal logic. Modal logic provides a way of talking about what is true in the actual world, in all possible worlds, or in at least one, unspecified world. The addition of the selection function to the semantics and the conditional connective to the object language of modal logic provides a way of talking also about what is true in *particular* non-actual possible situations. This is what counterfactuals are: statements about particular counterfactual worlds.

But the world selected cannot be just any world. The *s*-function must meet at least the following conditions. I shall use the following terminology for talking about the arguments and values of *s*-functions: where $f(A, \alpha)=\beta$, A is the *antecedent*, α is the *base world*, and β is the *selected world*.

(1) For all antecedents A and base worlds α, A must be true in $f(A,\alpha)$.

(2) For all antecedents A and base worlds α, $f(A,\alpha)=\lambda$ only if there is no world possible with respect to α in which A is true.

The first condition requires that the antecedent be true in the selected world. This ensures that all statements like 'if snow is white, then snow is white' are true. The second condition requires that the absurd world be selected only when the antecedent is impossible. Since everything is true in the absurd world, including contradictions, if the selection function were to choose it for the antecedent A, then 'if A, then B and not B' would be true. But one cannot legitimately reach an impossible conclusion from a consistent assumption.

The informal truth conditions that were suggested above required that the world selected *differ minimally* from the actual world. This implies, first that there are no differences between the actual world and the selected world except those that are required, implicitly or explicitly, by the antecedent. Further, it means that among the alternative ways of making the required changes, one must choose one that does the least violence to the correct description and explanation of the actual world. These are vague conditions which are largely dependent on pragmatic considerations for their application. They suggest, however, that the selection is based on an ordering of possible worlds with respect to their resemblance to the base world. If this is correct, then there are two further formal constraints which must be imposed on the s-function.

(3) For all base worlds α and all antecedents A, if A is true in α, then $f(A,\alpha)=\alpha$.

(4) For all base worlds α and all antecedents B and B', if B is true in $f(B',\alpha)$ and B' is true in $f(B,\alpha)$, then $f(B,\alpha)=f(B',\alpha)$.

The third condition requires that the base world be selected if it is among the worlds in which the antecedent is true. Whatever the criteria for evaluating resemblance among possible worlds, there is obviously no other possible world as much like the base world as the base world itself. The fourth condition ensures that the ordering among possible worlds is consistent in the following sense: if any selection established β as prior to β' in the ordering (with respect to a particular base world α), then no other selection (relative to that α) may establish β' as prior to β.[8] Conditons (3) and (4) together ensure that the s-function establishes a total ordering of all selected worlds with respect to each possible world, with the base world preceding all others in the order.

These conditions on the selection function are necessary in order that this account be recognizable as an explication of the conditional, but they are of course far from sufficient to determine the function uniquely. There may be further formal constraints that can plausibly be imposed on the selection principle, but we should not expect to find semantic conditions sufficient to guarantee that there will be a unique s-function for each valuation of non-conditional formulas on a model structure. The questions,

[8] If $f(A, \alpha) = \beta$, then β is established as prior to all worlds possible with respect to α in which A is true.

'On what basis do we select a selection function from among the acceptable ones?' and 'What are the criteria for ordering possible worlds?' are reformulations of the pragmatic problem of counterfactuals, which is a problem in the application of conditional logic. The conditions that I have mentioned above are sufficient, however, to define the semantical notions of validity and consequence for conditional logic.

3. THE FORMAL SYSTEM

The class of valid formulas of conditional logic according to the definitions in the preceding section, is coextensive with the class of theorems of a formal system, C2. The primitive connectives of C2 are the usual $\supset$ and $\sim$ (with v, &, and $\equiv$ defined as usual), as well as a conditional connective, $>$ (called the corner). Other modal and conditional concepts can be defined in terms of the corner as follows:

$$\Box A =_{DF} \sim A > A$$
$$\Diamond A =_{DF} \sim (A > \sim A)$$
$$A \gtreqless B =_{DF} (A>)B \ \& \ (B>A)$$

The rules of inference of C2 are *modus ponens* (if A and $A \supset B$ are theorems, then B is a theorem) and the Gödel rule of necessitation (if A is a theorem, then $\Box A$ is a theorem). There are seven axiom schemata:

(a1) Any tautologous wff (well-formed formula) is an axiom.
(a2) $\Box(A \supset B) \supset (\Box A \supset \Box B)$
(a3) $\Box(A \supset B) \supset (A>B)$
(a4) $\Diamond A \supset .(A>B) \supset \sim(A>\sim B)$
(a5) $A>(BvC) \supset .(A>B)v(A>C)$
(a6) $(A>B) \supset (A \supset B)$
(a7) $A \gtreqless B \supset .(A>C) \supset (B>C)$

The conditional connective, as characterized by this formal system, is intermediate between strict implication and the material conditional, in the sense that $\Box(A \supset B)$ entails $A>B$ by (a3) and $A>B$ entails $A \supset B$ by (a6). It cannot, however, be analysed as a modal operation performed on a material conditional (like Burks's causal implication, for example).[9] The corner lacks certain properties shared by the two traditional implication concepts, and in fact these differences help to explain some peculiarities of counterfactuals. I shall point out three unusual features of the conditional connective.

(1) Unlike both material and strict implication, the conditional corner is a non-transitive connective. That is, from $A>B$ and $B>C$, one cannot infer $A>C$. While this may at first seem surprising, consider the following example: *Premisses*. 'If J. Edgar Hoover were today a communist, then he would be a traitor.' 'If J. Edgar Hoover had been born a Russian, then he would today be a communist.' *Conclusion*. 'If J. Edgar Hoover had been born a Russian, he would be a traitor.' It seems reasonable to affirm these premisses and deny the conclusion.

If this example is not sufficiently compelling, note that the following rule follows from the transitivity rule: From $A>B$ to infer $(A \& C)>B$. But it is obvious that the former rule is invalid; we cannot always strengthen the antecedent of a true conditional and have it remain true. Consider 'If this match were struck, it would light', and 'If this match had been soaked in water overnight *and* it were struck, it would light.'[10]

(2) According to the formal system, the denial of a conditional is equivalent to a conditional with the same antecedent and opposite consequent (provided that the antecedent is not impossible). This is, $\Diamond A \supset {\sim} (A>B) \equiv (A>{\sim}B)$. This explains the fact, noted by both Goodman and Chisholm in their early papers on counterfactuals, that the normal way to contradict a counterfactual is to contradict the consequent, keeping the same antecedent. To deny 'If Kennedy were alive today, we wouldn't be in this Vietnam mess', we say, 'If Kennedy were alive today, we would so be in this Vietnam mess.'

[9] A. W. Burks, 'The Logic of Causal Propositions', *Mind*, 60 (1951): 363–82. The casual implication connective characterized in this article has the same structure as strict implication. For an interesting philosophical defence of this modal interpretation of conditionals, see B. Mayo, 'Conditional Statements', *Philosophical Review*, 66 (1957): 291–303.

[10] Although the transitivity inference fails, a related inference is of course valid. From $A>B$, $B>C$, and A, one can infer C. Also, note that the biconditional connective is transitive. From $A \lessgtr B$ and $B \gtrless C$, one can infer $A \gtrless C$. Thus the biconditional is an equivalence relation, since it is also symmetrical and reflexive.

(3) The inference of contraposition, valid for both the truth-functional horseshoe and the strict implication hook, is invalid for the conditional corner. $A>B$ may be true while $\sim B>\sim A$ is false. For an example in support of this conclusion, we take another item from the political opinion survey: 'If the US halts the bombing, then North Vietnam will not agree to negotiate.' A person would believe that this statement is true if he thought that the North Vietnamese were determined to press for a complete withdrawal of US troops. But he would surely deny the contrapositive, 'If North Vietnam agrees to negotiate, then the US will not have halted the bombing'. He would believe that a halt in the bombing, and much more, is required to bring the North Vietnamese to the negotiating table.[11]

Examples of these anomalies have been noted by philosophers in the past. For instance, Goodman pointed out that two counterfactuals with the same antecedent and contradictory consequents are 'normally meant' as direct negations of each other. He also remarked that we may sometimes assert a conditional and yet reject its contrapositive. He accounted for these facts by arguing that semifactuals—conditionals with false antecedent and consequent. . . . the practical import of a taken literally. 'In practice,' he wrote, 'full counterfactuals affirm, while semifactuals deny, that a certain connection obtains between antecedent and consequent. . . . The practical import of a semifactual is thus different from its literal import.'[12] Chisholm also suggested paraphrasing semifactuals before analysing them. 'Even if you were to sleep all morning, you would be tired' is to be read 'It is false that if you were to sleep all morning, you would not be tired.'[13]

A separate and non-conditional analysis for semifactuals is necessary to save the 'connection' theory of counterfactuals in the face of the anomalies we have discussed, but it is a baldly *ad hoc* manoeuvre. Any analysis can be saved by paraphrasing the counter-examples. The theory presented in Sect. 2 avoids this

---

[11] Although contraposition fails, *modus tollens* is valid for the conditional: from $A>B$ and $\sim B$, one can infer $\sim A$.

[12] Goodman, *Fact, Fiction, and Forecast*, 15, 32.

[13] Chisholm, 'The Contrary-to-Fact Conditional', 492.

difficulty by denying that the conditional can be said, in general, to assert a connection of any particular kind between antecedent and consequent. It is, of course, the structure of inductive and relations and casual connections which make counterfactuals and semifactuals true or false, but they do this by determining the relationships among possible worlds, which in turn determine the truth values of conditionals. By treating the relation between connection and conditionals as an indirect relation in this way, the theory is able to give a unified account of conditionals which explains the variations in their behaviour in different contexts.

4. THE LOGICAL PROBLEM: GENERAL CONSIDERATIONS

The traditional strategy for attacking a problem like the logical problem of conditionals was to find an *analysis*, to show that the unclear or objectionable phrase was dispensable, or replaceable by something clear and harmless. Analysis was viewed by some as an *unpacking*—a making manifest of what was latent in the concept; by others it was seen as the *replacement* of a vague idea by a precise one, adequate to the same purposes as the old expression, but free of its problems. The semantic theory of conditionals can also be viewed either as the construction of a concept to replace an unclear notion of ordinary language, or as an *explanation* of a commonly used concept. I see the theory in the latter way: no recommendation or stipulation is intended. This does not imply, however, that the theory is meant as a description of linguistic usage. What is being explained is not the rules governing the use of an English word, but the structure of a concept. Linguistic facts—what we would say in this or that context, and what sounds odd to the native speaker—are relevant as evidence, since one may presume that concepts are to some extent mirrored in language.

The 'facts', taken singly, need not be decisive. A recalcitrant counter-example may be judged a deviant use or a different sense of the word. We can claim that a paraphrase is necessary, or even that ordinary language is systematically mistaken about the concept we are explaining. There are, of course, different senses and times when 'ordinary language' goes astray, but such *ad hoc* hypotheses and qualifications diminish both the plausibility and the explanatory force of a theory. While we are not irrevocably bound to the linguistic facts, there are no 'don't cares'—contexts of use with which we are not concerned, since any context can be relevant as evidence for or against an analysis. A general interpretation which avoids dividing senses and accounts for the behaviour of a concept in many contexts fits the familiar pattern of scientific explanation in which diverse, seemingly unlike surface phenomena are seen as deriving from some common source. For these reasons, I take it as a strong point in favour of the semantic theory that it treats the conditional as a univocal concept.

5. PRAGMATIC AMBIGUITY

I have argued that the conditional connective is semantically unambiguous. It is obvious, however, that the context of utterance, the purpose of the assertion, and the beliefs of the speaker or his community may make a difference to the interpretation of a counterfactual. How do we reconcile the ambiguity of conditional sentences with the univocity of the conditional concept? Let us look more closely at the notion of ambiguity.

A sentence is ambiguous if there is more than one proposition which it may properly be interpreted to express. Ambiguity may be syntactic (if the sentence has more than one grammatical structure), semantic (if one of the words has more than one meaning), or pragmatic (if the interpretation depends directly on the context of use). The first two kinds of ambiguity are perhaps more familiar, but the third kind is probably the most common in natural languages. Any sentence involving pronouns, tensed verbs, articles, or quantifiers is pragmatically ambiguous. For example, the proposition expressed by 'L'état, c'est moi' depends on who says it; 'Do it now' may be good or bad advice depending on when is is said; 'Cherchez la femme' is ambiguous since it contains a definite description, and the truth conditions for 'All's well that ends well' depends on the domain of discourse. If the theory presented above is correct, then we may add conditional sentences to this list. The truth conditions for 'If wishes were horses, then beggars would ride' depend on the specification of an s-function.[14]

The grounds for treating the ambiguity of conditional sentences as pragmatic rather than semantic are the same as the grounds for treating the ambiguity of quantified sentences as pragmatic: simplicity and systematic coherence. The truth conditions for quantified statements vary with a change in the domain of discourse, but there is a single structure to these truth conditions which remains constant for every domain. The semantics for classical predicate logic brings out this common structure by giving the universal quantifier a single meaning and making the domain a parameter of the interpretation. In a similar fashion, the semantics for conditional logic brings out the common structure of the truth conditions for conditional statements by giving the connective a single meaning and making the selection function a parameter of the interpretation.

Just as we can communicate effectively using quantified sentences without explicitly specifying a domain, so we can communicate effectively using conditional sentences without explicity specifying an s-function. This suggests that there are further rules beyond those set down in the semantics, governing the use of conditional sentences. Such rules are the subject-matter of a *pragmatics* of conditionals. Very little can be said, at this point, about pragmatic rules for the use of conditionals since the logic has not advanced beyond the propositional stage, but I shall make a few speculative remarks about the kinds of research which may provide a framework for treatment of this problem, and related pragmatic problems in the philosophy of science.

(1) If we had a functional logic with a conditional connective, it is likely that $(\forall x) (Fx > Gx)$ would be a plausible candidate for the form of a law of nature. A law of nature says, not just that every actual F is a G, but further that for every possible F, if it were an F, it would be a G. If this is correct, then Hempel's confirmation paradox does not arise, since 'All ravens are black' is not logically equivalent to 'All non-black things are non-ravens.' Also, the

[14] I do not wish to pretend that the notions needed to define ambiguity and to make the distinction between pragmatic and semantic ambiguity (e.g. 'proposition', and 'meaning') are precise. They can be made precise only in the context of semantic and pragmatic theories. But even if it is unclear, in general, what pragmatic ambiguity is, it is clear, I hope, that my examples are cases of it.

relation between counterfactuals and laws becomes clear: laws support counterfactuals because they entail them. 'If this dove were a raven, it would be black' is simply an instantiation of 'All ravens are black.'[15]

(2) Goodman has argued that the pragmatic problem of counterfactuals is one of a cluster of closely related problems concerning induction and confirmation. He locates the source of these difficulties in the general problem of projectability, which can be stated roughly as follows: when can a predicate be validly projected from one set of cases to others? or when is a hypothesis confirmed by its positive instances? Some way of distinguishing between natural predicates and those which are artificially constructed is needed. If a theory of projection such as Goodman envisions were developed, it might find a natural place in a pragmatics of conditionals. Pragmatic criteria for measuring the inductive properties of predicates might provide pragmatic criteria for ordering possible worlds.[16]

(3) There are some striking structural parallels between conditional logic and conditional probability functions, which suggests the possibility of a connection between inductive logic and conditional logic. A probability assignment and an s-function are two quite different ways to describe the inductive relations among propositions; a theory which draws a connection between them might be illuminating for both.[17]

VI. CONCLUSION:
EMPIRICISM AND POSSIBLE WORLDS

Writers of fiction and fantasy sometimes suggest that imaginary worlds have a life of their own beyond the control of their creators.

---

[15] For a discussion of the relation of laws to counterfactuals, see E. Nagel, *Structure of Science* (New York, 1961): 47–78. For a recent discussion of the paradoxes of confirmation by the man who discovered them, see C. G. Hempel, 'Recent Problems of Induction' in *Mind and Cosmos*, ed. R. G. Colodny (Pittsburg, 1966): 112–34.

[16] Goodman, *Fact, Fiction, and Forecast*, esp. ch. 4.

[17] Several philosophers have discussed the relation of conditional propositions to conditional probabilities. See R. C. Jeffrey, 'If', *Journal of Philosophy*, 61 (1964): 702–3, and E. W. Adams, 'Probability and the Logic of Conditionals' in *Aspects of Inductive Logic*, ed. J. Hintikka and P. Suppes (Amsterdam, 1966): 256–316. I hope to present elsewhere my method of drawing the connection between the two notions, which differs from both of these.

Pirandello's six characters, for example, rebelled against their author and took the story out of his hands. The sceptic may be inclined to suspect that this suggestion is itself fantasy. He believes that nothing goes into a fictional world, or a possible world, unless it is put there by decision or convention; it is a creature of invention and not discovery. Even the fabulist Tolkien admits that Faërie is a land 'full of wonder, but not of information'.[18]

For similar reasons, the empiricist may be uncomfortable about a theory which treats counterfactuals as literal statements about non-actual situations. Counterfactuals are often contingent, and contingent statements must be supported by evidence. But evidence can be gathered, by us at least, only in this universe. To satisfy the empiricist, I must show how possible worlds, even if the product of convention, can be subjects of empirical investigation.

There is no mystery to the fact that I can partially define a possible world in such a way that I am ignorant of some of the determinate truths in that world. One way I can do this is to attribute to it features of the actual world which are unknown to me. Thus I can say, 'I am thinking of a possible world in which the population of China is just the same, on each day, as it is in the actual world.' *I* am making up this world—it is a pure product of my intentions—but there are already things true in it which I shall never know.

Conditionals do implicitly, and by convention, what is done explicitly by stipulation in this example. It is because counterfactuals are generally about possible worlds which are very much like the actual one, and defined in terms of it, that evidence is so often relevant to their truth. When I wonder, for example, what would have happened if I had asked my boss for a raise yesterday, I am wondering about a possible world that I have already roughly picked out. It has the same history, up to yesterday, as the actual world, the same boss with the same dispositions and habits. The main difference is that in that world, yesterday I asked the boss for a raise. Since I do not know everything about the boss's habits and dispositions in the actual world, there is a lot that I do not know about how he acts in the possible world that I have chosen, although I might find out by

[18] J. R. Tolkien, 'On Fairy Stories' in *The Tolkien Reader* (New York, 1966): 3.

watching him respond to a similar request from another, or by asking his secretary about his mood yesterday. These bits of information about the actual world would not be decisive, of course, but they would be relevant, since they tell me more about the non-actual situation that I have selected.

If I make a conditional statement—subjunctive or otherwise—and the antecedent turns out to be true, then whether I know it or not, I have said something about the actual world, namely that the consequent is true in it. If the antecedent is false, then I have said something about a particular counterfactual world, even if I believe the antecedent to be true. The conditional provides a set of conventions for selecting possible situations which have a specified relation to what actually happens. This makes it possible for statements about unrealized possibilities to tell us, not just about the speaker's imagination, but about the world.

III

COUNTERFACTUAL DEPENDENCE
AND TIME'S ARROW*

DAVID LEWIS

THE ASYMMETRY OF COUNTERFACTUAL
DEPENDENCE

TODAY I am typing words on a page. Suppose today were different. Suppose I were typing different words. Then plainly tomorrow would be different also; for instance, different words would appear on the page. Would yesterday also be different? If so, how? Invited to answer, you will perhaps come up with something. But I do not think there is anything you can say about how yesterday would be that will seem clearly and uncontroversially true.

The way the future is depends counterfactually on the way the present is. If the present were different, the future would be different; and there are counterfactual conditionals, many of them as unquestionably true as counterfactuals ever get, that tell us a good deal about how the future would be different if the present were different in various ways. Likewise the present depends

David Lewis, 'Counterfactual Dependence and Time's Arrow', first published *Noûs* XIII (1979), 455–76, copyright *Noûs* 1979 and used with their permission. Postscripts A, B, and C appeared for the first time in David Lewis, *Philosophical Papers*, vol. II (OUP, 1986) and are reprinted by permission of the author.

* I am grateful to many friends for discussion of these matters, and especially to Jonathan Bennett, Robert Goble, Philip Kitcher, Ernest Loevinsohn, John Perry, Michael Slote, and Robert Stalnaker. I am grateful to seminar audiences at several universities in New Zealand for comments on an early version of this essay, and to the New Zealand–United States Educational Foundation for making those seminars possible. I also thank Princeton University and the American Council of Learned Societies for research support at earlier stages. An earlier version of this essay was presented at the 1976 Annual Conference of the Australasian Association of Philosophy.

counterfactually on the past, and in general the way things are later depends on the way things were earlier.

Not so in reverse. Seldom, if ever, can we find a clearly true counterfactual about how the past would be different if the present were somehow different. Such a counterfactual, unless clearly false, normally is not clear one way or the other. It is at best doubtful whether the past depends counterfactually on the present, whether the present depends on the future, and in general whether the way things are earlier depends on the way things will be later.

Often, indeed, we seem to reason in a way that takes it for granted that the past is counterfactually independent of the present: that is, that even if the present were different, the past would be just as it actually is. In reasoning from a counterfactual supposition, we use auxiliary premises drawn from (what we take to be) our factual knowledge. But not just anything we know may be used, since some truths would not be true under the given supposition. If the supposition concerns the present, we do not feel free to use all we know about the future. If the supposition were true, the future would be different and some things we know about the actual future might not hold in this different counterfactual future. But we do feel free, ordinarily, to use whatever we know about the past. We evidently assume that even if our supposition about the present were true, the past would be no different. If I were acting otherwise just now, I would revenge a wrong done me last year—it is absurd even to raise the question whether the past wrong would have taken place if I were acting otherwise now! More generally, in reasoning from a counterfactual supposition about any time, we ordinarily assume that facts about earlier times are counterfactually independent of the supposition and so may freely be used as auxiliary premisses.

I would like to present a neat contrast between counterfactual dependence in one direction of time and counterfactual independence in the other direction. But until a distinction is made, the situation is not as neat as that. There are some special contexts that complicate matters. We know that present conditions have their past causes. We can persuade ourselves, and sometimes do, that if the present were different then these past causes would have to be different, else they would have caused the present to be as it actually is. Given such an argument—call it a *back-tracking argument*—we willingly grant that if the present were different, the past would be different too. I borrow an example from Downing (1959). Jim and Jack quarrelled yesterday, and Jack is still hopping mad. We conclude that if Jim asked Jack for help today, Jack would not help him. But wait: Jim is a prideful fellow. He never would ask for help after such a quarrel; if Jim were to ask Jack for help today, there would have to have been no quarrel yesterday. In that case Jack would be his usual generous self. So if Jim asked Jack for help today, Jack would help him after all.

At this stage we may be persuaded (and rightly so, I think) that if Jim asked Jack for help today, there would have been no quarrel yesterday. But the persuasion does not last. We very easily slip back into our usual sort of counterfactual reasoning, and implicitly assume once again that facts about earlier times are counterfactually independent of facts about later times. Consider whether pride is costly. In this case, at least, it costs Jim nothing. It would be useless for Jim to ask Jack for help, since Jack would not help him. We rely once more on the premiss we recently doubted: if Jim asked Jack for help today, the quarrel would nevertheless have taken place yesterday.

What is going on, I suggest, can best be explained as follows. (1) Counterfactuals are infected with vagueness, as everyone agrees. Different ways of (partly) resolving the vagueness are appropriate in different contexts. Remember the case of Caesar in Korea: had he been in command, would he have used the atom bomb? Or would he have used catapults? It is right to say either, though not to say both together. Each is true under a resolution of vagueness appropriate to some contexts. (2) We ordinarily resolve the vagueness of counterfactuals in such a way that the counterfactual dependence is asymmetric (except perhaps in cases of time travel or the like). Under this standard resolution, back-tracking arguments are mistaken: if the present were different the past would be the same, but the same past causes would fail somehow to cause the same present effects. If Jim asked Jack for help today, somehow Jim would have overcome his pride and asked despite yesterday's quarrel. (3) Some special contexts favour a different resolution of vagueness, one under which the past depends counterfactually on the present and some back-tracking arguments are correct. If someone propounds a back-tracking argument, for instance, his co-operation partners in conversation will switch to a resolution that gives him a chance to be right. (This sort of accommodating shift in abstract features of context is common; see Lewis (1979).) But when the need for a special resolution of vagueness comes to an end, the standard resolution returns. (4) A counterfactual saying that the past would be different if the present were somehow different may come out true under the special resolution of its vagueness, but false under the standard resolution. If so, call it a *back-tracking counter-factual*. Taken out of context, it will not be clearly true or clearly false. Although we tend to favour the standard resolution, we also charitably tend to favour a resolution which gives the sentence under consideration a chance of truth.

(Back-tracking counterfactuals, used in a context that favours their truth, are marked by a syntactic peculiarity. They are the ones in which the usual subjunctive conditional constructions are readily replaced by more complicated constructions: 'If it were that . . . then it would have to be that . . .' or the like. A suitable context may make it acceptable to say 'If Jim asked Jack for help today, there would have been no quarrel yesterday', but it would be more natural to say '. . . there would have to have been no quarrel yesterday'. Three paragraphs ago, I used such constructions to lure you into a context that favours back-tracking.)

I have distinguished the standard resolution of vagueness from the sort that permits back-tracking only so that I can ask you to ignore the latter. Only under the standard resolution do we have the clear-cut asymmetry of counterfactual dependence that interests me.

I do not claim that the asymmetry holds in all possible, or even all actual, cases. It holds for the sorts of familiar cases that arise in everyday life. But it well might break down in the different conditions that might obtain in a time machine, or at the edge of a black hole, or before the Big Bang, or after the Heat Death, or at a possible world consisting of one solitary atom in the void. It may also break down with respect to the immediate past. We shall return to these matters later.

Subject to these needed qualifications, what I claim is as follows. Consider those counterfactuals of the form 'If it were that A, then it would be that C' in which the supposition A is indeed false, and in which A and C are entirely about the states of affairs at two times t_A and t_C respectively. Many such counterfactuals are true in which C also is false, and in which t_C is later than t_A. These are counterfactuals that say how the way things are later depends on the way things were earlier. But if t_C is earlier than t_A, then such counterfactuals are true if and only if C is true. These are the counterfactuals that tell us how the way things are earlier does not depend on the way things will be later.

ASYMMETRIES OF CAUSATION AND OPENNESS

The asymmetry of counterfactual dependence has been little discussed. (However, see Downing (1959), Bennett (1974), and Slote (1978).) Some of its consequences are better known. It is instructive to see how the asymmetry of counterfactual dependence serves to explain these more familiar asymmetries.

Consider the temporal asymmetry of causation. Effects do not precede their causes, or at least not ordinarily. Elsewhere (Lewis, 1973c) I have advocated a counterfactual analysis of causation: (1) the relation of cause to effect consists in their being linked by a causal chain; (2) a causal chain is a certain kind of chain of counterfactual dependences; and (3) the counterfactuals involved are to be taken under the standard resolution of vagueness. If anything of the sort is right, there can be no backward causation without counterfactual dependence of past on future. Only where the asymmetry of counterfactual dependence breaks down can there possibly be exceptions to the predominant futureward direction of causation.

Consider also what I shall call the *assymmetry of openness*: the obscure contrast we draw between the 'open future' and the 'fixed past'. We tend to regard the future as a multitude of alternative possibilities, a 'garden of forking paths' in Borges's phrase, whereas we regard the past as a unique, settled, immutable

actuality. These descriptions scarcely wear their meaning on their
sleeves, yet do seem to capture some genuine and important
difference between past and future. What can it be? Several
hypotheses do not seem quite satisfactory.

Hypothesis 1: Asymmetry of Epistemic Possibility. Is it just
that we know more about the past than about the future, so that
the future is richer in epistemic possibilities? I think that's not it.
The epistemic contrast is a matter of degree, not a difference in
kind, and sometimes is not very pronounced. There is a great deal
we know about the future, and a great deal we don't know about
the past. Ignorance of history has not the least tendency to make
(most of) us think of the past as somewhat future-like, multiple,
open, or unfixed.

Hypothesis 2: Asymmetry of Multiple Actuality. Is it that all
our possible futures are equally actual? It is possible, I think, to
make sense of multiple actuality. Elsewhere I have argued for two
theses (in Lewis 1968 and 1970): (1) any inhabitant of any possible
world may truly call his own world actual; (2) we ourselves inhabit
this one world only, and are not identical with our other-worldly
counterparts. Both theses are controversial, so perhaps I am right
about one and wrong about the other. If (1) is true and (2) is false,
here we are inhabiting several worlds at once and truly calling all
of them actual. (Adams argues contrapositively in his (1974),
arguing from the denial of multiple actuality and the denial of (2)
to the denial of (1).) That makes sense, I think, but it gives us no
asymmetry. For in some sufficiently broad sense of possibility, we
have alternative possible pasts as well as alternative possible
futures. But if (1) is true and (2) is false, that means that *all* our
possibilities are equally actual, past as well as future.

Hypothesis 3: Asymmetry of Indeterminism. Is it that we think
of our world as governed by indeterministic laws of nature, so that
the actual past and present are nomically compossible with various
alternative future continuations? I think this hypothesis also fails.

For one thing, it is less certain that our world is indeterministic
than that there is an asymmetry between open future and fixed
past—whatever that may turn out to be. Our best reason to believe
in indeterminism is the success of quantum mechanics, but that

reason is none too good until quantum mechanics succeeds in giving a satisfactory account of processes of measurement.

For another thing, such reason as we have to believe in indeterminism is reason to believe that the laws of nature are indeterministic in both directions, so that the actual future and present are nomically compossible with various alternative pasts. If there is a process of reduction of the wave-packet in which a given superposition may be followed by any of many eigenstates, equally this is a process in which a given eigenstate may have been preceded by any of many superpositions. Again we have no asymmetry.

I believe that indeterminism is neither necessary nor sufficient for the asymmetries I am discussing. Therefore I shall ignore the possibility of indeterminism in the rest of this essay, and see how the asymmetries might arise even under strict determinism. A *deterministic* system of laws is one such that, whenever two possible worlds both obey the laws perfectly, then either they are exactly alike throughout all of time, or else they are not exactly alike through any stretch of time. They are alike always or never. They do not diverge, matching perfectly in their initial segments but not thereafter; neither do they converge. Let us assume, for the sake of the argument, that the laws of our actual world are in their sense deterministic.

(My definition of determinism derives from Montague (1962), but with modifications. (1) I prefer to avoid his use of mathematical constructions as *ersatz* possible worlds. But should you prefer *ersatz* worlds to the real thing, that will not matter for the purposes of this essay. (2) I take exact likeness of worlds at times as a primitive relation; Montague instead uses the relation of having the same complete description in a certain language, which he leaves unspecified.

My definition presupposes that we can identify stretches of time from one world to another. That presupposition is questionable, but it could be avoided at the cost of some complication.)

Hypothesis 4: Asymmetry of Mutability. Is it that we can change the future, but not the past? Not so, if 'change' has its literal meaning. It is true enough that if t is any past time, then we cannot bring about a difference between the state of affairs at t at time t_1 and the (supposedly changed) state of affairs at t at a later time t_2. But the pastness of t is irrelevant; the same would be true if t were present or future. Past, present, and future are alike immutable. What explains the impossibility is that such phrases as 'the state of affairs at t at t_1' or 'the state of affairs at t at t_2', if they mean anything, just mean: the state of affairs at t. Of course we cannot bring about a difference between that and itself.

Final Hypothesis: Asymmetry of Counterfactual Dependence. Our fourth hypothesis was closer to the truth than the others. What we *can* do by way of 'changing the future' (so to speak) is to bring it about that the future is the way it actually will be, rather than any of the other ways it would have been if we acted differently in the present. That is something like change. We make a difference. But it not literally change, since the difference we make is between actuality and other possibilities, not between successive actualities. The literal truth is just that the future depends counterfactually on the present. It depends, partly, on what we do now.

Likewise, something we ordinarily *cannot* do by way of 'changing the past' is to bring it about that the past is the way it actually was, rather than some other way it would have been if we acted differently in the present. The past would be the same, however we acted now. The past does not all depend on what we do now. It is counterfactually independent of the present.

In short, I suggest that the mysterious asymmetry between open future and fixed past is nothing else than the asymmetry of counterfactual dependence. The forking paths into the future—the actual one and all the rest—are the many alternative futures that would come about under various counterfactual suppositions about the present. The one actual, fixed past is the one past that would remain actual under this same range of suppositions.

TWO ANALYSES OF COUNTERFACTUALS

I hope I have now convinced you that an asymmetry of counterfactual dependence exists; that it has important consequences; and therefore that it had better be explained by any satisfactory semantic analysis of counterfactual conditionals. In the rest of this essay, I shall consider how that explanation ought to work.

It might work by fiat. It is an easy matter to build the asymmetry into an analysis of counterfactuals, for instance as follows.

ANALYSIS 1. *Consider a counterfactual 'If it were that A, then it would be that C' where A is entirely about affairs in a stretch of time t_A. Consider all those possible worlds w such that:*

(1) *A is true at w;*
(2) *w is exactly like our actual world at all times before a transition period beginning shortly before t_A;*
(3) *w conforms to the actual laws of nature at all times after t_A; and*
(4) *during t_A and the preceding transition periods, w differs no more from our actual world than it must to permit A to hold.*

The counterfactual is true if and only if C holds at every such world w.

In short, take the counterfactual present (if t_A is now), avoiding gratuitous difference from the actual present; graft it smoothly on to the actual past; let the situation evolve according to the actual laws; and see what happens. An analysis close to Analysis 1 has been put forward by Jackson (1977). Bennett (1974), Bowie (1979), and Weiner (1979) have considered, but not endorsed, similar treatments.

Analysis 1 guarantees the asymmetry of counterfactual dependence, with an exception for the immediate past. Let C be entirely about a stretch of time t_C. If t_C is later than t_A, then C may very well be false at our world, yet true at the worlds that meet the conditions listed in Analysis 1. We have the counterfactuals whereby the affairs of later times depend on those of earlier times. But if t_C is before t_A, and also before the transition period, then C holds at worlds that meet condition (2) if and only if C is true at our actual world. Since C is entirely about something that does not differ at all from one of these worlds to another, its truth value cannot vary. Therefore, except for cases in which t_C falls in the transition period, we have the counterfactuals whereby the affairs of earlier times are independent of those of later times.

We need the transition period, and should resist any temptation to replace (2) by the simpler and stronger

(2*) w is exactly like our actual world at all times before t_A.

(2*) makes for abrupt discontinuities. Right up to t, the match was stationary and a foot away from the striking surface. If it had been struck at t, would it have travelled a foot in no time at all? No; we should sacrifice the independence of the immediate past to provide an orderly transition from actual past to counterfactual present and future. That is not to say, however, that the immediate past depends on the present in any very definite way. There may be a variety of ways the transition might go, hence there may be no true counterfactuals that say in any detail how the immediate past would be if the present were different. I hope not, since if there were a definite and detailed dependence, it would be hard for me to say why some of this dependence should not be interpreted— wrongly, of course—as backward causation over short intervals of time in cases that are not at all extraordinary.

Analysis 1 seems to fit a wide range of counterfactuals; and it explains the asymmetry of counterfactual dependence, though with one rather plausible exception. Should we be content? I fear not, for two reasons.

First, Analysis 1 is built for a special case. We need a supposition about a particular time, and we need a counterfactual taken under the standard resolution of vagueness. What shall we do with suppositions such as

If kangaroos had no tails . . .

If gravity went by the inverse cube of distance . . .

If Collett had ever designed a Pacific . . .

which are not about particular times? Analysis 1 cannot cope as it stands, nor is there any obvious way to generalize it. At most we could give separate treatments of other cases, drawing on the cases handled by Analysis 1. (Jackson (1977) does this to some extent.) Analysis 1 is not much of a start toward a uniform treatment of counterfactuals in general.

Second, Analysis 1 gives us more of an asymmetry than we ought to want. No matter how special the circumstances of the case be, no provision whatever is made for actual or possible exceptions to the asymmetry (except in the transition period). That is too inflexible. Careful readers have thought they could make sense of stories of time travel (see my (1976) for further discussion); hard-headed psychical researchers have believed in precognition; speculative physicists have given serious consideration to tachyons, advanced potentials, and cosmological models with closed timelike curves. Most or all these phenomena would involve special exceptions to the normal asymmetry of counterfactual dependence. It will not do to declare them impossible a priori.

The asymmetry-by-fiat strategy of Analysis 1 is an instructive error, not a dead loss. Often we do have the right sort of supposition, the standard resolution of vagueness, and no extraordinary circumstances. Then Analysis 1 works as well as we could ask. The right analysis of counterfactuals needs to be both more general and more flexible. But also it needs to agree with Analysis 1 over the wide range of cases for which Analysis 1 succeeds.

The right general analysis of counterfactuals, in my opinion, is one based on comparative similarity of possible worlds, Roughly, a counterfactual is true if every world that makes the antecedent true without gratuitous departure from actuality is a world that also makes the consequent true. Such an analysis is given in my (1973*a*,*b*); here is one formulation.

ANALYSIS 2. *A counterfactual 'If it were that A, then it would be that C' is (non-vacuously) true if and only if some (accessible) world where both A and C are true is more similar to our actual world, overall, than is any world where A is true but C is false.*

This analysis if fully general: *A* can be a supposition of any sort. It is also extremely vague. Overall similarity among worlds is some sort of resultant of similarities and differences of many different kinds, and I have not said what system of weights or priorities should be used to squeeze these down into a single relation of overall similarity. I count that a virtue. Counterfactuals are both vague and various. Different resolutions of the vagueness of overall similarity are appropriate in different contexts.

Analysis 2 (plus some simple observations about the formal character of comparative similarity) is about all that can be said in full generality about counterfactuals. While not devoid of testable content—it settles some questions of logic—it does little to predict the truth values of particular counterfactuals in particular contexts. The rest of the study of counterfactuals is not fully general. Analysis 2 is only a skeleton. It must be fleshed out with an account of the appropriate similarity relation, and this will differ from context to context. Our present task is to see what sort of similarity relation can be combined with Analysis 2 to yield what I have called the standard resolution of vagueness: one that invalidates back-tracking arguments, one that yields an asymmetry of counterfactual dependence except perhaps under special circumstances, one that agrees with Analysis 1, our asymmetry-by-fiat analysis, whenever it ought to.

But first, a word of warning! Do not assume that just any respect of similarity you can think of must enter into the balance of overall similarity with positive weight. The point is obvious for some respects of similarity, if such they be. It contributes nothing to the similarity of two gemstones that both are grue. (To be *grue* is to be green and first examined before 2000 AD or blue and not first examined before 2000 AD.) But even some similarities in less gruesome respects may count for nothing. They may have zero weight, at least under some reasonable resolutions of vagueness. To what extent are the philosophical writings of Wittgenstein similar, overall, to those of Heidegger? I don't know. But here is one respect of comparison that does not enter into it at all, not even with negligible weight: the ratio of vowels to consonants.

(Bowie (1979) has argued that if some respects of comparison counted for nothing, my assumption of 'centring' in my (1973*a, b*) would be violated: worlds differing from ours only in the respects that don't count would be as similar to our world as our world is to itself. I reply that there may not be any worlds that differ from ours only in the respects that don't count, even if there are some respects that don't count. Respects of comparison may not be entirely separable. If the writings of two philosophers were alike in every respect that mattered, they would be word-for-word the same; then they would have the same ratio of vowels to consonants.)

And next, another word of warning! It is all too easy to make offhand similarity judgements and then assume that they will do for all purposes. But if we respect the extreme shiftiness and context-dependence of similarity, we will not set much store by offhand judgements. We will be prepared to distinguish between the similarity relations that guide our offhand explicit judgements and those that govern our counterfactuals in various contexts.

Indeed, unless we are prepared so to distinguish, Analysis 2 faces immediate refutation. Sometimes a pair of counterfactuals of the following form seem true: 'If A, the world would be very different; but if A and B, the world would not be very different.' Only if the similarity relation governing counterfactuals disagrees with that governing explicit judgements of what is 'very different' can such a pair be true under Analysis 2. (I owe this argument to Pavel Tichý and, in a slightly different form, to Richard J. Hall.) It seems to me no surprise, given the instability even of explicit judgements of similarity, that two different comparative similarity relations should enter into the interpretation of a single sentence.

The thing to do is not to start by deciding, once and for all, what we think about similarity of worlds, so that we can afterwards use these decisions to test Analysis 2. What that would test would be the combination of Analysis 2 with a foolish denial of the shiftiness of similarity. Rather, we must use what we know about the truth and falsity of counterfactuals to see if we can find some sort of similarity relation—not necessarily the first one that springs to mind—that combines with Analysis 2 to yield the proper truth conditions. It is this combination that can be tested against our knowledge of counterfactuals, not Analysis 2 by itself. In looking for a combination that will stand up to the test, we must use what we know about counterfactuals to find out about the appropriate similarity relation—not the other way around.

THE FUTURE SIMILARITY OBJECTION

Several people have raised what they take to be a serious objection against Analysis 2. (It was first brought to my attention by Michael Slote; it occurs, in various forms, in Bennett (1974), Bowie (1979), Creary and Hill (1975), Fine (1975), Jackson (1977), Richards

(1975), Schlossberger (1978), and Slote (1978). Kit Fine (1975: 452) states it as follows.

The counterfactual 'If Nixon had pressed the button there would have been a nuclear holocaust' is true or can be imagined to be so. Now suppose that there never will be a nuclear holocaust. Then that counterfactual is, on Lewis's analysis, very likely false. For given any world in which antecedent and consequent are both true it will be easy to imagine a closer world in which the antecedent is true and the consequent false. For we need only imagine a change that prevents the holocaust but that does not require such a great divergence from reality.

The presence or absence of a nuclear holocaust surely does contribute with overwhelming weight to some prominent similarity relations. (For instance, to one that governs the explicit judgement of similarity in the consequent of 'If Nixon had pressed the button, the world would be very different.') But the relation that governs the counterfactual may not be one of these. It may nevertheless be a relation of overall similarity—not because it is likely to guide our explicit judgements of similarity, but rather because it is a resultant, under some system of weights or priorities, of a multitude of relations of similarity in particular respects.

Let us take the supposition that Nixon pressed the button as implicitly referring to a particular time t—let it be the darkest moment of the final days. Consider w_0, a world that may or may not be ours. At w_0, Nixon does not press the button at t and no nuclear holocaust ever occurs. Let w_0 also be a world with deterministic laws, since we have confined our attention here to counterfactual dependence under determinism. Let w_0 also be a world that fits our worst fantasies about the button: there is such a button, it is connected to a fully automatic command-and-control system, the wired-in war plan consists of one big salvo, everything is in faultless working order, there is no way for anyone to stop the attack, and so on. Then I agree that Fine's counterfactual is true at w_0: if Nixon had pressed the button, there would have been a nuclear holocaust.

There are all sorts of worlds where Nixon (or rather, a counterpart of Nixon) presses the button at t. We must consider which of these differ least, under the appropriate similarity relation, from w_0. Some are non-starters. Those where the payload of the rockets consists entirely of confetti depart gratuitously from w_0 by any reasonable standards. The more serious candidates fall into several classes.

One class is typified by the world w_1. Until shortly before t, w_1 is exactly like w_0. The two match perfectly in every detail of particular fact, however minute. Shortly before t, however, the spatio-temporal region of perfect match comes to an end as w_1 and w_0 begin to diverge. The deterministic laws of w_0 are violated at w_1 in some simple, localized, inconspicuous way. A tiny miracle takes place. Perhaps a few extra neurons fire in some corner of Nixon's brain. As a result of this, Nixon presses the button. With no further miracles events take their lawful course and the two worlds w_1 and w_0 go their separate ways. The holocaust takes place. From that point on, at least so far as the surface of this planet is concerned, the two worlds are not even approximately similar in matters of particular fact. In short, the worlds typified by w_1 are the worlds that meet the conditions listed in Analysis 1, our asymmetry-by-fiat analysis. What is the case throughout these worlds is just what we think would have been the case if Nixon had pressed the button (assuming that we are at w_0, and operating under the standard resolution of vagueness). Therefore, the worlds typified by w_1 should turn out to be more similar to w_0, under the similarity relation we seek, than any of the other worlds where Nixon pressed the button.

(When I say that a miracle takes place at w_1, I mean that there is a violation of the laws of nature. But note that the violated laws are not laws of the same world where they are violated. That is impossible; whatever else a law may be, it is at least an exceptionless regularity. I am using 'miracles' to express a relation between different worlds. A miracle at w_1, relative to w_0, is a violation at w_1 of the laws of w_0, which are at best the almost-laws of w_1. The laws of w_1 itself, if such there be, do not enter into it.)

A second class of candidates is typified by w_2. This is a world completely free of miracles: the deterministic laws of w_0 are obeyed perfectly. However, w_2 differs from w_0 in that Nixon pressed the button. By definition of determinism, w_2 and w_0 are alike always or alike never, and they are not alike always.

Therefore, they are not exactly alike through any stretch of time. They differ even in the remote past. What is worse, there is no guarantee whatever that w_2 can be chosen so that the differences diminish and eventually become negligible in the more and more remote past. Indeed, it is hard to imagine how two deterministic worlds anything like ours could possibly remain just a little bit different for very long. There are altogether too many opportunities for little differences to give rise to bigger differences.

Certainly such worlds as w_2 should not turn out to be the most similar words to w_0 where Nixon pressed the button. That would lead to back-tracking unlimited. (And as Bennett (1974) observes, it would make counterfactuals useless; we know far too little to figure out which of them are true under a resolution of vagueness that validates very much back-tracking.) The lesson we learn by comparing w_1 and w_2 is that under the similarity relation we seek, a lot of perfect match of particular fact is worth a little miracle.

A third class of candidates is typified by w_3. This world begins like w_1. Until shortly before t, w_3 is exactly like w_0. Then a tiny miracle takes place, permitting divergence. Nixon presses the button at t. But there is no holocaust, because soon after t a second tiny miracle takes place, just as simple and localized and inconspicuous as the first. The fatal signal vanishes on its way from the button to the rockets. Thereafter events at w_3 take their lawful course. At least for a while, worlds w_0 and w_3 remain very closely similar in matters of particular fact. But they are no longer exactly alike. The holocaust has been prevented, but Nixon's deed has left its mark on the world w_3. There are his fingerprints on the button. Nixon is still trembling, wondering what went wrong—or right. His gin bottle is depleted. The click of the button has been preserved on tape. Light waves that flew out the window, bearing the image of Nixon's finger on the button, are still on their way into outer space. The wire is ever so slightly warmed where the signal current passed through it. And so on, and on, and on. The differences between w_3 and w_0 are many and varied, although no one of them amounts to much.

I should think that the close similarity between w_3 and w_0 could not last. Some of the little differences would give rise to bigger differences sooner or later. Maybe Nixon's memoirs are more sanctimonious at w_3 than at w_0. Consequently they have a different impact on the character of a few hundred out of the millions who read them. A few of these few hundred make different decisions at crucial moments of their lives—and we're off! But if you are not convinced that the differences need increase, no matter. My case will not depend on that.

If Analysis 2 is to succeed, such worlds as w_3 must not turn out to be the most similar worlds to w_0 where Nixon pressed the button. The lesson we learn by comparing w_1 and w_3 is that under the similarity relation we seek, close but approximate match of particular fact (especially if it is temporary) is not worth even a little miracle. Taking that and the previous lesson of w_2 together, we learn that perfect match of particular facts counts for much more than imperfect match, even if the imperfect match is good enough to give us similarity in respects that matter very much to us. I do not claim that this pre-eminence of perfect match is intuitively obvious. I do not claim that it is a feature of the similarity relations most likely to guide our explicit judgements. It is not; else the objection we are considering never would have been put forward. (See also the opinion survey reported by Bennett (1974).) But the pre-eminence of perfect match is a feature of some relations of overall similarity, and it must be a feature of any similarity relation that will meet our present needs.

A fourth class of candidates is typified by w_4. This world begins like w_1 and w_3. There is perfect match with w_0 until shortly before t, there is a tiny divergence miracle, the button is pressed. But there is a widespread and complicated and diverse second miracle after t. It not only prevents the holocaust but also removes all traces of Nixon's button-pressing. The cover-up job is miraculously perfect. Of course the fatal signal vanishes, just as at w_3, but there is much more. The fingerprint vanishes, and the sweat returns to Nixon's fingertip. Nixon's nerves are soothed, his memories are falsified, and so he feels no need of the extra martini. The click on the tape is replaced by innocent noises. The receding light waves cease to bear their incriminating images. The wire cools down, and not by heating its surroundings in the ordinary way. And so on, and on, and on. Not only are there no traces that any human detective could read; in every detail of particular fact, however minute, it is just as if the button-pressing had never been. The world w_4 and w_0 reconverge. They are exactly alike again soon after t, and exactly alike for evermore. All it takes is enough of a reconvergence miracle: one involving enough different sorts of violations of the laws of w_0, in enough different places. Because there are many different sorts of traces to be removed, and because the traces spread out rapidly, the cover-up job divides into very many parts. Each part requires a miracle at least on a par with the small miracle required to prevent the holocaust, or the one required to get the button pressed in the first place. Different sorts of unlawful process are needed to remove different sorts of traces; the miraculous vanishing of a pulse of current in a wire is not like the miraculous rearrangement of magnetized grains on a recording tape. The big miracle required for perfect reconvergence consists of a multitude of little miracles, spread out and diverse.

Such worlds as w_4 had better not turn out to be the most similar worlds to w_0 where Nixon pressed the button. The lesson we learn by comparing w_1 and w_4 is that under the similarity relation we seek, perfect match of particular fact even through the entire future is not worth a big, widespread, diverse miracle. Taking that and the lesson of w_2 together, we learn that avoidance of big miracles counts for much more than avoidance of little miracles. Miracles are not all equal. The all-or-nothing distinction between worlds that do and that do not ever violate the laws of w_0 is not sensitive enough to meet our needs.

This completes our survey of the leading candidates. There are other candidates, but they teach us nothing new. There are some worlds where approximate reconvergence to w_0 is secured by a second small miracle before t, rather than afterward as at w_3: Haig has seen fit to disconnect the button. Likewise there are worlds where a diverse and widespread miracle to permit perfect reconvergence takes place mostly before and during t: Nixon's fingers leave no prints, the tape recorder malfunctions, and so on.

Under the similarity relation we seek, w_1 must count as closer to w_0 than any of w_2, w_3, and w_4. That means that a similarity relation that combines with Analysis 2 to give the correct truth conditions for counterfactuals such as the one we have considered, taken under the standard resolution of vagueness, must be governed by the following system of weights or priorities.

(1) It is of the first importance to avoid big, widespread, diverse violations of law.

(2) It is of the second importance to maximize the spatio-temporal region throughout which perfect match of particular fact prevails.

(3) It is of the third importance to avoid even small, localized, simple violations of law.

(4) It is of little or no importance to secure approximate similarity of particular fact, even in matters that concern us greatly.

(It is a good question whether approximate similarities of particular fact should have little weight or none. Different cases come out differently, and I would like to know why. Tichý (1976) and Jackson (1977) give cases which appear to come out right under Analysis 2 only if approximate similarities count for nothing; but Morgenbesser has given a case, reported in Slote (1978), which appears to go the other way. This problem was first brought to my attention by Ernest Loevinsohn.)

Plenty of unresolved vagueness remains, of course, even after we have distinguished the four sorts of respect of comparison and ranked them in decreasing order of importance. But enough has been said to answer Fine's objection; and I think other versions of the future similarity objection may be answered in the same way.

THE ASYMMETRY OF MIRACLES

Enough has been said, also, to explain why there is an asymmetry of counterfactual dependence in such a case as we have just considered. If Nixon had pressed the button, the future would have been of the sort found at w_1: a future very different, in matters of particular fact, from that of w_0. The past also would have been of the sort found at w_1: a past exactly like that of w_0 until shortly before t. Whence came this asymmetry? It is not built into Analysis 2. It is not built into the standards of similarity that we have seen fit to combine with Analysis 2.

It came instead from an asymmetry in the range of candidates. We considered worlds where a small miracle permitted divergence from w_0. We considered worlds where a small miracle permitted approximate convergence to w_0 and worlds where a big miracle permitted perfect convergence to w_0. But we did not consider any worlds where a small miracle permitted perfect convergence to w_0. If we had, our symmetric standards of similarity would have favoured such worlds no less than w_1.

But are there any such worlds to consider? What could they be like: how could one small, localized, simple miracle possibly do all that needs doing? How could it deal with the fatal signal, the fingerprints, the memories, the tape, the light waves, and all the rest? I put it to you that it can't be done! Divergence from a world such as w_0 is easier than perfect convergence to it. Either takes a miracle, since w_0 is deterministic, but convergence takes very much more of a miracle. The asymmetry of counterfactual dependence arises because the appropriate standards of similarity, themselves symmetric, respond to this asymmetry of miracles.

It might be otherwise if w_0 were a different sort of world. I do not mean to suggest that the asymmetry of divergence and convergence miracles holds necessary or universally. For instance, consider a simple world inhabited by just one atom. Consider the worlds that differ from it in a certain way at a certain time. You will doubtless conclude that convergence to this world takes no more of a varied and widespread miracle than divergence from it. That means, if I am right, that no asymmetry of counterfactual dependence prevails at this world. Asymmetry-by-fiat analyses go wrong for such simple worlds. The asymmetry of miracles, and hence of counterfactual dependence, rests on a feature of worlds like w_0 which very simple worlds cannot share.

ASYMMETRY OF OVERDETERMINATION

Any particular fact about a deterministic world is predetermined throughout the past and post-determined throughout the future. At any time, past or future, it has at least one *determinant*: a minimal set of conditions jointly sufficient, given the laws of nature, for the fact in question. (Members of such a set may be causes of the fact, or traces of it, or neither.) The fact may have only one determinant at a given time, disregarding inessential differences in a way I shall not try to make precise. Or it may have two or more essentially different determinants at a given time, each sufficient by itself. If so, it is *overdetermined* at that time. Overdetermination is a matter of degree: there might be two determinants, or there might be very many more than two.

I suggest that what makes convergence take so much more of a miracle than divergence, in the case of a world such as w_0, is an asymmetry of overdetermination at such a world. How much overdetermination of later affairs by earlier ones is there at our world, or at a deterministic world which might be ours for all we know? We have our stock examples—the victim whose heart is simultaneously pierced by two bullets, and the like. But those cases seem uncommon. Moreover, the overdetermination is not very extreme. We have more than one determinant, but still not a very great number. Extreme overdetermination of earlier affairs by later ones, on the other hand, may well be more or less universal at a world like ours. Whatever goes on leaves widespread and varied traces at future times. Most of these traces are so minute or so dispersed or so complicated that no human detective could ever read them; but no matter, so long as they exist. It is plausible that very many simultaneous disjoint combinations of traces of any present fact are determinants thereof; there is no lawful way for the combination to have come about in the absence of the fact. (Even if a trace could somehow have been faked, traces of the absence of the requisite means of fakery may be included with the trace itself to form a set jointly sufficient for the fact in question). If so, the abundance of future traces makes for a like abundance of future determinants. We may reasonably expect overdetermination toward the past on an altogether different scale from the occasional case of mild overdetermination toward the future.

That would explain the asymmetry of miracles. It takes a miracle to break the link between any determinant and that which it determines. Consider our example. To diverge from w_0, a world where Nixon presses the button need only break the links whereby certain past conditions determine that he does not press it. To converge to w_0, a world where Nixon presses the button must break the links whereby a varied multitude of future conditions vastly overdetermine that he does not press it. The more overdetermination, the more links need breaking and the more widespread and diverse must a miracle be if it is to break them all.

An asymmetry noted by Popper (1956) is a special case of the asymmetry of overdetermination. There are processes in which a spherical wave expands outward from a point source to infinity. The opposite processes, in which a spherical wave contrasts inward from infinity and is absorbed, would obey the laws of nature equally well. But they never occur. A process of either sort exhibits extreme overdetermination in one direction. Countless tiny samples of the wave each determine what happens at the space-time point where the wave is emitted or absorbed. The processes that occur are the ones in which this extreme overdetermination goes toward the past, not those in which it goes toward the future. I suggest that the same is true more generally.

Let me emphasize, once more, that the asymmetry of overdetermination is a contingent, *de facto* matter. Moreover, it may be a local matter, holding near here but not in remote parts of time and space. If so, then all that rests on it—the asymmetries of miracles, of counterfactual dependence, of causation and openness—may likewise be local and subject to exceptions.

I regret that I do not know how to connect the several asymmetries I have discussed and the famous asymmetry of entropy.

REFERENCES

Adams, Robert M., 'Theories of Actuality', *Noûs*, 8 (1974): 211–31.

Bennett, Jonathan, review of Lewis (1973*a*), *Canadian Journal of Philosophy*, 4 (1974): 381–402.

Bowie, G. Lee, 'The Similarity Approach to Counterfactuals: Some Problems', *Noûs*, 13 (1979): 477–98.

Creary, Lewis, and Hill, Christopher, review of Lewis (1973*a*), *Philosophy of Science*, 42 (1975): 341–4.

Downing, P. B., 'Subjunctive Conditionals, Time Order, and Causation', *Proceedings of the Aristotelian Society* 59 (1959): 125–40.

Fine, Kit, review of Lewis (1973*a*), *Mind*, 84 (1975): 451–8.

Jackson, Frank, 'A Causal Theory of Counterfactuals', *Australasian Journal of Philosophy*, 55 (1977): 3–21.

Lewis, David, 'Counterpart Theory and Quantified Modal Logic', *Journal of Philosophy*, 65 (1968): 113–26.

—— 'Anselm and Actuality', *Noûs*, 4 (1970): 175–88.

—— *Counterfactuals* (Oxford: Blackwell, 1973*a*).

—— Counterfactuals and Comparative Possibility', *Journal of Philosophical Logic*, 2 (1973*b*): 418–46.

—— 'Causation', *Journal of Philosophy*, 70 (1973*c*): 556–67; repr. in Ernest Sosa (ed.), *Causation and Conditionals* (London: OUP, 1975).

—— 'The Paradoxes of Time Travel', *American Philosophical Quarterly*, 13 (1976): 145–52.

—— 'Scorekeeping in a Language Game', *Journal of Philosophical Logic*, 8 (1979): 339–59.

Montague, Richard, 'Deterministic Theories', in *Decisions, Values and Groups* (Oxford: Pergamon Press, 1962); repr. in Montague, *Formal Philosophy* (New Haven: Yale University Press, 1974).

Popper, Karl, 'The Arrow of Time', *Nature*, 177 (1956): 538.

Richards, Tom, 'The Worlds of David Lewis', *Australasian Journal of Philosophy*, 53 (1975): 105–18.

Schlossberger, Eugene, 'Similarity and Counterfactuals', *Analysis*, 38 (1978): 80–2.

Slote, Michael A., 'Time in Counterfactual', *Philosophical Review*, 87 (1978): 3–27.

Tichý, Pavel, 'A Counterexample to the Stalnaker–Lewis Analysis of Counterfactuals', *Philosophical Studies*, 29 (1976): 271–3.

Weiner, Joan, 'Counterfactual Conundrum', *Noûs*, 13 (1979): 499–509.

Postscripts

A. New Theory and Old?

From time to time I have been told, much to my surprise, that this essay presents a 'new theory' of counterfactuals, opposed to the 'old theory' I had advanced in earlier writings.[1]

[1] Principally *Counterfactuals* (Oxford, 1973); also 'Counterfactuals and Comparative Possibility', *Journal of Philosophical Logic* 2 (1973): 418–46.

I would have thought, rather, that the truth of the matter was as follows. In the earlier writings I said that counterfactuals were governed in their truth conditions by comparative overall similarity of worlds, but that there was no one precisely fixed relation of similarity that governed all counterfactuals always. To the contrary, the governing similarity relation was both vague and context-dependent. Different contexts would select different ranges of similarity relations, probably without ever reaching full determinacy. In this essay I reiterate all that. Then I focus attention on some contexts in particular, and on the range of similarity relations that apply in such contexts. Thereby I add to my earlier discussion, but do not at all subtract from it. Yet not a few readers think I have taken something back. Why?

The trouble seems to be that a comparative relation of the sort that I now put forward—one that turns to some extent on the size of regions of perfect match, and to some extent on the scarcity in one world of events that violate the laws of another—is not at all what my earlier writings led these readers to expect. But why not? I think the trouble has three sources.

One source, I think, is entrenched doubt about the very idea of similarity. It is widely thought that every shared property, in the most inclusive possible sense of that word, is prima facie a respect of similarity: that things can be similar in respect of satisfying the same miscellaneously disjunctive formula, or in respect of belonging to the same utterly miscellaneous class. If so, then there's little to be said about comparative similarity. Any two things, be they two peas in a pod or be they a raven and a writing-desk, are alike in infinitely many respects and unlike in equally many.

Against this scepticism, I observed that we undeniably do make judgements of comparative overall similarity. And readers took the point—but in far too limited a way. 'Yes,' I think they thought, 'there is indeed a comparative relation that is special in the way it governs our explicit snap judgements. We can scarcely doubt that—we have an operational test. But leave that firm ground, and we're as much at sea as ever. Apart from that one special case, we do not understand how one shared property can be more or less of a similarity-maker than another; or how it can be that some orderings are comparisons of similarity and others aren't.' And so

I speak of similarity, and these sceptics understand me in the only way they can: they seize on the one discrimination they regard as unproblematic, since they can understand how to pick out one similarity relation operationally in terms of snap judgements. Then they observe, quite rightly, that the 'similarity relation' I now put forward as governing counterfactuals isn't *that* one.

The right lesson would have been more far-reaching. Our ability to make the snap judgement is one reason, among others, to reject the sceptical, egalitarian orthodoxy. It just isn't so that all properties (in the most inclusive sense) are equally respects of similarity. Then it is by no means empty to say as I do that a relation of overall similarity is any weighted resultant of respects of similarity and dissimilarity. (To which I add that the weighting might be non-Archimedean; that is, we might have a system of priorities rather than trade-offs.) Here we have a class of comparative relations that can go far beyond the one that governs the snap judgements; and that yet falls far short of the class delineated just by the formal character of comparative similarity.

Once we reject egalitarianism, what shall we put in its place? An analysis, somehow, of the difference between those properties that are respects of similarity and those that aren't? A primitive distinction? A distinction built into our ontology, in the form of a denial of the very existence of the alleged properties that aren't respects of similarity? A fair question; but one it is risky to take up, lest we put the onus on the wrong side. What we know best on this subject, I think, is that egalitarianism is prima facie incredible. We are entitled to reject it without owing any developed alternative.[2]

A second source of trouble, I suspect, is that some readers think of imperfect similarity always as imperfect match, and neglect the case of perfect match over a limited region. To illustrate, consider three locomotives: 2818, 4018, and 6018. 2818 and 4018 are alike

---

[2] In this area I am indebted to Michael Slote; I long ago defended the egalitarian orthodoxy against his good sense, not entirely to my own satisfaction. More recently I have benefited from extensive discussions with D. M. Armstrong, which have helped me to distinguish and relate the question of egalitarianism and the traditional problem of universals. For further discussion, see my 'New Work for a Theory of Universals', *Australasian Journal of Philosophy*, 61 (1983): 343–77.

in this way: they have duplicate boilers, smoke-boxes, and fire-boxes (to the extent that two of a kind from an early twentieth-century production line ever are duplicates), and various lesser fittings also are duplicated. But 2818 is a slow, small-wheeled, two-cylindered 2–8–0 coal-hauler—plenty of pull, little speed—whereas 4018 is the opposite, a fast, large-wheeled, four-cylindered 4–6–0 express passenger locomotive. So is 6018; but 6018, unlike 2818, has few if any parts that duplicate the corresponding parts of 4018. (6018 is a scaled-up and modernized version of 4018.) Anyone can see the way in which 6018 is more similar to 4018 than 2818 is. But I would insist that there is another way of comparing similarity, equally deserving of that name, on which the duplicate standard parts make 2818 the stronger candidate.

A third source of trouble may be a hasty step from similarity with respect to laws of nature to similarity *of* the laws—or, I might even say, to similarity of the linguistic codifications of laws. Consider three worlds. The first has some nice, elegant system of uniform laws. The second does not: the best way to write down its laws would be to write down the laws of the first world, then to mutilate them by sticking in clauses to permit various exceptions in an unprincipled fashion. Yet almost everything that ever happens in the second world conforms perfectly to the laws of the first. The third world does have a nice, elegant, uniform system; its laws resemble those of the first world except for a change of sign here, a switch from inverse square to inverse cube there, and a few other such minor changes. Consequently, the third world constantly violates the laws of the first; any little thing that goes on in the third would be prohibited by the laws of the first. Focus on the linguistic codification of the laws, and it may well seem that the third world resembles the first with respect to laws far more than the second does. But I would insist that there is another way of comparing similarity with respect to laws, equally deserving of that name, on which the second world resembles the first very well, and the third resembles the first very badly. That is the way that neglects linguistic codifications, and looks instead at the classes of lawful and of outlawed events.

B. Big and Little Miracles

It has often been suggested, not often by well-wishers, that I should distinguish big and little miracles thus: big miracles are other-worldly events that break many of the laws that actually obtain, whereas little miracles break only a few laws. I think this proposal is thoroughly misguided. It is a good thing that I never endorsed it, and a bad thing that I am sometimes said to have endorsed it.

Consider two cases. (1) By 'laws' we might mean *fundamental* laws: those regularities that would come out as axioms in a system that was optional among true systems in its combination of simplicity and strength. If the hopes of physics come true, there may be only a few of these fundamental laws altogether. Then *no* miracle violates many fundamental laws; *any* miracle violates the Grand Unified Field equation, the Schrödinger equation, or another one of the very few, very sweeping fundamental laws.

Or (2) by 'laws' we might rather mean fundamental or *derived* laws: those regularities that would come out as axioms *or theorems* in an optimal system. Then any miracle violates infinitely many laws; and again it doesn't seem that big miracles violate more laws than little ones.

It's a blind alley to count the violated laws. What to do instead? Take the laws collectively; distinguish lawful events from unlawful ones. (For example, lawful pair-annihilations with radiation from unlawful quiet disappearings of single particles without a trace.) In whatever way events can be spread out or localized, unlawful events can be spread out or localized. In whatever way several events can be alike or varied, several unlawful events can be alike or varied. In whatever way we can distinguish one simple event from many simple events, or from one complex event consisting of many simple parts, we can in particular distinguish one simple unlawful event from many, or from one complex event consisting of many simple unlawful parts. A big miracle consists of many little miracles together, preferably not all alike. What makes the big miracle more of a miracle is not that it breaks more laws; but that it is divisible into many and varied parts, any one of which is on a par with the little miracle.

C. Worlds to which Convergence is Easy

Begin with our base world w_0, the deterministic world something like our own. Proceed to w_1, the world which starts out just like w_0, diverges from it by a small miracle, and therefore evolves in accordance with the laws of w_0. Now extrapolate the later part of w_1 backward in accordance with the laws of w_0 to obtain what I shall call a *Bennett world*.[3] This Bennett world is free of miracles, relative to w_0. That is, it conforms perfectly to the laws of w_0; and it seems safe to suppose that these are the laws of the Bennett world also. From a certain time onward, the Bennett world and world w_1 match perfectly, which is to say that w_1 converges to the Bennett world. Further, this convergence is accomplished by a small miracle: namely the very same small miracle whereby w_1 diverges from w_0. For we had already settled that this small divergence miracle was the only violation by w_1 of the laws of w_0, and those are the same as the laws of the Bennett world. Thus the Bennett world is a world to which convergence is easy, since w_1 converges to it by only a small miracle.

What then becomes of my asymmetry of miracles? I said that 'divergence from such a world as w_0 is easier than perfect convergence to it. Either takes a miracle . . . but convergence takes very much more of a miracle.' To be sure, I said that it might be otherwise for a different sort of world. But the Bennett world seems to be a world of the same sort as w_0. After all, it has the very same laws.

No. Same laws are not enough. If there are *de facto* asymmetries of time, not written into the laws, they could be just what it takes to make the difference between a world to which the asymmetry of miracles applies and a world to which it does not; that is, between a world like w_0 (or ours) to which convergence is difficult and a Bennett world to which convergence is easy. Consider, for instance, Popper's asymmetry.[4] That is not a matter of law, so it could obtain in one and not the other of two worlds with exactly

[3] So-called to acknowledge my indebtedness to Jonathan Bennett, who first brought the possibility of such worlds to my attention. See his 'Counterfactuals and Temporal Direction', *Philosophical Review*, 93 (1984): 57–91, esp. 63–4. I am indebted also to David Sanford for helpful correspondence on the subject.

[4] Karl Popper, 'The Arrow of Time', *Nature*, 177 (1956): 538.

the same laws. Likewise in general for the asymmetry of overdetermination.

A Bennett world is deceptive. After the time of its convergence with w_1, it contains exactly the same apparent traces of its past that w_1 does; and the traces to be found in w_1 are such as to record a past exactly like that of the base world w_0. So the Bennett world is full of traces that seem to record a past like that of w_0. But the past of the Bennett world is not like the past of w_0: under the laws that are common to both worlds, the past of the Bennett world predetermines that Nixon presses the button, whereas the past of w_0 predetermines that he does not. Further, we cannot suppose that the two pasts are even close. As I noted in discussing world w_2, there is no reason to think that two lawful histories can, before diverging, remain very close throughout a long initial segment of time. To constrain a history to be lawful in its own right, and to constrain it also to stay very close to a given lawful history for a long time and then swerve off, is to impose two very strong constraints. There is not the slightest reason to think the two constraints are compatible.

To be sure, any complete cross-section of the Bennett world, taken in full detail, is a truthful record of its past; because the Bennett world is lawful, and its laws are *ex hypothesi* deterministic (in both directions), and any complete cross-section of such a world is lawfully sufficient for any other. But in a world like w_0, one that manifests the ordinary *de facto* asymmetries, we also have plenty of very *incomplete* cross-sections that post-determine incomplete cross-sections at earlier times. It is these incomplete post-determinants that are missing from the Bennett world. Not throughout its history; but the post-determination across the time of convergence with w_1 is deficient.

Popper's pond is deceptive in just the same way. Ripples rise around the edge; they contract inward and get higher; when they reach the centre a stone flies out of the water—and then the pond is perfectly calm. What has happened is the time-reversed mirror image of what ordinarily happens when a stone falls into a pond. It is no less lawful; the violated asymmetries are not a matter of law. There would be no feasible way to detect what had happened. For there would be no trace on the water of its previous agitation;

and the rock would be dry, the air would bear no sound of a splash, the nearby light would bear no tell-tale image, . . . In short, a perfect cover-up job—and without any miracle! But not a world like w_0, and not in a world like ours. To be sure, if the laws are deterministic, the event is post-determined by any complete cross-section afterward. But we lack the usual abundance of lesser post-determinants.

IV

PROBABILITIES OF CONDITIONALS
AND CONDITIONAL PROBABILITIES*

DAVID LEWIS

THE truthful speaker wants not to assert falsehoods, wherefore he
is willing to assert only what he takes to be very probably true. He
deems it permissible to assert that A only if $P(A)$ is sufficiently
close to 1, where P is the probability function that represents his
system of degrees of belief at the time. Assertability goes by
subjective probability.

At least, it does in most cases. But Ernest Adams has pointed
out an apparent exception.[1] In the case of ordinary indicative
conditionals, it seems that assertability goes instead by the
conditional subjective probability of the consequent, given the
antecedent. We define the conditional probability function $P(-/-)$
by a quotient of absolute probabilities, as usual:

(1) $P(C/A) = \mathrm{df}\ P(CA)/P(A)$, if $P(A)$ is positive.

(If the denominator $P(A)$ is zero, we let $P(C/A)$ remain
undefined.) The truthful speaker evidently deems it permissible to
assert the indicative conditional that if A, then C (for short,
$A \to C$) only if $P(C/A)$ is sufficiently close to 1. Equivalently: only
if $P(CA)$ is sufficiently much greater than $P(\bar{C}A)$.

Adams offers two sorts of evidence. There is direct evidence,

David Lewis, 'Probabilties of Conditionals and Conditional Probabilities', first
published in *Philosophical Review*, 85 (1976): 297–315, reprinted with postscript in
Philosophical Papers, vol. ii (OUP, 1986). Used by permission of the author.

* An earlier version of this paper was presented at a Canadian Philosophical
Association colloquium on probability semantics for conditional logic at Montreal
in June 1972. I am grateful to many friends and colleagues, especially to Ernest
Adams and Robert Stalnaker, for valuable comments.

[1] Ernest Adams, 'The Logic of Conditionals', *Inquiry*, 8 (1965): 166–97; and
'Probability and the Logic of Conditionals', *Aspects of Inductive Logic*, ed. Jaakko
Hintikka and Patrick Suppes (Dordrecht, 1966). I shall not here consider Adam's
subsequent work, which differs at least in emphasis.

obtained by contrasting cases in which we would be willing or unwilling to assert various indicative conditionals. There also is indirect evidence, obtained by considering various inferences with indicative conditional premisses or conclusions. The ones that seem valid turn out to be just the ones that preserve assertability, if assertability goes by conditional probabilities for conditionals and by absolute probabilities otherwise.[2] Our judgements of validity are not so neatly explained by various rival hypothesis. In particular, they do not fit the hypothesis that the inferences that seem valid are just the ones that preserve truth if we take the conditionals as truth-functional.

Adams has convinced me. I shall take it as established that the assertability of an ordinary indicative conditional $A \rightarrow C$ does indeed go by the conditional subjective probability $P(C/A)$. But why? Why not rather by the absolute probability $P(A \rightarrow C)$?

The most pleasing explanation would be as follows: The assertability of $A \rightarrow C$ does go by $P(A \rightarrow C)$ after all; indicative conditionals are not exceptional. But also it goes by $P(C/A)$, as Adams says, for the meaning of $\rightarrow$ is such as to guarantee that $P(A \rightarrow C)$ and $P(C/A)$ are always equal (if the latter is defined). For short: *probabilities of conditionals are conditional probabilities*. This thesis has been proposed by various authors.[3]

If this is so, then of course the ordinary indicative conditional $A \rightarrow C$ cannot be the truth-functional conditional $A \supset C$. $P(A \supset C)$ and $P(C/A)$ are equal only in certain extreme cases. The indicative conditional must be something else: call it a *probability conditional*. We may or may not be able to give truth conditions for probability conditionals, but at least we may discover a good deal about their meaning and their logic just by using what we know about conditional probabilities.

Alas, this most pleasing explanation cannot be right. We shall see that there is no way to interpret a conditional connective so

[2] More precisely, just the ones that satisfy this condition: for any positive ε there is a positive δ such that if any probability function gives each premiss an assertability within δ of 1 then it also gives the conclusion an assertability within δ of 1.

[3] Richard Jeffrey, 'If' (abstract), *Journal of Philosophy*, 61 (1964): 702–3; Brian Ellis, 'An Epistemological Concept of Truth', *Contemporary Philosophy in Australia*, ed. Robert Brown and C. D. Rollins, London, 1969; Robert Stalnaker, 'Probability and Conditionals', *Philosophy of Science*, 37 (1970): 64–80. We shall consider later whether to count Adams as another adherent of the thesis.

that, with sufficient generality, the probabilities of conditionals will equal the appropriate conditional probabilities. If there were, probabilities of conditionals could serve as links to establish relationships between the probabilities of non-conditionals, but the relationships thus established turn out to be incorrect. The quest for a probability conditional is futile, and we must admit that assertability does not go by absolute probability in the case of indicative conditionals.

PRELIMINARIES

Suppose we are given an interpreted formal language equipped at least with the usual truth-functional connectives and with the further connective $\rightarrow$. These connectives may be used to compound any sentences in the language. We think of the interpretation as giving the truth value of every sentence at every possible world. Two sentences are *equivalent* iff they are true at exactly the same worlds, and *incompatible* iff there is no world where both are true. One sentence *implies* another iff the second is true at every world where the first is true. A sentence is *necessary, possible, or impossible* iff it is true at all worlds, at some, or at none. We may think of a probability function P as an assignment of numerical values to all sentences of this language, obeying these standard laws of probability:

(2) $1 \geqslant P(A) \geqslant 0,$

(3) if A and B are equivalent, then $P(A) = P(B),$

(4) if A and B are incompatible, then $P(A \vee B) = P(A) + P(B),$

(5) if A is necessary, then $P(A) = 1.$

The definition (1) gives us the multiplication law for conjunctions.

Whenever $P(B)$ is positive, there is a probability function P' such that $P'(A)$ always equals $P(A/B)$; we say that P' *comes from P by conditionalizing on B.* A class of probability functions is *closed under conditionalizing* iff any probability function that comes by conditionalizing from one in the class is itself in the class.

Suppose that $\rightarrow$ is interpreted in such a way that, for some particular probability function P, and for any sentences A and C,

(6) $P(A \rightarrow C) = P(C/A),$ if $P(A)$ is positive;

iff so, let us call → a *probability conditional for P*. Iff → is a probability conditional for every probability function in some class of probability functions, then let us call → a *probability conditional* for the class. And iff → is a probability conditional for all probability functions, so that (6) holds for any *P*, *A*, and *C*, then let us call → a *universal probability conditional*, or simply a *probability conditional*.

Observe that if → is a universal probability conditional, so that (6) holds always, then (7) also holds always:

(7) $P(A{\rightarrow}C/B) = P(C/AB)$, if $P(AB)$ is positive.

To derive (7), apply (6) to the probability function *P'* that comes from *P* by conditionalizing on *B*; such a *P'* exists if $P(AB)$ and hence also $P(B)$ are positive. Then (7) follows by several applications of (1) and the equality between $P'(-)$ and $P(-/B)$. In the same way, if → is a probability conditional for a class of probability functions, and if that class is closed under conditionalizing, then (7) holds for any probability function *P* in the class, and for any *A* and C. (It does not follow, however, that if (6) holds for a particular probability function *P*, then (7) holds for the same *P*.)

FIRST TRIVIALITY RESULT

Suppose by way of *reductio* that → is a universal probability conditional. Take any probability function *P* and any sentences *A* and *C* such that $P(AC)$ and $P(A\bar{C})$ both are positive. Then $P(A)$, $P(C)$, and $P(\bar{C})$ also are positive. By (6) we have:

(8) $P(A \rightarrow C) = P(C/A)$.

By (7), taking *B* as *C* or as $\bar{C}$ and simplifying the right-hand side, we have:

(9) $P(A \rightarrow C/C) = P(C/AC) = 1$,
(10) $P(A \rightarrow C/\bar{C}) = P(C/A\bar{C}) = 0$.

For any sentence *D*, we have the familiar expansion by cases:

(11) $P(D) = P(D/C) \cdot P(C) + P(D/\bar{C}) \cdot P(\bar{C})$.

In particular, take D as $A \to C$. Then we may substitute (8), (9), and (10) into (11) to obtain:

(12) $P(C/A) = 1 \cdot P(C) + 0 \cdot P(\bar{C}) = P(C)$.

With the aid of the supposed probability conditional, we have reached the conclusion that if only $P(AC)$ and $P(A\bar{C})$ both are positive, then A and C are probabilistically independent under P. That is absurd. For instance, let P be the subjective probability function of someone about to throw what he takes to be a fair die, let A mean that an even number comes up, and let C mean that the six comes up. $P(AC)$ and $P(A\bar{C})$ are positive. But, *contra* (12), $P(C/A)$ is ½ and $P(C)$ is ⅙; A and C are not independent. More generally, let C, D, and E be possible but pairwise incompatible. There are probability functions that assign positive probability to all three: let P be any such. Let A be the disjunctive $C \vee D$. Then $P(AC)$ and $P(A\bar{C})$ are positive but $P(C/A)$ and $P(C)$ are unequal.

Our supposition that $\to$ is a universal probability conditional has led to absurdity, but not quite to contradiction. If the given language were sufficiently weak in expressive power, then our conclusion might be unobjectionable. There might not exist any three possible but pairwise incompatible sentences to provide a counter-example to it. For all I have said, such a weak language might be equipped with a universal probability conditional. Indeed, consider the extreme case of a language in which there are none but necessary sentences and impossible ones. For this very trivial language, the truth-functional conditional itself is a universal probability conditional.

If an interpreted language cannot provide three possible but pairwise incompatible sentences, then we may justly call it a *trivial language*. We have proved this theorem: *any language having a universal probability conditional is a trivial language.*

SECOND TRIVIALITY RESULT

Since our language is not a trivial one, our indicative conditional must not be a universal probability conditional. But all is not yet lost for the thesis that probabilities of conditionals are conditional probabilities. A much less than universal probability conditional might be good enough. Our task, after all, concerns subjective probability: probability functions used to represent people's systems of beliefs. We need not assume, and indeed it seems rather implausible, that any probability function whatever represents a system of beliefs that it is possible for someone to have. We might set aside those probability functions that do not. If our indicative conditional were a probability conditional for a limited class of probability functions, and if that class were inclusive enough to contain any probability function that might ever represent a speaker's system of beliefs, that would suffice to explain why assertability of indicative conditionals goes by conditional subjective probability.

Once we give up on universality, it may be encouraging to find that probability conditionals for particular probability functions, at least, commonly do exist. Given a probability function P, we may be able to tailor the interpretation of $\rightarrow$ to fit.[4] Suppose that for any A and C there is some B such that $P(B/\bar{A})$ and $P(C/A)$ are equal if both defined; this should be a safe assumption when P is a probability function rich enough to represent someone's system of beliefs. If for any A and C we arbitrarily choose such a B and let $A \rightarrow C$ be interpreted as equivalent to $AC \vee \bar{A}B$, then $\rightarrow$ is a probability conditional for P. But such piecemeal tailoring does not yet provide all that we want. Even if there is a probability conditional for each probability function in a class, it does not follow that there is one probability conditional for the entire class. Different members of the class might require different interpretations of $\rightarrow$ to make the probabilities of conditionals and the conditional probabilities come out equal. But presumably our indicative conditional has a fixed interpretation, the same for speakers with different beliefs, and for one speaker before and after a change in his beliefs. Else how are disagreements about a conditional possible, or changes of mind? Our question, therefore, is whether the indicative conditional might have one fixed

<hr />

[4] I am indebted to Bas van Fraassen for this observation, He has also shown that by judicious selection of the Bs we can give $\rightarrow$ some further properties that might seem appropriate to a conditional connective. See Bas van Fraassen, 'Probabilities of Conditionals', in *Foundations of Probability Theory, Statistical Inference and Statistical Theories of Science*, i, ed. W. Harper and C. A. Hooker (Dordrecht, 1976): 261.

interpretation that makes it a probability conditional for the entire class of all those probability functions that represent possible systems of beliefs.

This class, we may reasonably assume, is closed under conditionalizing. Rational change of belief never can take anyone to a subjective probability function outside the class; and there are good reasons why the change of belief that results from coming to know an item of new evidence should take place by conditionalizing on what was learned.[5]

Suppose by way of *reductio* that $\rightarrow$ is a probability conditional for a class of probability functions, and that the class is closed under conditionalizing. The argument proceeds much as before. Take any probability function P in the class and any sentences A and C such that $P(AC)$ and $P(A\bar{C})$ are positive. Again we have (6) and hence (8); (7) and hence (9) and (10); (11) and hence by substitution (12): $P(C/A)$ and $P(C)$ must be equal. But if we take three pairwise incompatible sentences C, D, and E such that $P(C)$, $P(D)$, and $P(E)$ are all positive and if we take A as the disadjunction $C \vee D$, then $P(AC)$ and $P(A\bar{C})$ are positive but $P(C/A)$ and $P(C)$ are unequal. So there are no such three sentences. Further, P has at most four different values. Else there would be two different values of P, x and y, strictly intermediate between 0 and 1 and such that $x + y \neq 1$. But then if $P(F) = x$ *and* $P(G) = y$ it follows that at least three of $P(FG)$, $P(\bar{F}G)$, $P(F\bar{G})$, and $P(\bar{F}\bar{G})$ are positive, which we have seen to be impossible.

If a probability function never assigns positive probability to more than two incompatible alternatives, and hence is at most four-valued, then we may call it *a trivial probability function*. We have proved this theorem: *if a class of probability functions is closed under conditionalizing, then there can be no probability conditional for that class unless the class consists entirely of trivial probability functions.* Since some probability functions that represent possible systems of belief are not trivial, our indicative conditional is not a probability conditional for the class of all such probability functions. Whatever it may mean, it cannot possibly have a meaning such as to guarantee, for all possible subjective

[5] These reasons may be found in Paul Teller, 'Conditionalization and Observation', *Synthese*, 26 (1973): 218–58.

probability functions at once, that the probabilities of conditionals equal the corresponding conditional probabilities. There is no such meaning to be had. We shall have to grant that the assertability of indicative conditionals does not go by absolute probability, and seek elsewhere for an explanation of the fact that it goes by conditional probability instead.

THE INDICATIVE CONDITIONAL AS
NON-TRUTH-VALUED

Assertability goes in general by probability because probability is probability of truth and the speaker wants to be truthful. If this is not so for indicative conditionals, perhaps the reason is that they have no truth values, no truth conditions, and no probabilities of truth. Perhaps they are governed not by a semantic rule of truth but by a rule of assertability.

We might reasonably take it as the goal of semantics to specify our prevailing rules of assertability. Most of the time, to be sure, that can best be done by giving truth conditions plus the general rule that speakers should try to be truthful, or in other words that assertability goes by probability of truth. But sometimes the job might better be done another way: for instance, by giving truth conditions for antecedents and for consequents, but not for whole conditionals, plus the special rule that the assertability of an indicative conditional goes by the conditional subjective probability of the consequent given the antecedent. Why not? We are surely free to institute a new sentence form, without truth conditions, to be used for making it known that certain of one's conditional subjective probabilities are close to 1. But then it should be no surprise if we turn out to have such a device already.

Adams himself seems to favour this hypothesis about the semantics of indicative conditionals.[6] He advises us, at any rate, to set aside questions about their truth and to concentrate instead on their assertability. There is one complication: Adams does *say* that conditional probabilities are probabilities of conditionals. Nevertheless he does not mean by this that the indicative conditional is what I have called here a probability conditional; for

[6] 'The Logic of Conditionals.'

he does not claim that the so-called 'probabilities' of conditionals are probabilities of truth, and neither does he claim that they obey the standard laws of probability. They are probabilities only in name. Adams's position is therefore invulnerable to my triviality results, which were proven by applying standard laws of probability to the probabilities of conditionals.

Would it make sense to suppose that indicative conditionals *do not* have truth values, truth conditions, or probabilities of truth, but that they *do* have probabilities that obey the standard laws? Yes, but only if we first restate those laws to get rid of all mention of truth. We must continue to permit unrestricted compounding of sentences by means of the usual connectives, so that the domain of our probability functions will be a Boolean algebra (as is standardly required); but we can no longer assume that these connectives always have their usual truth-functional inter-pretations, since truth-functional compounding of non-truth-valued sentences makes no sense. Instead we must choose some deductive system—any standard formalization of sentential logic will do—and characterize the usual connectives by their deductive role in this system. We must replace mention of equivalence, incompatibility, and necessity in laws (3) through (5) by mention of their syntactic substitutes in the chosen system: inter-deducibility, deductive inconsistency, and deducibility. In this way we could describe the probability functions for our language without assuming that all probabilities of sentences, or even any of them, are probabilities of truth. We could still hold that assertability goes in most cases by probability, though we could no longer restate this as a rule that speakers should try to tell the truth.

Merely to deny that probabilities of conditionals are probabilities of truth, while retaining all the standard laws of probability in suitably adapted form, would not yet make it safe to revive the thesis that probabilities of conditionals not conditional probabilities. It was not the connection between truth and probability that led to my triviality results, but only the application of standard probability theory to the probabilities of conditionals. The proofs could just as well have used versions of the laws that mentioned deducibility instead of truth. Whoever still wants to say that probabilities of conditionals are conditional probabilities had better also employ a non-standard calculus of 'probabilities'. He might drop the requirement that the domain of a probability function is a Boolean algebra, in order to exclude conjunctions with conditional conjuncts from the language. Or he might instead limit (4), the law of additivity, refusing to apply it when the disjuncts A and B contain conditional conjuncts. Either manœuvre would block my proofs. But if it be granted that the 'probabilities' of conditionals do not obey the standard laws, I do not see what is to be gained by insisting on calling them 'probabilities'. It seems to me that a position like Adams's might best be expressed by saying that indicative conditionals have neither truth values nor probabilities, and by introducing some neutral term such as 'assertability' or 'value' which denotes the probability of truth in the case of non-conditionals and the appropriate conditional probability in the case of indicative conditionals.

I have no conclusive objection to the hypothesis that indicative conditionals are non-truth-valued sentences, governed by a special rule of assertability that does not involve their non-existent probabilities of truth. I have an inconclusive objection, however: the hypothesis requires too much of a fresh start. It burdens us with too much work still to be done, and wastes too much that has been done already. So far, we have nothing but a rule of assertability for conditionals with truth-valued antecedents and consequents. But what about compound sentences that have such conditionals as constituents? We think we know how the truth conditions for compound sentences of various kinds are determined by the truth conditions of constituent subsentences, but this knowledge would be useless if any of those subsentences lacked truth conditions. Either we need new semantic rules for many familiar connectives and operators when applied to indicative conditionals—perhaps rules of truth, perhaps special rules of assertability like the rule for conditionals themselves—or else we need to explain away all seeming examples of compound sentences with conditional constituents.

THE INDICATIVE CONDITIONAL AS
TRUTH-FUNCTIONAL

Fortunately a more conservative hypothesis is at hand. H. P. Grice has given an elegant explanation of some qualitative rules governing the assertability of indicative conditionals.[7] It turns out that a quantitative hypothesis based on Grice's ideas gives us just what we want: the rule that assertability goes by conditional subjective probability.

According to Grice, indicative conditionals *do* have truth values, truth conditions, and probabilities of truth. In fact, the indicative conditional $A \rightarrow C$ is simply the truth-functional conditional $A \supset C$. But the assertability of the truth-functional conditional does not go just by $P(A \supset C)$, its subjective probability of truth. It goes by the resultant of that and something else.

It may happen that a speaker believes a truth-functional conditional to be true, yet he ought not to assert it. Its assertability might be diminished for various reasons, but let us consider one in particular. The speaker ought not to assert the conditional if he believes it to be true predominantly because he believes its antecedent to be false, so that its probability of truth consists mostly of its probability of vacuous truth. In this situation, why assert the conditional instead of denying the antecedent? It is pointless to do so. And if it is pointless, then also it is worse than pointless: it is misleading. The hearer, trusting the speaker not to assert pointlessly, will assume that he has not done so. The hearer may then wrongly infer that the speaker has additional reason to believe that the conditional is true, over and above his disbelief in the antecedent.

This consideration detracts from the assertability of $A \supset C$ to the extent that both of two conditions hold: first, that the probability $P(\bar{A})$ of vacuity is high; and second, that the probability $P(\bar{C}A)$ of falsity is a large fraction of the total probability $P(A)$ of non-vacuity. The product

(13) $P(\bar{A}) \cdot (P(\bar{C}A)/P(A))$

[7] H. Grice, 'Logic and Conversation', William James Lectures, given at Harvard University in 1967, and repr. in this volume (Essay VIII).

of the degrees to which the two conditions are met is therefore a suitable measure of diminution of assertability. Taking the probability $P(A \supset C)$ of truth, and subtracting the diminution of assertability as measured by (13), we obtain a suitable measure of resultant assertability:

(14) $P(A \supset C) - P(\bar{A}) \cdot (P(\bar{C}A)/P(A))$.

But (14) may be simplified, using standard probability theory; and so we find that the resultant assertability, probability of truth minus the diminution given by (13), is equal to the conditional probability $P(C/A)$. That is why assertability goes by conditional probability.

Diminished assertability for such reasons is by no means special to conditionals. It appears also with uncontroversially truth-functional constructions such as negated conjunction. We are gathering mushrooms; I say to you 'You won't eat that one and live.' A dirty trick: I thought that one was safe and especially delicious, I wanted it myself, so I hoped to dissuade you from taking it without actually lying. I thought it highly probable that my trick would work, that you would not eat the mushroom, and therefore that I would turn out to have told the truth. But though what I said had a high subjective probability of truth, it had a low assertability and it was a misdeed to assert it. Its assertability goes not just by probability but by the resultant of that and a correction term to take account of the pointlessness and misleadingness of denying a conjunction when one believes it false predominantly because of disbelieving one conjunct. Surely few would care to explain the low assertability of what I said by rejecting the usual truth-functional semantics for negation and conjunction, and positing instead a special probabilistic rule of assertability.

There are many considerations that might detract from assertability. Why stop at (14)? Why not add terms to take account of the diminished assertability of insults, of irrelevancies, of long-winded pomposities, of breaches of confidence, and so forth? Perhaps part of the reason is that, unlike the diminution of assertability when the probability of a conditional is predominantly due to the improbability of the antecedent, these other diminutions depend heavily on miscellaneous features of the

conversational context. In logic we are accustomed to consider
sentences and inferences in abstraction from context. Therefore it
is understandable if, when we philosophize, our judgements of
assertability or of assertability-preserving inference are governed
by a measure of assertability such as (14), that is $P(C/A)$, in
which the more context-dependent dimensions of assertability are
left out.

There is a more serious problem, however. What of conditionals
that have a high probability predominantly because of the
probability of the consequent? If we are on the right track, it
seems that there should be a diminution of assertability in this case
also, and one that should still show up if we abstract from context:
we could argue that in such a case it is pointless, and hence also
misleading, to assert the conditional rather than the consequent.
This supposed diminution is left out, and I think rightly so, if we
measure the assertability of a conditional $A \supset C$ (in abstraction
from context) by $P(C/A)$. If A and C are probabilistically
independent and each has probability 0.9, then the probability of
the conditional (0.91) is predominantly due to the probability of
the consequent (0.9), yet the conditional probability $P(C/A)$ is
high (0.9) so we count the conditional as assertable. And it does
seem so, at least in some cases: 'I'll probably flunk, and it doesn't
matter whether I study; I'll flunk if I do and I'll flunk if I don't.'

The best I can do to account for the absence of a marked
diminution in the case of the probable consequent is to concede
that considerations of conversational pointlessness are not
decisive. They create only tendencies towards diminished
assertability, tendencies that may or may not be conventionally
reinforced. In the case of the improbable antecedent, they are
strongly reinforced. In the case of the probable consequent,
apparently they are not.

In conceding this, I reduce the distance between my present
hypothesis that indicative conditionals are truth-functional and the
rival hypothesis that they are non-truth-valued and governed by a
special rule of assertability. Truth conditions plus general
conversational considerations are not quite the whole story. They
go much of the way toward determining the assertability of
conditionals, but a separate convention is needed to finish the job.
The point of ascribing truth conditions to indicative conditionals is

not that we can thereby get rid entirely of special rules of assertability.

Rather, the point of ascribing truth conditions is that we thereby gain at least a prima-facie theory of the truth conditions and assertability of compound sentences with conditional constituents. We need not waste whatever general knowledge we have about the way the truth conditions of compounds depend on the truth conditions of their constituents. Admittedly we might go wrong by proceeding in this way. We have found one explicable discrepancy between assertability and probability in the case of conditionals themselves, and there might be more such discrepancies in the case of various compounds of conditionals. (For instance, the assertability of a negated conditional seems not to go by its probability of truth, but rather to vary inversely with the assertability of the conditional.) It is beyond the scope of this essay to survey the evidence, but I think it reasonable to hope that the discrepancies are not so many, or so difficult to explain, that they destroy the explanatory power of the hypothesis that the indicative conditional is truth-functional.

PROBABILITIES OF STALNAKER CONDITIONALS

It is in some of the writings of Robert Stalnaker that we find the fullest elaboration of the thesis that conditional probabilities are probabilities of conditionals.[8] Stalnaker's conditional connective $>$ has truth conditions roughly as follows: a conditional $A > C$ is true iff the least drastic revision of the facts that would make A true would make C true as well. Stalnaker conjectures that this interpretation will make $P(A > C)$ and $P(C/A)$ equal whenever $P(A)$ is positive. He also lays down certain constraints on $P(A > C)$ for the case that $P(A)$ is zero, explaining this by means of an extended concept of conditional probability that need not concern us here.

Stalnaker supports his conjecture by exhibiting a coincidence

[8] 'Probabilities and Conditionals.' The Stalnaker conditional had been introduced in Robert Stalnaker, 'A Theory of Conditionals', *Studies in Logical Theory*, ed. Nicholas Rescher (Oxford, 1968), and repr. in this volume (Essay II). I have discussed the Stalnaker conditional in *Counterfactuals* (Oxford, 1973): 77–83, arguing there that an interpretation quite similar to Stalnaker's is right for counterfactuals but wrong for indicative conditionals.

between two sorts of validity. The sentences that are true no matter what, under Stalnaker's truth conditions, turn out to be exactly those that have positive probability no matter what, under his hypothesis about probabilities of conditionals. Certainly this is weighty evidence, but it is not decisive. Cases are known in modal logic, for instance, in which very different interpretations of a language happen to validate the very same sentences. And indeed our triviality results show that Stalnaker's conjecture cannot be right, unless we confine our attention to trivial probability functions.[9]

But it is almost right, as we shall see. Probabilities of Stalnaker conditionals do not, in general, equal the corresponding conditional probabilities.[10] But they do have some of the characteristic properties of conditional probabilities.

A possible totality of facts corresponds to a possible world; so a revision of facts corresponds to a transition from one world to another. For any given world W and (possible) antecedent A, let W_A be the world we reach by the least drastic revision of the facts of W that makes A true. There is to be no gratuitous revision: W_A may differ from W as much as it must to permit A to hold, but no more. Balancing off respects of similarity and difference against each other according to the importance we attach to them, W_A is to be the closest in overall similarity to W among the worlds where A is true. Then the Stalnaker conditional $A > C$ is true at the world W iff C is true at W_A, the closest A-world to W. (In case the

---

[9] Once it is recognized that the Stalnaker conditional is not a probability conditional, the coincidence of logics has a new significance. The hypothesis that assertability of indicative conditionals goes by conditional probabilities, though still sufficiently well supported by direct evidence, is no longer unrivalled as an explanation of our judgements of validity for inferences with indicative conditional premises or conclusions. The same judgements could be explained instead by the hypothesis that the indicative conditional is the Stalnaker conditional and we judge valid those inferences that preserve truth.

[10] Although the probabilities of Stalnaker conditionals and the corresponding conditional probabilities cannot always be equal, they often are. They are equal whenever the conditional (and perhaps some non-conditional state of affairs on which it depends) is probabilistically independent of the antecedent, e.g. my present subjective probabilities are such that the conditional probability of finding a penny in my pocket, given that I look for one, equals the probability of the conditional 'I look for a penny > I find one.' The reason is that both are equal to the absolute probability that there is a penny in my pocket now.

antecedent A is impossible, so that there is no possible A-world to serve as W_A, we take $A > C$ to be vacuously true at all worlds. For simplicity I speak here only of absolute impossibility; Stalnaker works with impossibility relative to worlds.) Let us introduce this notation:

(15) $W(A) = \text{df} \begin{cases} 1 \text{ if } A \text{ is true at the world } W \\ 0 \text{ if } A \text{ is false at } W \end{cases}$.

Then we may give the truth conditions for non-vacuous Stalnaker conditionals as follows:

(16) $W(A > C) = W_A(C)$, if A is possible.

It will be convenient to pretend, from this point on, that there are only finitely many possible worlds. That will trivialize the mathematics but not distort our conclusions. Then we can think of a probability function P as a distribution of probability over the worlds. Each world W has a probability $P(W)$, and these probabilities of worlds sum to 1. We return from probabilities of worlds to probabilities of sentences by summing the probabilities of the worlds where a sentence is true:

(17) $P(A) = \Sigma_W P(W) \cdot W(A)$.

I shall also assume that the worlds are distinguishable: for any two, some sentence of our language is true at one but not the other. Thus we disregard phenomena that might result if our language were sufficiently lacking in expressive power.

Given any probability function P and any possible A, there is a probability function P' such that, for any world W',

(18) $P'(W') = \Sigma_W P(W) \cdot \begin{cases} 1 \text{ if } W_A \text{ is } W' \\ 0 \text{ otherwise} \end{cases}$.

Let us say that P' *comes from P by imaging on A*, and call P' the *image of P on A*. Intuitively, the image on A of a probability function is formed by shifting the original probability of each world W over to W_A, the closest A-world to W. Probability is moved around but not created or destroyed, so the probabilities of worlds still sum to 1. Each A-world keeps whatever probability it had originally, since if W is an A-world then W_A is W itself, and it

may also gain additional shares of probability that have been
shifted away from $\bar{A}$-worlds. The $\bar{A}$-worlds retain none of their
original probability, and gain none. All the probability has been
concentrated on the A-worlds. And this has been accomplished
with no gratuitous movement of probability. Every share stays as
close as it can to the world where it was originally located.

Suppose that P' comes from P by imaging on A, and consider
any sentence C.

(19) $P'(C)$

$$= \Sigma_{w'} P'(W') \cdot W'(C), \text{ by (17) applied to } P';$$

$$= \Sigma_{w'}\left(\Sigma_w P(W) \cdot \left\{\begin{matrix} 1 \text{ if } W_A \text{ is } W' \\ 0 \text{ otherwise} \end{matrix}\right\}\right) \cdot W'(C), \text{ by (18);}$$

$$= \Sigma_w P(W) \cdot \left(\Sigma_{w'}\left\{\begin{matrix} 1 \text{ if } W_A \text{ is } W' \\ 0 \text{ otherwise} \end{matrix}\right\} \cdot W'(C)\right), \text{ by algebra;}$$

$$= \Sigma_w P(W) \cdot W_A(C), \text{ simplifying the inner sum;}$$

$$= \Sigma_w P(W) \cdot W(A > C), \text{ by (16);}$$

$$= P(A > C), \text{ by (17).}$$

We have proved this theorem: *the probability of a Stalnaker
conditional with a possible antecedent is the probability of the
consequent after imaging on the antecedent.*

Conditionalizing is one way of revising a given probability
function so as to confer certainty—probability of 1—on a given
sentence. Imaging is another way to do the same thing. The two
methods do not in general agree. (Example: let $P(W)$, $P(W')$, and
$P(W'')$ each equal $\frac{1}{3}$; let A hold at W and W' but not W''; and let
W' be the closest A-world to W''. Then the probability function
that comes from P by conditionalizing on A assigns probability $\frac{1}{2}$
to both W and W'; whereas the probability function that comes
from P by imaging on A assigns probability $\frac{1}{3}$ to W and $\frac{2}{3}$ to W'.)
But though the methods differ, either one can plausibly be held to
give minimal revisions: to revise the given probability function as
much as must be done to make the given sentence certain, but no
more. Imaging P on A gives a minimal revision in this sense:
unlike all other revisions of P to make A certain, it involves no
gratuitous movement of probability from worlds to dissimilar
worlds. Conditionalizing P on A gives a minimal revision in this

different sense: unlike all other revisions of P to make A certain, it does not distort the profile of probability ratios, equalities, and inequalities among sentences that imply A.[11]

Stalnaker's conjecture divides into two parts. This part is true: the probability of a non-vacuous Stalnaker conditional is the probability of the consequent, after minimal revision of the original probability function to make the antecedent certain. But it is not true that this minimal revision works by conditionalizing. Rather it must work by imaging. Only when the two methods give the same result does the probability of a Stalnaker conditional equal the corresponding conditional probability.

Stalnaker gives the following instructions for deciding whether or not you believe a conditional.[12]

> First, add the antecedent (hypothetically) to your stock of beliefs; second, make whatever adjustments are required to maintain consistency (without modifying the hypothetical belief in the antecedent); finally, consider whether or not the consequent is true.

That is right, for a Stalnaker conditional, if the feigned revision of beliefs works by imaging. However the passage suggests that the thing to do is to feign the sort of revision that would take place if the antecedent really were added to your stock of beliefs. That is wrong. If the antecedent really were added, you should (if possible) revise by conditionalizing. The reasons in favour of responding to new evidence by conditionalizing are equally reasons against responding by imaging instead.

PROBABILITY-REVISION CONDITIONALS

Suppose that the connective $\rightarrow$ is interpreted in such a way that for any probability function P, and for any sentences A and C,

(20) $P(A \rightarrow C) = P_A(C)$, if A is possible,

where P_A is (in some sense) the minimal revision of P that raises the probability of A to 1. Iff so, let us call $\rightarrow$ a *probability-revision*

---

[11] Teller, 'Conditionalization and Observation'.
[12] 'A Theory of Conditionals', Essay II in this volume.

conditional. Is there such a thing? We have seen that it depends on the method of revision. Conditionalizing yields revisions that are minimal in another sense; and if P_A is obtained by imaging then the Stalnaker conditional is a probability-revision, conditional. (unless the language is trivial). Imaging yields revisions that are minimal in another sense; and if P_A is obtained by imaging then the Stalnaker conditional is a probability-revision conditional. Doubtless there are still other methods of revision, yielding revisions that are minimal in still other senses than we have yet considered. Are there any other methods which, like imaging and unlike conditionalizing, can give us a probability-revision conditional? There are not, as we shall see. The only way to have a probability-revision conditional is to interpret the conditional in Stalnaker's way and revise by imaging.

Since we have not fixed on a particular method of revising probability functions, our definition of a probability-revision conditional should be understood as tacitly relative to a method. To make this relativity explicit, let us call → a *probability-revision conditional for* a given method iff (20) holds in general when P_A is taken to be the revision obtained by that method.

Our definition of a Stalnaker conditional should likewise be understood as tacitly relative to a method of revising worlds. Stalnaker's truth conditions were deliberately left vague at the point where they mention the minimal revision of a given world to make a given antecedent true. With worlds, as with probability functions, different methods of revision will yield revisions that are minimal in different senses. We can indeed describe any method as selecting the antecedent world closest in overall similarity to the original world; but different methods will fit this description under different resolutions of the vagueness of similarity, resolutions that stress different respects of comparison. To be explicit, let us call → a *Stalnaker conditional for* a given method of revising worlds iff (16) holds in general when W_A is taken to be the revision obtained by that method (and $A \rightarrow C$ is true at all worlds if A is impossible). I spoke loosely of 'the' Stalnaker conditional, but henceforth it will be better to speak in the plural of the Stalnaker conditionals for various methods of revising worlds.

We are interested only in those methods of revision, for worlds and for probability functions, that can be regarded as giving revisions that are in some reasonable sense minimal. We have no hope of saying in any precise way just which methods those are, but at least we can list some formal requirements that such a method must satisfy. The requirements were given by Stalnaker for revision of worlds, but they carry over *mutatis mutandis* to revision of probability functions also. First, a minimal revision to reach some goal must be one that does reach it. For worlds, W_A must be a world where A is true; for probability functions, P_A must assign to A a probability of 1. Second, there must be no revision when none is needed. For worlds, if A is already true at W then W_A must be W itself; for probability functions, if $P(A)$ is already 1, then P_A must be P. Third, the method must be consistent in its comparisons. For worlds, if B is true at W_A and A is true at W_B then W_A and W_B must be the same; else W_A would be treated as both less and more of a revision of W than is W_B. Likewise for probability functions, if $P_A(B)$ and $P_B(A)$ both are 1, then P_A and P_B must be the same.

Let us call any method of revision of worlds or of probability functions *eligible* if it satisfies these three requirements. We note that the methods of revising probability functions that we have considered are indeed eligible. Conditionalizing is an eligible method; or, more precisely, conditionalizing can be extended to an eligible method applicable to any probability function P and any possible A. (Choose some fixed arbitrary well-ordering of all probability functions. In case P_A cannot be obtained by conditionalizing because $P(A)$ is zero, let it be the first, according to the arbitrary ordering, of the probability functions that assign to A a probability of 1.) Imaging is also an eligible method. More precisely, imaging on the basis of any eligible method of revising worlds is an eligible method of revising probability functions.

Our theorem of the previous section may be restated as follows. *If $\rightarrow$ is a Stalnaker conditional for any eligible method of revising worlds, then $\rightarrow$ is also a probability-revision conditional for an eligible method of revising probability functions; namely for the method that works by imaging on the basis of the given method of revising worlds.* Now we shall prove the converse: *if $\rightarrow$ is a probability-revision conditional for an eligible method of revising* *probability functions, then → is also a Stalnaker conditional for an eligible method of revising worlds.* In short, the *probability-revision conditionals are exactly the Stalnaker conditionals.*

Suppose that we have some eligible methods of revising probability functions; and suppose that → is a probability-revision conditional for this method.

We shall need to find a method of revising worlds; therefore let us consider the revision of certain special probability functions that stand in one-to-one correspondence with the worlds. For each world W, there is a probability function P that gives all the probability to W and none to any other world. Accordingly, by (17),

$$(21) \quad P(A) = \begin{Bmatrix} 1 \text{ if } A \text{ is true at } W \\ 0 \text{ if } A \text{ is false at } W \end{Bmatrix} = W(A)$$

for any sentence A. Call such a probability function *opinionated*, since it would represent the beliefs of someone who was absolutely certain that the world W was actual and who therefore held a firm opinion about every question; and call the world W where P concentrates all the probability the *belief of world of P.*

Our given method of revising probability functions preserves opinionation. Suppose P were opinionated and P_A were not, for some possible A. That is to say that P_A gives positive probability to two or more worlds. We have assumed that our language has the means to distinguish the worlds, so there is some sentence C such that $P_A(C)$ is neither 0 nor 1. But since P is opinionated, $P(A \to C)$ is either 0 or 1, contradicting the hypothesis that → is a probability-revision conditional so that $P_A(C)$ and $P(A \to C)$ are equal.

Then we have the following method of revising worlds. Given a world W and possible sentence A, let P be the opinionated probability function with belief world W, revise P according to our given method of revising probability functions, and let W_A be the belief world of the resulting opinionated probability function P_A. Since the given method of revising probability functions is eligible, so is the derived method of revising worlds.

Consider any world W and sentences A and C. Let P be the opinionated probability function with belief world W, and let W_A be as above. Then if A is possible,

$$(22) \quad W(A \to C) = P(A \to C), \text{ by (21)};$$
$$= P_A(C), \text{ by (20)};$$
$$= W_A(C), \text{ by (21) applied to } W_A.$$

So $\to$ is a Stalnaker conditional for the derived method of revising worlds. *Quod erat demonstrandum.*

Postscript

Indicative Conditionals better Explained

I retract the positive theory of indicative conditionals that I proposed in the essay. I now prefer the alternative theory advanced by Frank Jackson.[1]

The two theories have much in common. Both agree (1) that the indicative conditional has the truth conditions of the truth-functional conditional $A \supset C$, yet (2) its assertability goes by the conditional subjective probability $P(C/A)$, provided that we abstract from special considerations—of etiquette, say—that apply in special cases. Both theories further agree, therefore, (3) that there is a discrepancy between truth- and assertability-preserving inference involving indicative conditionals; and (4) that our intuitions about valid reasoning with conditionals are apt to concern the latter, and so to be poor evidence about the former. (As to whether 'validity' should be the word for truth- or for assertability-preservation, that seems a non-issue if ever there was one.) Further, the theories agree (5) that the discrepancy between the assertability $P(C/A)$ and the probability of truth $P(A \supset C)$ is due to some sort of Gricean implicature, and (6) that an adequate account of this implicature must use the premiss that the conditional has the truth conditions of $A \supset C$. I still hold these six theses.

---

[1] 'On Assertion and Indicative Conditionals', *Philosophical Review*, 88 (1979): 565–89, and repr. in this volume (Essay VI); 'Conditionals and Possibilia', *Proceedings of the Aristotelian Society*, 81 (1981): 125–37.

But what sort of implicature is involved? Formerly, I thought it was predominantly a conversational implicature, akin to the implicature from 'Here, you have a good point' to 'Elsewhere, you mostly don't.' According to Jackson, it is a conventional implicature, akin to the implicature from 'She votes Liberal but she's no fool' to 'Liberal voters mostly are fools.'

I said, following Grice: if $P(A \supset C)$ is high mostly because $P(A)$ is low, what's the sense of saying $A \supset C$? Why not say the stronger thing that's almost as probable, not-A? If you say the weaker thing, you will be needlessly uninformative. Besides, you will mislead those who rely on you not to be needlessly uninformative, and who will infer that you were not in a position to say the stronger thing.

To which Jackson replies that we often do say weaker things than we believe true, and for a very good reason. I speak to you (or to my future self, via memory) in the expectation that our belief systems will be much alike, but not exactly alike. If there were too little in common, my attempts to convey information would fail; if there were too much in common, they would serve no purpose. I do not know quite what other information you (or I in future) may possess from other sources. Maybe you (or I in future) know something that now seems to me improbable. I would like to say something that will be useful even so. So let me not say the strongest thing I believe. Let me say something a bit weaker, if I can thereby say something that will not need to be given up, that will remain useful, even if a certain hypothesis that I now take to be improbable should turn out to be the case. If I say something that I would continue to believe even if I should learn that the improbable hypothesis is true, then that will be something that I think you can take my word for even if you already believe the hypothesis.

Let us say that A is robust with respect to B (according to someone's subjective probabilities at a certain time) iff the unconditional probability of A and the probability of A conditionally on B are close together, and both are high; so that even if one were to learn that B, one would continue to find A probable. Then Jackson's point is that one might say the weaker thing rather than the stronger for the sake of robustness. The weaker might be more robust with respect to some case that one judges to be improbable, but that one nevertheless does not wish to ignore.

If it is pointless to say the weaker instead of the stronger, how much more pointless to say the weaker and the stronger both! And yet we do. I might say: 'Bruce is asleep in the rag box, or anyway somewhere downstairs.' Jackson can explain that. There's point in saying the stronger, and there's point in saying the more robust, and they're different, so I say them both.

It could be useful to point out that one is saying something robust. One might say: 'I am saying A not because I do not believe anything stronger, but because I want to say something which is robust with respect to B—something you may rely on even if, unlike me, you believe that B.' But that's clumsy. It would be a good idea if we had conventional devices to signal robustness more concisely. So it would be no surprise to find out that we do. Jackson suggests that we have various such devices, and that the indicative conditional construction is one of them.

An indicative conditional is a truth-functional conditional that conventially implicates robustness with respect to the antecedent. Therefore, an indicative conditional with antecedent A and consequent C is assertable iff (or to the extent that) the probabilities $P(A \supset C)$ and $P(A \supset C/A)$ both are high. If the second is high, the first will be too; and the second is high if $P(C/A)$ is high; and that is the reason why the assertability of indicative conditionals goes by the corresponding conditional probability.

Jackson lists several advantages of his implicature-of-robustness theory over my assert-the-stronger theory. I will mention only one (which is not to suggest that I find the rest unpersuasive). I can say: 'Fred will not study, and if he does he still won't pass.' If the conditional is assertable only when the denial of its antecedent is not, as the assert-the-stronger theory predicts, then how can it happen that the conditional and the denial of its antecedent *both* are assertable? As already noted, Jackson can explain such things. The conditional was added for the sake of robustness, so that even if you happen to think I'm wrong about Fred not studying, you can still take my word for it that if he studies he still won't pass.

So far, I have just been retailing Jackson. But I think that one complication ought to be added. (Jackson tells me that he agrees.)

Above, I introduced robustness by what was in effect a double definition: first in terms of probability, then in terms of what would happen if something were learned. Let us distinguish more carefully:

> A is robust$_1$ with respect to B iff $P(A)$ and $P(A/B)$ are close, and both are high.
> A is robust$_2$ with respect to B iff $P(A)$ is high, and would remain high even if one were to learn that B.

Robustness$_1$ is robustness as Jackson officially defines it; and it is the implicature of robustness$_1$ that explains why assertability of conditionals goes by conditional probability. But our reasons for wanting to say what's robust, and for needing signals of robustness, seem to apply to robustness$_2$. Most of the time, fortunately, the distinction doesn't matter. Suppose that if one were to learn that B, one would learn only that B, and nothing else (or nothing else relevant). And suppose that one would then revise one's beliefs by conditionalizing. Then we have robustness$_2$ of A with respect to B iff we have robustness$_1$. In this normal case, the distinction makes no difference.

However, there may be abnormal cases: cases in which B could not be learned all by itself, but would have to be accompanied by some extra information E. Suppose A is robust$_1$ with respect to B alone; but not with respect to B and E in conjunction. Then A will not be robust$_2$ with respect to B. Example: A is 'I'll never believe that Reagan works for the KGB'; B is 'Reagan works for the KGB'; and E is not-A. My thought is that if the KGB were successful enough to install their man as president, surely they'd also be successful enough to control the news completely. So $P(A)$ and $P(A/B)$ are both high; but of course $P(A/BE) = 0$. Yet if I did learn that Reagan worked for the KGB, I'd *ipso facto* learn that I believed it—despite my prior expectation that the KGB would be able to keep me from suspecting. So A is not at all robust$_2$ with respect to B.[2]

---

[2] A closely related point appears in Bas van Fraassen's review of Brian Ellis, *Rational Belief Systems, Canadian Journal of Philosophy*, 10 (1980): 497–511, with an illustrative example due to Richmond Thomason: a man accepts 'If my wife were deceiving me, I would believe that she was not (because she is so clever)', but that doesn't mean that if he were to come to believe the antecedent he would then believe the consequent.

When the two senses of robustness come apart in special cases, which one does the indicative conditional signal? What really matters is robustness$_2$, so it would be more useful to signal that. On the other hand, it would be much easier to signal robustness$_1$. Robustness$_2$ with respect to B amounts roughly to robustness$_1$ with respect to the whole of what would be learned if B were learned. (The two are equivalent under the assumption that the learner would conditionalize.) But it might be no easy thing to judge what would be learned if B were learned, in view of the variety of ways that something might be learned. For the most part, robustness$_1$ is a reasonable guide to the robustness$_2$ that really matters—a fallible guide, as we've seen, but pretty good most of the time. So it's unsurprising if what we have the means to signal is the former rather than the latter. And if this gets conventionalized, it should be unsurprising to find that we signal robustness$_1$ even when that clearly diverges from robustness$_2$. That is exactly what happens. Example: I can perfectly well say 'If Reagan works for the KGB, I'll never believe it.'

V

PROBABILITIES OF CONDITIONALS AND CONDITIONAL PROBABILITIES II

DAVID LEWIS

ADAMS'S thesis about indicative conditionals is that their assertability goes by the conditional subjective probability of the consequent given the antecedent, in very much the same way that assertability normally goes by the subjective probability of truth.[1] The thesis is well established; the remaining question is how it may best be explained. The nicest explanation would be that the truth conditions of indicative conditionals are such as to guarantee the equality

(*) $P(A \rightarrow C) = P(C/A) = \mathrm{df}\ P(CA)/P(A)$

whenever $P(A)$ is positive. In a previous essay,[2] I argued that this nicest explanation cannot be right. After reviewing my previous argument, I shall here extend it in order to plug some loopholes.

1

I began with a *first triviality result*, as follows. Except in a trivial case, there is no way to interpret $\rightarrow$ uniformly[3] so that (*) holds

David Lewis, 'Probabilities of Conditionals and Conditional Probabilities II', *Philosophical Review*, 95 (October 1986): 581–9. Used with permission.

[1] See Ernest W. Adams, 'The Logic of Conditionals', *Inquiry*, 8 (1965): 166–97; *The Logic of Conditionals* (Dordrecht: Reidel, 1975).

[2] 'Probabilities of Conditionals and Conditional Probabilities', *Philosophical Review*, 85 (1976): 297–315; repr. (with postscripts) in my *Philosophical Papers*, ii (Oxford: OUP, 1986) and repr. in this volume (Essay IV).

[3] I take it to be part of the 'nicest explanation' now under attack that $\rightarrow$ is to be interpreted uniformly, the same way in the context of one probability function as in the context of another. The proposal that $\rightarrow$ has a non-uniform interpretation, so that for each P we have a $\rightarrow_P$ that satisfies (*), but in general a different $\rightarrow_P$ for

universally, for every probability function P (as well as for every antecedent A and consequent C).

But you might say the (*) doesn't have to hold universally, throughout the class of all probability functions whatever. To explain Adams's thesis, it is good enough if (*) holds only throughout the class of *belief functions*: probability functions that represent possible systems of belief.

I agree. However I cited reasons why the change of belief that results from coming to know an item of new evidence should take place by conditionalizing on what was learned; I concluded that the class of belief functions is closed under conditionalizing; and I appealed to a *second triviality result*, as follows. Except in a trivial case, there is no way to interpret $\rightarrow$ uniformly so that (*) holds throughout a class of probability functions closed under conditionalizing.

In the previous essay, that was the end of my argument. But I now think the end came too soon. I owe you answers to two more objections.

2

You might say that not just any proposition[4] could be an item of evidence. Even granted that change of belief takes place (at least sometimes) by conditionalizing on one's total evidence, that does not mean that the class of belief functions must be closed under conditionalizing generally. It is enough that the class should be closed under conditionalizing on those propositions that could be someone's total evidence.

In proving the second triviality result, I did not use the full

different P, is a rival hypothesis, an alternative way to explain Adams's thesis. It is unscathed by my arguments here and in the previous paper. See Robert Stalnaker, 'Indicative Conditionals', *Philosophia*, 5 (1975): 269–86, reprinted in W. L. Harper *et al.* (eds.), *Ifs* (Dordrecht: Reidel, 1981) and repr. in this volume (Essay VII); and Bas van Fraassen, 'Probabilities of Conditionals', in W. L. Harper and C. A. Hooker (eds.), *Foundations of Probability Theory, Statistical Inference and Statistical Theories of Science*, i (Dordrecht: Reidel, 1976).

[4] Here I switch from sentences (in the previous essay) to propositions as the bearers of subject probability. The reason is that our items of evidence might be propositions that have no accurate expression in any language we are capable of using.

strength of my assumption that the class in question was closed under conditionalizing. I only conditionalized twice: once on a proposition C, once on its negation $-C$. But that, you might well say, was bad enough. A proposition that could be someone's total evidence must be, in certain respects, highly specific. But to the extent that a proposition is specific, its negation is unspecific. So one time or the other, whether on C or on $-C$, I conditionalized on a proposition of the wrong sort; and the result may well have been a probability function that was not a belief function.

I agree. I did not give any good reason why belief functions should be closed under conditionalizing generally. I should only have assumed that they are closed under conditionalizing on a certain special class of *evidence propositions*.

Consider a limited class of evidence propositions: those that characterize the total evidence available to a particular subject at a particular time, as it is or as it might have been, in a maximally specific way. These propositions—as always with the maximally specific alternatives for a single subject-matter—comprise a partition: they are mutually exclusive and jointly exhaustive. Further, the subject's limited powers of discrimination will ensure that this partition is a finite one.

So the hypothesis now before us says that (*) holds throughout the class of belief functions, and that this class is closed under conditionalizing on the members of a certain finite partition of evidence propositions. Against this I appeal to a *third triviality result*, as follows. Except in a trivial case, there is no way to interpret $\rightarrow$ uniformly so that (*) holds throughout a class of probability functions closed under conditionalizing on the propositions in some finite partition.

The proof differs little from my previous proofs of the first and second results. Let P be a probability function in the class. Let C, D, . . . be all the propositions in the partition to which P assigns positive probability; we assume that there are at least two such propositions. Let A be a proposition such that $P(A/C)$, $P(A/D)$, . . ., are all positive, and such that $P(C/A) \neq P(C)$. If there are no such P, C, D, . . ., and A, that is the case I am here calling 'trivial'. We may be sure that the case of the class of belief functions and a partition of evidence propositions will not be thus trivial.

By finite additivity, the definition of conditional probability, and the imcompatibility of $C, D, \ldots$, we have that

$$P(A \to C) = P(A \to C/C)P(C) + P(A \to C/D)P(D) + \ldots$$

Suppose for *reductio* that (*) holds throughout the class. By applying it in turn to P and to all the functions $P(-/C)$, $P(-/D)$, $\ldots$ that come from P by conditionalizing on $D, C, \ldots$ respectively, we have

$$\frac{P(CA)}{P(A)} = \frac{P(CA/C)P(C)}{P(A/C)} + \frac{P(CA/D)P(D)}{P(A/D)} + \ldots$$

The first term of the right-hand sum simplifies and the other terms vanish, so we have

$$P(C/A) = P(C),$$

which contradicts our choice of A and thereby completes the *reductio*.

3

So if you grant that change of belief takes place (at least sometimes) by conditionalizing, and only insist that the conditionalizing must be on evidence propositions, then I take your point but I can make my case against (*) despite it. However you might go further. You might say that conditionalizing never yields one belief function from another.

Why? You might say it because you run my own argument in reverse.[5] Adams's thesis is compelling; it needs to be explained; it turns out that even a modicum of closure under conditionalizing would wreck the explanation; therefore even that modicum of closure is to be rejected. I reply that if (*) does not hold throughout the belief functions, that wrecks only one explanation of Adams's thesis. Other hypotheses remain.[6]

[5] Thus Wayne Davis, in discussion.

[6] Of several available proposals to explain Adams's thesis without the aid of (*), I now favour that of Frank Jackson, 'On Assertion and Indicative Conditionals', *Philosophical Review*, 87 (1979): 565–89, and repr. in this volume (Essay VI). In particular, I take it to be better (for the reasons Jackson gives) than the explanation of Adams's thesis that I proposed in 'Probabilities of Conditionals and Conditional Probabilities'.

You might better say it for a more direct reason.[7] If one belief function came from another by conditionalizing on the evidence, it would be *irregular*. It would not spread its probability over all the possibilities there are, but would assign probability zero to all possibilities that conflict with the evidence. You might insist that an irregular probability function cannot represent a reasonable system of belief. It would be over-confident to respond to evidence by conditionalizing and thereby falling into irregularity. To do so is to dismiss the genuine possibility that one has mistaken the evidence. It is to be ready to bet against that possibility at any odds, no matter how high the stakes. And it is to dismiss the possibility forever, no matter how much later evidence may call for reconsideration. For once a proposition gets probability zero, no subsequent conditionalizing ever can restore it to positive probability. (And neither can the generalized conditionalizing we shall soon consider.) Surely it would be more reasonable to respond to evidence in a slightly more moderate way, almost conditionalizing but not quite. If a possibility conflicts with the evidence, by all means bring its probability down very low—but never quite to zero.

It's one thing to say, as you have, that an irregular probability function cannot represent a reasonable system of belief; it's something else to say that it cannot represent a system of belief at all. The latter is what you need if, despite my triviality results so far, you still say that (*) holds throughout the class of all belief functions. But you can cross the gap by appealing to a theory of intentionality according to which—roughly speaking—the content of a total mental state is the system of belief and desire that best rationalizes the behaviour to which that state would tend to dispose one. How could an unreasonable belief function ever be part of the system that best rationalizes anything? If it cannot, it never is suited to be part of the content of any mental state, in which case it is not a belief function after all. This theory of reason as constitutive of content must be handled with care, lest it prove

[7] Thus Anthony Appiah, 'The Importance of Triviality', *Philosophical Review*, 95 (1986): 209–31. But Appiah is no upholder of (*), although he faults my argument against it. He rejects it on the strength of an argument advanced by I. F. Carlstrom and C. S. Hill in their review of Adams, 'The Logic of Conditionals', *Philosophy of Science*, 45 (1978): 155–8.

too much—namely that there is no such thing as unreason—but it may well be that a sufficiently qualified form of it would meet your needs.

(What if some state would dispose one to behaviour that would indeed suggest a complete and irrevocable dismissal of the possibility that one has mistaken the evidence? Even so, it is not clear that an irregular belief function is called for. If a system is to do well at rationalizing behaviour, of course one *desideratum* is that the behaviour should fit the prescriptions of the system. But another *desideratum*, you may plausibly say, is that the system itself should be reasonable. Even if an irregular function does best on fit, a not-quite irregular function may yet do better on balance.)

For what it is worth, I would insist that the ideally rational agent does conditionalize on his total evidence, and thereby falls into irregularity. He never does mistake the evidence, wherefore he may and he must dismiss the possibility that he has mistaken it. Else there is a surefire way to drain his pockets: sell him insurance against the mistakes he never makes, collect the premium, never pay any claims.[8] This surprising conclusion does nothing to show that we, the imperfect folk who do run the risk of mistaking our evidence, would be reasonable to conditionalize ourselves into irregularity. Not at all—rather, it shows that we differ more from the ideally rational agent than might have been thought. After all, many of our virtues consist of being good at coping with our limitations. (Whatever the divine virtues may be, they can scarcely include curiosity, fortitude, or gumption.) Likewise our cautious refusal to conditionalize quite all the way helps us to cope with our fallibility. One departure from the perfection of ideal rationality demands another.

(If I am right that the ideally rational agent conditionalizes, then

---

[8] In other words, if the ideally rational agent did not conditionalize, and reserved some probability for the hypothesis that he had mistaken his evidence, then he would be vulnerable to a 'diachronic Dutch book'—which, by definition of ideal rationality, he is not. See Paul Teller, 'Conditionalization and Observation', *Synthese*, 26 (1973): 218–58, and Bas van Fraassen, 'Belief and the Will', *Journal of Philosophy*, 81 (1984): 235–56, for discussion of diachronic Dutch books. However, Teller and van Fraassen would accept the conclusion I draw only in much-qualified form, if at all.

I have shown at least that (*) does not hold throughout the class of *his* belief functions. So if Adams's thesis applies to his indicative conditionals, it must be otherwise explained. But what does that show about us? You might well doubt whether Adams's thesis does apply to the ideally rational agent, given that we differ from him more than might have been thought.)

But if we are talking of everyday, less-than-ideal rationality, then I agree that it is unreasonable to conditionalize, reasonable to shun irregularity. Nor can I challenge your further conclusion that no belief function—anyhow, none suited to ordinary folk—is irregular. I accept it, if not wholeheartedly, at least for the sake of the argument.

If we do not conditionalize on our evidence, what do we do instead? To this question, Jeffrey has offered a highly plausible answer.[9] In conditionalizing, the probability of the evidence proposition is exogenously raised to one; the probability of anything else conditional on that evidence is left unchanged. Jeffrey generalizes this in a natural way, as follows. The probability of the evidence proposition is exogenously raised, not to one but to some less extreme value; the probability of the negation of the evidence proposition is lowered by an equal amount, as must be done to preserve additivity; and the probabilities of anything else conditional on the evidence and conditional on its negation both are left unchanged. So if P is the original probability function and the probability of proposition C is exogenously raised by amount x, we get a new probability function P_x given by the schema

$$(GC) \quad P_x(B) = P(B) + x[P(B/C) - P(B/-C)]$$

whenever $P(C)$ and $P(-C)$ and x are positive, C is an evidence proposition, and x is less than $P(-C)$. (The final restriction excludes the case that $x = P(-C)$, which reduces to ordinary conditionalizing on C and engenders irregularity; and also the case that x is greater than $P(-C)$, in which P_x would assign negative

[9] Richard C. Jeffrey, *The Logic of Decision* (New York, 1965, and Chicago, 1983), ch. 11. Jeffrey actually describes a more general case, in which there may be exogenous change to the probabilities of several evidence propositions simultaneously, but for the argument to follow it is enough to consider the simpler case. For further discussion, see Paul Teller, 'Conditionalization and Observation'.

values and so would not be a genuine probability function.) I shall assume that change of belief under the impact of evidence takes place (at least sometimes) in conformity to schema (GC).

So the hypothesis now before us says that (*) holds throughout the class of belief functions, and that this class is closed under change in conformity to schema (GC). Against this I appeal to a *fourth triviality result*, as follows. Except in a trivial case, there is no way to interpret $\rightarrow$ uniformly so that (*) holds throughout a class of probability functions closed under change in conformity to (GC).

Let P be a probability function in the class. Let C be an evidence proposition such that $P(C)$ and $P(-C)$ are positive. Let A be a proposition such that $P(A/C)$ and $P(A/-C)$ are positive and unequal. If there are no such P, C, and A, that is the case I am now calling 'trivial'. We may be sure that the class of belief functions will not be trivial in this way.

Suppose for *reductio* that (*) holds throughout the class, hence both for P and for any P_x with x between 0 and $P(-C)$. So we have

$$P(A \rightarrow C) = P(CA)/P(A),$$
$$P_x(A \rightarrow C) = P_x(CA)/P_x(A);$$

where by (GC),

$$P_x(A \rightarrow C) = P(A \rightarrow C) + x[P(A \rightarrow C/C) - P(A \rightarrow C/-C)],$$
$$P_x(CA) = P(CA) + x[P(CA/C) - P(CA/-C)]$$
$$= P(CA) + xP(A/C),$$
$$P_x(A) = P(A) + x[P(A/C) - P(A/-C)].$$

From these equations, we can derive that whenever x is between 0 and $P(-C)$,

$$x[P(A/C) - P(A/-C)][P(A \rightarrow C/C) - P(A \rightarrow C/-C)]$$
$$= P(A/C) - P(A)[P(A \rightarrow C/C) - P(A \rightarrow C/-C)] -$$
$$P(C/A)[P(A/C) - P(A/-C)].$$

The only way this can hold for a range of values of x is that the coefficient of x on the left-hand side is zero, and the right-hand side also is zero. There are two cases.

Case 1. The coefficient is zero because $P(A/C) = P(A/-C)$. But that contradicts our choice of A.

Case 2. The coefficient is zero because $P(A \to C/C) = P(A \to C/-C)$. Then since the right-hand side also is zero, and since its second term vanishes, we have that

$$
\begin{aligned}
0 &= P(A/C) - P(C/A)[P(A/C) - P(A/-C)] \\
&= P(A/C)[1 - P(C/A)] + P(C/A)\,P(A/-C) \\
&= P(A/C)\,P(-C/A) + P(C/A)\,P(A/-C),
\end{aligned}
$$

which contradicts our choice of P, C, and A, whereby all of $P(A/C)$, $P(-C/A)$, $P(C/A)$, and $P(A/-C)$ must be positive. This completes the *reductio*.

VI

ON ASSERTION AND INDICATIVE CONDITIONALS*

FRANK JACKSON

INTRODUCTION

THE circumstances in which it is natural to assert the ordinary indicative conditional 'If P then Q' are those in which it is natural to assert 'Either not P or, P and Q', and conversely. For instance, the circumstances in which it is natural to assert 'If it rains, the match will be cancelled' are precisely those in which it is natural to assert 'Either it won't rain, or it will and the match will be cancelled.' Similarly, the circumstances in which it is natural to assert 'Not both P and Q' are precisely those in which it is natural to assert 'Either not P or not Q.' We explain the latter coincidence of assertion conditions by a coincidence of truth conditions. Why not do the same in the case of the conditional? Why not, that is, hold that 'If P then Q' has the same truth conditions as 'Either not P or, P and Q'?

This hypothesis—given the standard and widely accepted truth-functional treatments of 'not', 'or', and 'and'—amounts to the Equivalence thesis: the thesis that $(P \rightarrow Q)$ is equivalent to $(P \supset Q)$. (I will use '$\rightarrow$' for the indicative conditional, reserving '$\Box\rightarrow$' for the subjunctive or counterfactual conditional.) In this essay I defend a version of the Equivalence thesis.

As a rule, our intuitive judgements of assertability match up with our intuitive judgements of probability, that is, S is assertable to the extent that it has high subjective probability for its assertor.

Frank Jackson, 'On Assertion and Indicative Conditionals', *Philosophical Review*, 88 (1979): 565–89. Used with permission.

* I am conscious of a more than usually large debt to many discussions with Brian Ellis, Lloyd Humberstone, and Robert Pargetter; and also to comments from the referee.

Now it has been widely noted that when $(P \supset Q)$ is highly probable but both $-P$ and Q are not highly probable, it is proper to assert $(P \rightarrow Q)$.[1] The problem for the Equivalence thesis is to explain away the putative counter examples to '$P \vdash (P \rightarrow Q)$' and '$Q \vdash (P \rightarrow Q)$', the only too familiar cases where despite the high probability of $-P$ or of Q, and so of $(P \supset Q)$, $(P \rightarrow Q)$ is not highly assertable.

I will start in Sect. 1 by considering the usual way of trying to explain away these counter-examples and argue that it fails. An obvious reaction to this failure would be (is) to abandon the Equivalence thesis; but I argue in Sect. 2 that another is possible, namely that the general thought behind the usual way of explaining away the paradoxes of material implication is mistaken. This leads in Sect. 3 to the version of the Equivalence thesis I wish to defend. In Sect. 4 I point out some of the advantages of this account of indicative conditionals, and in Sect. 5 I reply to possible objections.

1. THE USUAL WAY OF EXPLAINING AWAY THE COUNTER-EXAMPLES

Suppose S_1 is logically stronger that S_2: S_1 entails S_2 but not conversely. And suppose S_1 is nearly as highly probable as S_2. (It cannot, of course, be quite as probable, except in very special cases.) Why then assert S_2 instead of S_1? There are many possible reasons: S_2 might read or sound better, S_1 might be unduly blunt or obscene, and so on. But if we concentrate on epistemic and semantic considerations widely construed, and put aside more particular, highly contextual ones like those just mentioned, it seems that there would be no reason to assert S_2 instead of S_1. There is no significant loss of probability in asserting S_1 and, by the transitivity of entailment, S_1 must yield everything and more than S_2 does. Therefore, S_1 is to be asserted rather than S_2, *ceteris paribus*.

This line of thought, which I will tag, 'Assert the stronger instead of the weaker (when probabilities are close)', has been

[1] Though the point is commonly put in terms of evidence, see e.g. Charles L. Stevenson, 'If-iculties', *Philosophy of Science*, 37 (1970): 27–49, and G. H. von Wright, 'On Conditionals' in *Logical Studies* (Routledge & Kegan Paul: London, 1957), see 139.

prominent in defences of the Equivalence thesis that the ordinary indicative conditional, $(P \rightarrow Q)$, is equivalent to the material conditional, $(P \supset Q)$.[2] The Equivalence theorist explains away the impropriety of asserting $(P \supset Q)$ when one of $-P$ or Q is highly probable by saying that in such a case you should come right out and assert the logically stronger statement, namely either $-P$ or Q as the case may be.

The same idea can be put in terms of evidence instead of probability.[3] If your evidence favours $(P \supset Q)$ by favouring one of $-P$ or Q you should simply assert $-P$ or Q, whichever it is, and not the needlessly weak conditional.[4] But I will concentrate in the main on the probabilistic formulation when presenting my objections.

My first objection is that a conditional like 'If the sun goes out of existence in ten minutes time, the earth will be plunged into darkness in about eighteen minutes' time' is highly assertable. However, the probability of the material conditional and the probability of the negation of its antecedent are both very close (if not equal) to one, and so at most the probability of the conditional is only marginally the greater. Hence this is a case where the

---

[2] Particularly in discussion, but see R. C. Jeffrey, *Formal Logic* (New York, 1967), ch. 3; David Lewis, 'Probabilities of Conditionals and Conditional Probabilities', *Philosophical Review*, 75 (1976): 297–315; and for support for the general idea and other arguments for the Equivalence thesis see Michael Clark, 'Ifs and Hooks', *Analysis*, 32.2 (1971): 33–9.

[3] I understand that this was the emphasis in H. P. Grice's influential, unpublished William James Lectures (since published as *Studies in the Way of Words* (Cambridge, Mass., 1989)), see L. Jonathan Cohen, 'Some Remarks on Grice's Views about the Logical Particles of Natural Language', in *Pragmatics of Natural Languages*, ed. Y. Bar-Hillel (Reidel: Dordrecht, 1971); Clark, 'Ifs and Hooks', and particularly 'Ifs and Hooks: A Rejoinder', *Analysis*, 34.3 (1974): 77–83; A. J. Ayer, *Probability and Evidence* (Macmillan: London, 1972); Stevenson, 'If-iculties'; and J. L. Mackie, *Truth, Probability and Paradox* (London, 1973).

[4] In their presentation of Grice's (tentative) views Cohen *et al.* sometimes use formulations that are ambiguous about whether it is all or part of your evidence that is meant. If it is all, things are as above; but if it is part, the view being reported is that $(P \rightarrow Q)$ is assertable if *part* of your total evidence favours $(P \supset Q)$ without favouring one of $-P$ or Q, even if your total evidence favours one of them. There is immediate trouble for such a view. Suppose I know that Fred and Bill both live in Oak Street. Even though my evidence strongly favours the material conditional, it would normally be wrong to assert 'If Fred lives in Elm Street, Bill lives in Elm Street' in such a case; nevertheless *part* of what I know, namely that they live in the same street, favours the material conditional without favouring its consequent and without favouring the negation of its antecedent.

weaker is assertable despite the absence of any appreciable gain in probability, contrary to the maxim 'Assert the stronger instead of the weaker.'

The second objection is that conditionals whose high probability is almost entirely due to that of their consequents may be highly assertable. Suppose we are convinced that Carter will be re-elected whether or not Reagan runs. We say both 'If Reagan runs, Carter will be re-elected' and 'If Reagan does not run, Carter will be re-elected.' The high subjective probability can only be due to that of the common consequent, yet the consequent is allegedly logically stronger and so by the maxim the conditionals ought not be assertable.

Moreover, such cases cannot be handled by a conventional exemption[5] from the maxim in the case of conditionals with very probable consequents. Both the following conditionals are highly *unassertable*, but have very probable consequents: 'If the history books are wrong, Caesar defeated Pompey in 48 BC', 'If the sun goes out of existence in ten minutes time, the earth will *not* be plunged into darkness in eighteen minutes' time.'

The third objection is that there is a third paradox of material implication. If the Equivalence thesis is true, then $((P \to Q) \vee (Q \to R))$ is a logical truth. But evidently it is not in general highly assertable. Of course logical truths are as logically weak as you can get, but nevertheless 'Assert the stronger instead of the weaker' is of no assistance in explaining away the third paradox. Whatever you think about this maxim in general, it does not apply universally to logical truths. 'If that's the way it is, then that's the way it is', 'George must either be here or not here', 'The part is not greater than the whole', and so on, are all highly assertable.

The fourth objection is that 'Assert the stronger instead of the weaker' is, of necessity, silent about divergences in assertability among logical equivalents simply because logical equivalents do not differ in strength. But the equivalence theorist must acknowledge some marked divergences among equivalents. According to him, $((-P \& (P \to R))$ and $(-P \& (P \to S))$ are logically equivalent, both being equivalent to $-P$. But their

---

[5] *Pace* what appears to be Lewis's suggestion, 'Probabilities of Conditionals and Conditional Probabilities', 308.

assertability can differ sharply. 'The sun will come up tomorrow but if it doesn't, it won't matter' is highly unassertable, while 'The sun will come up tomorrow but if it doesn't, that will be the end of the world' is highly assertable.

My final objection is that if the standard way of trying to explain away the paradoxes is right, 'or' and '$\rightarrow$' are on a par. It would, for instance, be just as wrong, and just as right, to assert 'P or Q' merely on the basis of knowing P as to assert $(P \supset Q)$ merely on the basis of knowing not P. And, more generally, '$P \vdash (P$ or $Q)$' and '$Q \vdash (P$ or $Q)$' should strike us as just as much a problem for the thesis that 'P or Q' is equivalent to $(P \vee Q)$ as do the paradoxes of material implication for the Equivalence thesis. It is a plain fact that they do not. The thesis that 'P or Q' is equivalent to $(P \vee Q)$ is relatively non-controversial, the thesis that $(P \rightarrow Q)$ is equivalent to $(P \supset Q)$ is highly controversial.

This objection, of course, applies not just to attempts to explain away the paradoxes in terms of 'Assert the stronger', but to any attempt which appeals simply to considerations of conversational propriety. It leaves it a mystery why we—who are after all reasonably normal language-users—find it so easy to swallow one thesis and so hard to swallow the other.

Should we respond to these objections by abandoning the Equivalence thesis or by looking for a different way of explaining away the paradoxes? An argument for the latter is that the thought behind 'Assert the stronger rather than the weaker' contains a serious lacuna, as I now argue.

2. A REASON FOR SOMETIMES ASSERTING THE WEAKER

Suppose, as before, that S_1 is logically stronger than S_2 and that S_1's probability is only marginally lower than S_2's. Consistent with this it may be that the impact of new information, I, on S_1 is very different from the impact of I on S_2; in particular it may happen that I reduces the probability of S_1 substantially without reducing S_2's to any significant extent (indeed S_2's may rise). I will describe such a situation as one where S_2 but not S_1 is *robust* with respect to I. If we accept Conditionalization, the plausible thesis that the impact of new information is given by the relevant conditional probability, then 'P is robust with respect to Γ' will be true just when both $Pr(P)$ and $Pr(P/I)$ are close and high.[6] (Obviously a more general account would simply require that $Pr(P)$ and $Pr(P/I)$ be close, but throughout we will be concerned only with cases where the probabilities are high enough to warrant assertion, other things being equal.)

We can now see the lacuna in the line of thought lying behind 'Assert the stronger instead of the weaker.' Despite S_1 and S_2 both being highly probable and S_1 entailing everything S_2 does, there may be a good reason for asserting S_2 either instead of or as well as S_1. It may be desirable that what you say should remain highly probable should I turn out to be the case, and further it may be that $Pr(S_2/I)$ is high while $Pr(S_1/I)$ is low. In short, robustness with respect to I may be desirable, and (consistent with S_1 entailing S_2) S_2 may have it while S_1 lacks it.

Examples bear this out. Robustness is an important ingredient in assertability. Here are two examples taken from those which might be (are) thought to be nothing more than illustrations of 'Assert the stronger instead of the weaker.'

Suppose I read in the paper that Hyperion won the 4.15. George asks me who won the 4.15. I say 'Either Hyperion or Hydrogen won.' Everyone agrees that I have done the wrong thing. Although the disjunction is highly probable, it is not highly assertable. Why? The standard explanation is in terms of 'Assert the stronger instead of the weaker.'[7] But is this the whole story? Consider the following modification to our case. What I read is that H___ won. The name is too blurred for me to do more than pick out the initial letter. However I happen to know that

[6] See e.g. Jeffrey, *Logic of Decision* (New York, 1965); and F. P. Ramsey, *Foundations of Mathematics* (London, 1931), ch. 7. Robustness is a notion I first heard about some years ago from Manfred von Thun in the context of *weight* in J. M. Keynes's sense, *Treatise on Probability* (London, 1921). Brian Skyrms uses 'resilience' for a similar notion, see his 'Physical Laws and Philosophical Reduction' in *Induction, Probability and Confirmation*, Minnesota Studies in Philosophy of Science, vi, ed. G. Maxwell and R. M. Anderson, Jr. (University of Minnesota Press: Minneapolis, 1975). Neither should be held responsible for my use of the notion in what follows.

[7] 'Standard' in that it is offered by non-equivalence theorists as well as equivalence theorists, see e.g. Mackie, *Truth, Probability and Paradox*, 76.

Hyperion and Hydrogen are the only two horses in the 4.15 whose names begin with 'H', and in addition I know that Hydrogen is a no-hoper from the bush. Clearly it is still the case that 'Hyperion won' is highly probable and it would be quite proper for me to say so. But it would *also* be quite proper for me to say 'Hyperion or Hydrogen won', despite its being weaker and only marginally more probable. Indeed the natural thing to do would be to say something like 'Either Hyperion or Hydrogen won. It can't have been Hydrogen—he's a no-hoper. So it must have been Hyperion.'

The obvious explanation for the marked change in the assertability of the disjunction is that in the original case it was not robust with respect to the negation of both its disjuncts taken separately, while in the modified case it is. In the original case, were I to learn that Hyperion was not the winner I would have to abandon the disjunction. In the modified case I would not, though I would have to abandon my low opinion of Hydrogen. Therefore, in the modified case there is point to asserting that Hyperion or Hydrogen won instead of simply that Hyperion won, even if the probabilities are very close. This disjunction possesses a relevant robustness that its left disjunct lacks.

Indeed surely there are many cases where disjunctions are highly assertable even though they have probabilities for their assertors only marginally greater than that of one of their disjuncts. Consider 'Either Oswald killed Kennedy or the Warren Commission was incompetent.' This is highly assertable even for someone convinced that the Warren Commission was not incompetent. Yet they are in a position to assert the stronger 'Oswald killed Kennedy.' The disjunction is nevertheless highly assertable for them, because it would still be probable were information to come to hand that refuted one or other disjunct. The disjunction is robust with respect to the negation of either of its disjuncts taken separately—and just this may make it pointful to assert it. Because it makes it acceptable to a possible hearer who denies one or other of the disjuncts.

Moreover, we can have highly probable disjunctions which are, unlike the two just considered, significantly more probable than either of their disjuncts and yet which are not highly assertable.

Suppose I propose to toss a fair coin five times in such a way that the tosses are probabilistically independent; then 'At least one of the five tosses will be a head' is probable enough (~97 per cent) to warrant assertion. Consequently so is the equivalent disjunction 'Either at least one of the first three tosses or at least one of the last two tosses will be a head', and moreover each disjunct is significantly less probable than the disjunction. But it would be highly misleading to assert the disjunction in preference to the equivalent sentence. For it would create in hearers the mistaken expectation that should the first three tosses fail to yield a head, they can be sure that at least one of the last two will.

The second example is one of David Lewis's.

We are gathering mushrooms; I say to you 'You won't eat that one and live.' A dirty trick: I thought that one was safe and especially delicious, I wanted it myself, so I hoped to dissuade you from taking it without actually lying. I thought it highly probable that my trick would work, that you would not eat the mushroom, and therefore I would turn out to have told the truth. But though what I said had a high subjective probability of truth, it had a low assertability and it was a misdeed to assert it. Its assertability goes not just by probability but by the resultant of that and a correction term to take account of the pointlessness and misleadingness of denying a conjunction when one believes it false predominantly because of disbelieving one conjunct.[8]

But this explanation faces two difficulties. First, suppose I am not *that* confident that my trick will work. I am pretty sure but not certain enough to warrant outright assertion. And further suppose that I am also pretty certain that you will die for reasons unconnected with mushrooms. The two factors combined bring the probability of 'You won't eat that one and live' up to a level sufficient to warrant assertion. In this case the probability of falsity of each conjunct contributes significantly to the probability that the negated conjunction is true, but nevertheless it would still be a misdeed to assert it. Second, suppose the mushroom really is dangerous and I say 'You won't eat that one and live' while crushing it under my foot for safety's sake. The difference in probability between the negated conjunction and 'You won't eat

[8] 'Probabilities of Conditionals and Conditional Probabilities', Essay IV in this volume.

that one' will then be minuscule. But the negated conjunction is nevertheless highly assertable in this case.

It seems to me, therefore, that a better explanation is one in terms of robustness. You take me to be providing information relevant to mushroom-eating pleasures, and so construct for yourself the following piece of practical reasoning. I won't eat that one and live. (Premiss supplied by me.) I eat that one. (Premiss you can make true.) Therefore, I won't live. The conclusion is undesirable, hence you are led to refrain from making the second premiss true.

Why were you tricked? The argument is valid, the premiss I supplied does have a high probability, and you are able to give the second premiss a high probability. But in order to infer the conclusion of a valid argument all premisses need to be highly probable *together*; and if you were to make the second premiss highly probable, the first premiss (supplied by me) would no longer be highly probable. In the circumstances you were entitled to take it that not only was 'You won't eat that one and live' highly probable, it was also robust with respect to 'You eat that one.' My misdeed lay in asserting something lacking appropriate robustness.

The upshot, then, is simply that when considering propriety of assertion we should take account of robustness *as well as* high probability, relevance, informativeness, and so on.

3. THE APPLICATION OF ROBUSTNESS TO CONDITIONALS

Robustness is a relative affair. A highly probable sentence may be very robust relative to one possible piece of information[9] and the opposite relative to another. Often the possible information relative to which robustness is desirable is given by the context. In the mushroom-gathering story it was obvious that the hearer expected sentences that were robust relative to his eating the mushroom. That is how he was tricked. But context will not always

[9] The possible information may be actual. Obviously we are often interested in robustness relative to what we might, but don't to date, know. But this is not part of the definition of robustness. If it was, P would automatically become non-robust with respect to I on learning I! When I is known at t, our definition makes P robust with respect to I if and only if P is highly probable at t.

be enough. It makes sense that we should have syntactical constructions which signal the possible information relative to which we take what we are saying to be robust.

Their role would be akin to that of 'but' in signalling or indicating a contrast without the obtaining of this contrast being a necessary condition for speaking truly.[10] Thus the truth conditions for 'P but Q' are the same as those for 'P & Q'. In familiar jargons[11] their literal content is the same, but the use of the first carries a conventional (not conversational) implicature that the second does not; or they differ in tone but are alike in sense. I will however talk mainly of signalling and indicating rather than implicature or tone. What follows does not depend crucially on the precise way such a distinction should be drawn.

It is, of course, vital that we allow the possibility of distinguishing signalling or indicating an attitude towards a sentence from making that attitude part of the truth-conditions, sense, or literal content of what we say. There is a great difference between producing a sentence S as something accepted and thereby asserted, and producing it as an example or as something granted for the sake of argument. It is thus important that we can signal this—perhaps by using Frege's assertion sign—and such a signal cannot be taken simply as part of the content of what is said. Because 'S and I accept (or assert) S' may as easily as S itself be produced as an example or granted for the sake of argument, rather than being asserted.[12]

I am suggesting, then, that when we assert a sentence it makes sense that we should have ways of indicating that as well as obeying the base rule that requires that S be highly probable, we also take it that, for some I, S is robust with respect to I.

One way of doing this is to put your sentence in disjunctive form when it would be shorter and simpler not to. Suppose I am asked what colour Harry's car is. It is perfectly acceptable for me to reply simply that it is blue, even if my ground for being confident that it

---

[10] See e.g. M. Dummett, *Frege* (Duckworth: London, 1973): 85–6.

[11] See e.g. Dummett, *Frege*, and various of Grice's papers, including 'Logic and Conversation', in *Syntax and Semantics*, iii, ed. Peter Cole and Jerry L. Morgan (New York, 1975), and 'Further Notes on Logic and Conversation' in *Syntax and Semantics*, ix, ed. Peter Cole (New York, 1978).

[12] Cf. Dummett, *Frege*, 316.

is blue is that it is light-blue. Unless there is reason to think that
the precise shade matters, near enough is good enough here.
Suppose however that I replied that Harry's car is either light-blue
or dark-blue. This reply is not acceptable in the circumstances
even if the precise shade does not matter, despite the fact that
(ignoring borderline cases) it is equivalent to the acceptable one
(and so incidentally the difference in assertability cannot be
explained by reference to 'Assert the stronger instead of the
weaker'). The reason that the second reply is not acceptable is that
in putting it in explicitly disjunctive form you signal robustness
with respect to the negation of each disjunct taken separately. The
reply would be proper only if both the (subjective) probability of
its being light-blue or dark-blue given it is not light-blue and the
probability of its being light-blue or dark-blue given it is not dark-
blue were high. And in our case the former is low.

In general we are happiest asserting disjunctions which are two-
sidedly robust. We most happily assert 'P or Q' when $Pr(P \vee Q)$,
$Pr(P \vee Q/-P)$, and $Pr(P \vee Q/Q-Q)$ are all high. (Thus, the oft-
noted 'exclusive feel' about the inclusive 'or'. Accordingly, when
we are not in a position to so assert, we should expect to have a
way of signalling merely one-sided robustness in order to avoid
misleading our hearers into assuming two-sided robustness. And it
seems that we do.

Consider the following, common enough kind of case. You are
pretty sure that George lives in Boston but not quite sure enough
to warrant outright assertion. You are, though, sure enough that
he lives somewhere in New England. You say 'He lives in Boston
or anyway somewhere in New England.' Likewise we say things
like 'He is a fascist (communist) or anyhow on the far right (left)'
and 'Caesar defeated Pompey in 48 BC, or at least that's what
George told me.' We use the 'P or anyway Q' construction to
indicate that '$P \vee Q$' is robust with respect to $-P$, but not with
respect to $-Q$. Should you learn against your expectation that
George does not live in Boston, the disjunction will still be highly
probable for you due to its right disjunct 'George lives in New
England' still being so; but obviously you will have to abandon the
disjunction altogether should you learn that George does not live
in New England after all.

A consequence of this asymmetry is that commutation can give strange-sounding results. 'He lives in Boston or anyway somewhere in New England' is a happy saying, whereas 'He lives somewhere in New England or anyway in Boston' is not. Nevertheless commutation is valid; for the truth-conditions of 'P or anyway Q' are just those of '$P \vee Q$'. 'George lives in Boston or anyway somewhere in New England' is true if and only if either 'George lives in Boston' is true or 'George lives somewhere in New England' is true. 'Caesar defeated Pompey in 48 BC, or at least that is what George told me' is true if either disjunct is true and false if neither is; and so on and so forth. Signalling robustness does not invade truth-conditions.

Before I apply these ideas to indicative conditionals, let me review the course of the argument. High probability is an important ingredient in assertability. Everyone accepts that. But so is robustness. Commonly, cases cited to illustrate 'Assert the stronger instead of the weaker' really illustrate the importance of robustness. The relevant robustness, however, is relative to statements other than the one being asserted. (Every highly probable statement is trivially robust with respect to itself.) Thus we need devices and conventions to signal which statements our assertions are robust relative to. We have just been looking at some of these devices and have noted that their presence does not alter truth-conditions. Accordingly, I suggest that the indicative conditional construction is such a device. It signals robustness with respect to its antecedent. Hence it is proper to assert $(P \rightarrow Q)$ when $(P \supset Q)$ is highly probable and robust with respect to P, that is, when $Pr(P \supset Q/P)$ is also high. But, by analogy with explicit disjunction and '$-$or anyway$-$', the truth-conditions of $(P \rightarrow Q)$ are those of $(P \supset Q)$. It is like 'Nevertheless P' in this regard. The use of 'nevertheless' signals the robustness of P with respect to what has gone before, but the whole sentence is true if and only if P is.

At first glance it may appear that this version of the Equivalence thesis is totally opposed to those theories which assign conditionals assertion and acceptance, but not truth, conditions.[13] But in fact it

---

[13] For recent examples see Ernest W. Adams, *The Logic of Conditionals* (Reidel: Dordrecht, 1975), and Mackie, *Truth, Probability and Paradox*.

is a half-way house. Consider again 'Nevertheless P'. Although the whole is true if and only if P is true; a part—'nevertheless'—contributes to assertion—conditions without affecting truth-conditions. We can give the conditions under which it is proper to use 'nevertheless', but not those under which using it is saying something true. Likewise with the signalling role of the indicative conditional construction. Our theory is thus a supplemented Equivalence theory. In the widest sense of 'meaning', $(P \to Q)$ and $(P \supset Q)$ do not mean the same. But their truth-conditions are the same—they agree in sense or literal content. The extra element is that in using $(P \to Q)$ you explicitly signal the robustness of $(P \supset Q)$ with respect to P, and this element affects assertion-conditions without affecting truth-conditions.

We could have gone further and made the robustness of $(P \supset Q)$ with respect to P a necessary condition for the truth of $(P \to Q)$. But this seems, as a simple fact of linguistic usage, too strong. For, first, we allow that a person may speak truly in the conditional mode without *deserving* to do so. Suppose it is highly probable that it will rain tomorrow and in consequence that the match will be cancelled. But, with the intention of misleading Fred, I say that if it rains, the match will go ahead. In this case 'It rains $\supset$ the match will go ahead' is neither probable nor robust with respect to 'It rains'. Further suppose that it does indeed rain, but against the odds, the match goes ahead. We allow that I have spoken truly without of course deserving to do so. And, secondly, we allow that *one* member of the set of conditionals of the form 'If I write down the number _____, I will write down the number of molecules in this room' is true. Yet *none* is robust with respect to its antecedent.

What is the point of signalling the robustness of $(P \supset Q)$ with respect to P? The answer lies in the importance of being able to use *modus ponens*. Although $(P \supset Q)$, P, $\therefore Q$ is certainly valid, there is a difficulty about using it in practice. Suppose my evidence makes $(P \supset Q)$ highly probable but that I have no evidence concerning P. Q is of interest to me, so I set about finding evidence for P if I can. The difficulty is that finding evidence that makes P highly probable is not enough in itself for me to conclude Q by *modus ponens*. For the evidence that makes P probable may make $(P \supset Q)$ improbable. Indeed it is easy to prove from the calculus that, except in special cases of extreme probability, $Pr(P \supset Q/P) < Pr(P \supset Q)$; that is, normally on learning P I must *lower* the probability I give $(P \supset Q)$ so endangering the inference to Q. It is thus of particular interest whether or not $(P \supset Q)$'s high probability would be unduly diminished by learning P; that is, it is important whether or not $(P \supset Q)$ is robust with respect to P. In sum, we must distinguish the *validity* of *modus ponens* from its *utility* in a situation where I know $(P \supset Q)$ but do not know P.[14] The robustness of $(P \supset Q)$ relative to P is what is needed to ensure the utility of *modus ponens* in such situations.

It does not, though, ensure the utility of *modus tollens*. $Pr(P \supset Q/P)$ can be high when $Pr(P \supset Q/-Q)$ is low. And this is how things should be. You may properly assert $(P \to Q)$ when you would *not* infer $-P$ on learning $-Q$. Suppose you say 'If he doesn't live in Boston, then he lives somewhere in New England' or 'If he works, he will still fail', you will — despite the validity of *modus tollens* — neither infer that he lives in Boston on learning (to your surprise) that he doesn't live in New England nor infer that he didn't work on learning (to your surprise) that he passed. Rather on learning either you would abandon the original conditional as mistaken.[15] Of course it is not only the robustness of material conditionals with respect to their antecedents that is important. Accordingly if our approach is along the right lines we should expect a linguistic device to signal the robustness of Q with respect to P, not merely of $(P \supset Q)$ with respect to P. But if the Supplemented Equivalence thesis is right, the latter is sufficient for the former. Consider $(Q \ \& \ (P \to Q))$. According to the Equivalence thesis it is equivalent to Q, and according to our supplementation the right-hand conjunct signals that $Pr(P \supset Q/P)$ is high. But $Pr(P \supset Q/P)$ simplifies to $Pr(Q/P)$. Hence asserting $(Q \ \& \ (P \to Q))$ is equivalent to asserting Q and also signals the robustness of Q with respect to P — just what we are looking for.

[14] In my view the objection to *disjunctive syllogism* in A. R. Anderson and N. D. Belnap, *Entailment* (Princeton, 1977), conflates these two questions. Note particularly the top paragraph of their p. 177.

[15] I here dissent from W. E. Johnson's illuminating remarks in ch. 3 of *Logic*, pt. 1 (New York, 1964). (Incidentally, saying P only if Q does seem to signal robustness of $P \supset Q$ with respect to $-Q$.)

When we assert both Q and $(P \to Q)$ we commonly use a 'still' construction: 'The match will be played, and it will still be played if it rains', 'Carter will be re-elected, and if the Camp David talks fail, he will still be re-elected.' And often we don't bother to repeat the common element, Q. Context makes it clear that we think that the match will be played or that Carter will be re-elected, and we simply say 'The match will still be played if it rains' or '(Even) if the Camp David talks fail, Carter will still be re-elected.' A stronger position is that 'If P, then still Q' entails Q.[16] But consider one who makes, all in one breath, the following perfectly acceptable remark. 'If it rains lightly, the match will still be played. But if it rains heavily, as it well may, the match will be cancelled.' Surely he is not asserting *inter alia* that the match will be played.

4. DEFENCE

I take for granted one negative argument for our Supplemented Equivalence thesis, namely that all its competitors face well-known objections. One obvious positive argument for it would consist in assembling a large number of examples of indicative conditionals and testing our intuitions concerning assertion against the results our theory predicts. Fortunately this is not necessary. Ernest Adams has provided a simple formula governing our intuitions, and the Supplemented Equivalence theory explains this formula.

Adams has shown that the (intuitively justified) assertability of $(P \to Q)$ is given by

$$Pr(Q/P) = df \ \frac{Pr(PQ)}{Pr(P)}.[17]$$

[16] Some have held the similar position that 'Q even if P' entails Q. See e.g. Mackie, *Truth, Probability and Paradox*, 72, and Pollock, *Logic of Conditionals*, 29. I would advance a similar objection to this position.

[17] Adams, *Logic of Conditionals*, and his earlier papers 'The Logic of Conditionals', *Inquiry*, 8/2 (1965): 166–97 and 'Probability and the Logic of Conditionals' in *Aspects of Inductive Logic*, ed. J. Hintikka and P. Suppes (Amsterdam, 1966): 265–316. Strong evidence that he is essentially right is the number of authors of very different philosophical persuasions who have found this general kind of thesis congenial, e.g. Brian Ellis, 'An Epistemological Concept of

Thus I assent to 'If it rains, the match will be cancelled' to the extent that my subjective probability of the match being cancelled given it rains is high.

We explain Adams's thesis as follows. On our theory, the assertability of $(P \rightarrow Q)$ will be the product of two factors: the extent to which $Pr(P \supset Q)$ is high and the extent to which $(P \supset Q)$ is robust with respect to P. But we have from the calculus that $Pr(P \supset Q/P) = Pr(Q/P)$, and that $Pr(P \supset Q) \geqslant Pr(Q/P)$. Consequently both conditions are satisfied to the extent that $Pr(Q/P)$ is high. QED.

An important recent result of Lewis's highlights the significance of this derivation. He *proves* that the obvious alternative explanation of Adams's thesis fails. He proves (by a *reductio* argument) that $(P \rightarrow Q)$ does not differ in truth-conditions from $(P \supset Q)$ in such a way as to make $Pr(P \rightarrow Q) = Pr(Q/P)$.[18]

Consequently, we can explain why $(P \rightarrow Q)$ and $(P \rightarrow -Q)$ are not assertable together when P is consistent. $Pr(Q/P)$ and $Pr(-Q/P)$ cannot (from the calculus) both be high.[19] Or, more precisely, they cannot both be high relative to the same body of evidence. Robustness, like probability in general, is relative to evidence, and of course $Pr(Q/P \& R)$ and $Pr(-Q/P \& S)$ can both be high. Accordingly our theory predicts that we should be happy to assert both $(P \rightarrow Q)$ and $(P \rightarrow -Q)$ when it is *explicit* that the relevant bodies of evidence are appropriately different. Exactly this happens. Harry and George are discussing whether Fred went to the rock concert. Harry says 'If Fred went, he must have gone by car, because there was a transport strike at the time.' George says 'But Fred regards the private car as exploitative and never goes

Truth' in *Contemporary Philosophy in Australia*, ed. R. Brown and C. D. Rollins (London, 1969); Jeffrey, 'If', *Journal of Philosophy*, 61 (1964): 702–3; Robert Stalnaker, 'Probability and Conditionals', *Philosophy of Science*, 37 (1970): 64–80; and Lewis, 'Probabilities of Conditionals and Conditional Probabilities', Essay IV in this volume. Adams's formula does not of course take into account the kind of 'local' sources of unassertability set to one side in section 1, like obscenity, rudeness, and long-windedness.

[18] 'Probabilities of Conditionals and Conditional Probabilities', Essay IV in this volume.

[19] When P is inconsistent, $Pr(P) = 0$, and $Pr(Q/P)$ is undefined; accordingly we need a ruling about the assertability of $(P \rightarrow Q)$ in such cases. The ruling I will follow is that all such conditionals are assertable. Others are possible.

anywhere by car on principle; so if he went, it cannot have been by car.' They conclude 'In that case, obviously Fred did not go to the rock concert.' Instead of regarding their statements as mutually inconsistent, Harry and George draw from them the conclusion that Fred did not go.[20]

Our theory, then, makes highly assertable just those conditionals intuition judges to be highly assertable. But what of our intuitive, judgements of validity? I am committed to taking $-P$, $\therefore$ $P \to Q$, and Q, $\therefore$ $P \to Q$ to be valid, and they notoriously lack intuitive appeal. But this lack of appeal seems to derive from our reluctance to assert $(P \to Q)$ merely because we are confident that $-P$ and our (less-marked) reluctance to assert $(P \to Q)$ merely because we are confident that Q, and our theory can explain these easily enough. Neither the fact that $Pr(-P)$ is high nor the fact that $Pr(Q)$ is high is sufficient for $Pr(P \supset Q/P)$ being high. The reason our reluctance is less marked in the case of asserting $(P \to Q)$ on the basis of our certainty that Q, is that $Pr(Q)$ being high together with P and Q being probabilistically independent *is* sufficient for $Pr(P \supset Q/P)$ being high.

Similarly, what I referred to earlier as the third paradox—that $((P \to Q) \vee (Q \to R))$ is a logical truth and yet is far from invariably highly assertable—is not a decisive objection to our supplemented version of the Equivalence thesis, because the presence of signals can make logical truths unassertable. We have already noted the plausibility of giving 'Nevertheless P' the same truth-conditions as P. Consequently 'Nevertheless P or nevertheless not P' is a logical truth, but it is not highly assertable.

What of *strengthening the antecedent, hypothetical syllogism*, and *contraposition*, all of which are of course valid on our theory. Take *contraposition* (similar points apply to all three). The problem is not that it seems invalid stated in symbols; exactly the reverse is the case, as is evinced by its appearance in *Natural* Deduction systems. The problem is rather a certain class of apparent counter-examples like: 'If George works hard, he will (still) fail; therefore, if he passes, he won't have worked hard', and 'If Carter is re-elected, it won't be by a large margin; therefore if Carter is re-elected by a large margin, he won't be re-elected.'

[20] For other examples of this kind see Clark, 'Ifs and Hooks: A Rejoinder'.

But these apparent counter-examples are paralleled by ones against the commutativity of '—or anyway—': for instance, 'It won't rain or anyway not heavily; therefore, it won't rain heavily or anyway it won't rain.' Despite this, we noted that it seemed clearly right to give the same truth-conditions to 'P or anyway Q' as are standardly given to 'P or Q'. The explanation for the counterintuitive feel must therefore lie not in the failure of *commutation* but in the failure of what is signalled by 'anyway' to 'commute'. Similarly *addition* is hardly appealing when applied to '—or at least—'. Consider 'Harry said that Caesar defeated Pompey in 48 BC; therefore Harry said that Caesar defeated Pompey in 48 BC or at least Caesar defeated Pompey in 48 BC.'

It seems therefore not unreasonable to attribute the counterintuitive feel of certain instances of *contraposition* to the failure of what is signalled by the indicative conditional construction to 'contrapose' (and likewise for *hypothetical syllogism*, and so on). And it may be confirmed by inspection that the putative counter-examples to *contraposition* are all ones where $Pr(P \supset Q/P) = Pr(Q/P)$ is high, and $Pr(-Q \supset -P/-Q) = Pr(-P/-Q)$ is low. For example, the probability of Carter not being re-elected by a large margin given he is re-elected may be high when the probability of Carter not being re-elected given he is re-elected by a large margin is minimal. Accordingly, we can explain our reluctance to assert 'If Carter is re-elected by a large margin, then Carter will not be re-elected' even when we are happy to assert 'If Carter is re-elected, then it will not be by a large margin' in terms, not of the first being false and the second true, but in terms of what is signalled by saying the first being false and what is signalled by saying the second being true.

5. ON THREE OBJECTIONS

(i) It may be objected that the account offered above is circular. The Equivalence thesis itself is not circular, obviously, but the supplemented thesis involves a story about the role of the indicative conditional construction as signalling robustness, and it might be objected that robustness can only be elucidated via a conditional construction. P is robust for person S relative to I just if P's high probability for S would not be substantially reduced *if S were* to acquire the information that I. One reply would be to urge that we simply define robustness in terms of conditional probability,

$$Pr(P/I) = \text{df } \frac{Pr(PI)}{Pr(I)}.$$

No conditionals there.

This reply is open to challenge. For the defence of so defining robustness must involve a defence of Conditionalization, the thesis that the impact of new information is given by the relevant conditional probability, and it might be urged that talk of the impact of new information can best be understood as talk of what one's probabilities would or should be *if* one were to acquire the new information. But another reply is possible. The conditionals involved here are essentially subjunctive and counterfactual in character, and as such are importantly distinct from indicative conditionals. It is not, therefore, uselessly circular to appeal to the former in one's story about the latter.

I take the case for separating out the problem of indicative conditionals from the problem of subjunctive conditionals to be familiar.[21] It derives from pairs like 'Carter is bald, no one knows it' and 'If Carter were bald, no one would know it', and 'If Oswald did not shoot Kennedy, someone else did' and 'If Oswald had not shot Kennedy, someone else would have.' For each pair we assent to the first and dissent from the second, and our dissent from the second member of each pair is accompanied by assent to, respectively, 'If Carter were bald, everyone would know it' and 'If Oswald had not shot Kennedy, no one would have.'

It sometimes seems to be thought that the contrast between indicative and subjunctive or counterfactual conditionals only shows up when (1) the consequents are *known* one way or the other and (2) they are not about the future.[22] But here is a pair involving a future, doubtful event. I have been told that Fred's

[21] From e.g. Lewis, *Counterfactuals* (Oxford, 1973), and Adams, 'Subjunctive and Indicative Conditionals', *Foundations of Language*, 6 (1970): 89–94.

[22] See e.g. Ellis, 'A Unified Theory of Conditionals', *Journal of Philosophical Logic,* 7 (1978): 107–24, and (with reservations) Adams, *Logic of Conditionals:* ch. 4.

birthday and George's birthday fall next week. But I cannot remember the exact days, only that Fred's is the day before George's. I say 'If Fred's is next Tuesday, George's will be next Wednesday', and I don't say 'If Fred's were next Tuesday, George's would be next Wednesday' (unless of course I know that the hospital specially arranged George's birth one day after Fred's, or something of that kind). Likewise, suppose that station *B* is half-way between *A* and *C*. A person at *B* observing a train passing through *on time* may well affirm 'If the train had been late leaving *A*, it would be late pulling into *C*' while denying 'If the train was late leaving *A*, it will be late pulling into *C*.'

It is nevertheless undeniable that the contrast between indicative and counterfactual conditionals is less marked in the case of conditionals pertaining to the future. For example, *before* the assassination of Kennedy we would say both 'If Oswald *were* not to shoot Kennedy, no one would' and 'If Oswald *does* not shoot Kennedy, no one will.' It is only now, after the event, that we say 'If Oswald did not shoot Kennedy, someone else did.' But this is a point in favour of our theory, for it can explain why the contrast is less marked in the case of the future.

It is a fact that we know more about the past than about the future. I know more about who won last year's election than I do about who will win next year's. In particular, our beliefs about the future by and large depend on relatively tenuous beliefs about what present and past conditions will give rise to, while our beliefs about the past are frequently independent of our beliefs about how the past came about. My beliefs about next year's election-winner rest on my beliefs about present conditions and their effect on electoral popularity, while my beliefs about last year's winner are by and large independent of my views as to what led to her success. Predicting election-winners calls for a theory of what makes for electoral popularity, retrodicting them only calls for an ability to read the newspapers. Consequently the probabilities we assign future events depend on our views about what would lead to what. But by our theory it is these very probabilities that settle the indicative conditionals we assert and it is these very views about what would lead to what that are expressed in subjunctive and counterfactual conditionals.[23] Hence the general match between the two in the case of the future. On the other hand, the probabilities we assign past events may be largely independent of our views about what would lead to what. When Q is past we may give $Pr(Q/P)$ a high value independently of what we believe gave rise to it, and so may assert $(P \to Q)$ largely independently of our stance on counterfactuals of the form $(- \Box \to Q)$, including in particular $(P \Box \to Q)$.

It might also be thought that the contrast between indicative and subjunctive conditionals is simply due to the different role of what is being taken for granted, presupposed, or regarded as common knowledge in the context.[24] When we consider indicative conditionals we 'hold on to' common knowledge, when we consider subjunctive conditionals we need not.[25] It is taken for granted that someone shot Kennedy, hence even under the indicatively expressed supposition that Oswald did not shoot Kennedy, we hold that someone (else) did. But under the subjunctively expressed supposition that Oswald had not, we may abandon this presupposition. Likewise with the other examples given. It is common knowledge that Carter is not bald and also (we were supposing) that Fred's birthday is the day before George's and that the train was on time at B, and these facts were what was being retained when the indicatives were in question and being abandoned when the subjunctives were in question.

However, the reverse happens with other examples. You and I

[23] I argue this in detail in 'A Casual Theory of Counterfactuals', *Australasian Journal of Philosophy*, 55 (1977): 3–21; but the general idea is widely accepted.

[24] I am indebted here in particular to the referee for drawing my attention to Stalnaker, 'Indicative Conditionals', in *Language in Focus*, ed. A. Kasher (Dordrecht, 1976).

[25] Ibid. 182–7, shows how to express this in terms of the familiar possible-worlds approach to counterfactuals (due to him, 'A Theory of Conditionals', in *Studies in Logical Theory*, ed. N. Rescher (Oxford, 1968), and Lewis, *Counterfactuals*). According to Stalnaker this approach works for both indicative and subjunctive conditionals, the difference between the two being due to the fact that in the case of the former but not the latter the similarity relation is constrained by the need to preserve common knowledge. When we consider $(P \to Q)$ at world i we are to look for the closest P-world *which shares with i what is being taken to be common knowledge in the context of assertion* and ask whether it is a Q-world. But see the counter-examples below.

have been taking the date of Caesar's defeat of Pompey as common knowledge; and it is just this we hold on to in asserting the *subjunctive* 'If the historians had reported the date of Caesar's victory as 50 BC, they would have been wrong' (not even historians can change the past), and it is just this we abandon in asserting the indicative 'If the historians do report the date as 50 BC, then I am wrong in giving it as 48 BC.' Perhaps it will be objected that what was taken as common knowledge was that the historians have the date right, rather than the date itself. But then my point can be made with a different pair. We *assert* 'If Caesar's victory was in 50 BC, the historians have the date wrong', while *denying* 'If Caesar's victory had been in 50 BC, the historians would have got the date wrong.' Likewise, it is common ground that the declared winner of a presidential election is the person with the most votes. Yet it is just this we are prepared to abandon when we consider indicative conditionals starting. 'If Ford got more votes than Carter, . . .', and just this we hold on to when considering subjunctive conditionals starting 'If Ford had got more votes than Carter, . . .'

(ii) Thus far I have focused on explaining assent patterns to conditionals in terms of the Supplemented Equivalence theory. What of dissent? Standardly you dissent from an assertion just when its subjective probability of falsity is high (neglecting, as before, highly contextual factors like obscenity). The probable falsity of what may be signalled by the assertion is by and large irrelevant.[26] You dissent from 'He is poor but happy' just when it is probable that he is either not poor or not happy, not when you dissent from the signalled contrast. Dissent is typically dissent from what is literally said. But it is clear and generally acknowledged that we dissent from conditionals in circumstances other than those where it is probable that the antecedent is true and the consequent false. Even anti-Warrenites dissent from 'If Oswald killed Kennedy, then the Warren Commission got the killer's identity wrong'; but they do not regard 'Oswald killed Kennedy and the Warren Commission got the killer's identity

---

[26] Cf. Cohen's report of Grice's views, 'Some Remarks on Grice's Views'.

right' as highly probable. They think rather that Oswald did not kill Kennedy and that the Warren Commission got the killer's identity wrong.

There are, however, exceptions to the rule that we dissent just when it is probable that what is literally said is false. Suppose I say in a serious tone of voice 'I believe that it will rain tomorrow.' There are *two* circumstances in which you naturally dissent. One is when you think I am lying, that is, when the probability of falsity of what is literally said is high (by your lights). The other is when you think it will not rain. In this case your dissent is not from what I literally say but from what I signal by saying it in a serious tone of voice, namely that its raining is highly probable.

Another example is when I say 'The winner of the election for club president will come from Tom, Dick, and Harry.' What I say counts as true if anyone of these three wins. But you won't dissent only if you think this improbable. You may grant it probable because of the excellent chance Tom has of winning but nevertheless dissent because I left out George, and in your view George has the best chance after Tom. In other words, you will dissent when what *you* would assert is that the winner will come from Tom and George, and not only when you are prepared to say that none of Tom, Dick, and Harry has a chance.

The explanation for these two cases being exceptions to the rule that dissent is prompted by low probability of literal truth, appears to lie in the peculiarly intimate relationship that obtains in them between what is said and what is signalled. In the second example what is signalled is sufficient for the high probability of what is said. In saying that the election is out of Tom, Dick, and Harry, I signal that the high probability for me of the triple disjunction is robust with respect to the conjunction of the negations of any two of the disjuncts (for example, that it is highly probable that Dick will be elected given that Harry won't and Tom won't). This is sufficient (by the calculus) for the high probability of the disjunction. In the first example what is signalled is arguably sufficient for the truth of what is said. If I say 'I believe it will rain tomorrow' in an appropriately serious tone it is arguable that I signal that I do indeed believe it will rain tomorrow, and I am not, say, producing the sentence merely as a handy example of a belief-sentence. At any rate, it can hardly be denied that there is a close connection between what is said and what is signalled in this case.

According to our account, conditionals are yet another example of the same general kind. What is singalled by the assertion of $(P \to Q)$ amounts to $Pr(Q/P)$ being high. This is sufficient for $Pr(P \supset Q)$ being high. So what is signalled is sufficient for the high probability of what is literally said. Hence, drawing on the moral of the two examples just discussed, dissent from $(P \to Q)$ may be prompted by the dissenter giving a low value to $Pr(Q/P)$ as much as by his giving a low value to $Pr(P \supset Q)$. Moreover, the latter is sufficient for the former by the calculus, so all cases of dissent from $(P \to Q)$ are ones where $Pr(Q/P)$ is low. This result squares with our intuitions. I dissent from 'If it rains, the match will be cancelled given rain is low. Further if $Pr(Q/P)$ is low, both $Pr(P \supset -Q)$ and $Pr(-Q/P)$ are high. So our theory predicts assent to $(P \to -Q)$ when you dissent from $(P \to Q)$.

And this is just how it turns out in practice. If you dissent from 'If Fred went, he went by car', you assent to 'If Fred went, he did not go by car', which of course is consistent with our earlier observation that in special cases you may assent to both. Indeed the earlier observation highlights the significance of the derivation of the result that if you dissent from $(P \to Q)$, you assent to $(P \to -Q)$. For the result cannot be explained in terms of the two being contradictories.

(iii) Conditionals like 'If he is speaking the truth, I'm a Dutchman' are often cited as being more hospitable to the Equivalence thesis than most. But they present a prima-facie objection to our version. 'He is speaking the truth $\supset$ I'm a Dutchman' is not robust with respect to 'He is speaking the truth.' Should he turn out to be speaking the truth, I won't conclude that I'm a Dutchman. The probability that I'm Dutch given he is speaking the truth is low. But there is good reason to hold that Dutchman conditionals are a very special case. For suppose what he is saying is that I am a Dutchman. Then 'If he is speaking the truth, I'm a Dutchman', standardly interpreted, is certainly true, but I would *not* use it in this case to express my utter disbelief in his truthfulness. Instead I would say something like 'If he's speaking the truth, pigs have wings.' Therefore the use of a Dutchman conditional to express disbelief in its antecedent is not the standard one. The very circumstances in which 'If he's speaking the truth, I'm a Dutchman', standardly interpreted is beyond doubt true are the very ones in which we would *not* use it in the way in question. Hence it is not an objection to our theory that it does not cover them. Our theory is a theory of the standard indicative conditional.

Postscript

Why not simply say the following about $(P \to Q)$? We can distinguish truth-conditions from assertion-conditions. The truth-conditions for $(P \to Q)$ are those of $(P \supset Q)$. There are good and well-known arguments for this. And the assertion-condition for $(P \to Q)$ is that $Pr(Q/P)$ be high. There are good and well-known arguments for this. End of story.

My reason is that conjoining is not explaining. The problem is to explain one in terms of the other. And given the widely accepted view that the best approach to meaning and analysis is via truth-conditions, we should hope for a theory which explains the assertion-conditions in terms of the truth-conditions. This is essentially what I have attempted. I have tried to show how *a* plausible thesis about $(P \to Q)$'s truth-conditions, namely the Equivalence thesis, can, in the light of the importance of robustness for assertability, explain *the* plausible thesis about $(P \to Q)$'s assertion-condition, namely Adams's thesis.

In my view this puts a very different complexion on certain putative counter-examples to the Equivalence thesis. We saw, for instance, how granting the validity of *contraposition* can force the equivalence theorist into holding that 'If Carter is re-elected by a large margin, then he will not be re-elected' is true. But what is it that is *immediately evident* about this putative counter-example? Surely that it has very low assertability. But the Supplemented Equivalence theory *explains* this, and what a theory well explains cannot be an objection to that theory.

VII

INDICATIVE CONDITIONALS*

ROBERT STALNAKER

'EITHER the butler or the gardener did it. Therefore, if the butler didn't do it, the gardener did.' This piece of reasoning—call it the *direct argument*—may seem tedious, but it is surely compelling. Yet if it is a valid inference, then the indicative conditional conclusion must be logically equivalent to the truth-functional material conditional,[1] and *this* conclusion has consequences that are notoriously paradoxical. The problem is that if one accepts the validity of the intuitively reasonable direct argument from the material conditional to the ordinary indicative conditional, then one must accept as well the validity of many arguments that are intuitively absurd. Consider, for example, 'the butler did it; therefore, if he didn't, the gardener did.' The premiss of this argument entails the premiss of the direct argument, and their conclusions are the same. Therefore, if the direct argument is valid, so is this one. But this argument has no trace of intuitive plausibility. Or consider what may be inferred from the *denial* of a conditional. Surely I may deny that if the butler didn't do it, the gardener did without affirming the butler's guilt. Yet if the conditional is material, its negation entails the truth of its antecedent. It is easy to multiply paradoxes of the material

Robert Stalnaker, 'Indicative Conditionals' first published in *Philosophia* 5 (1975): 269–86, reprinted in *Ifs*, ed. W. L. Harper, R. Stalnaker and, G. Pearce, copyright © 1976 by D. Reidel Publishing Company. Reprinted by permission of Kluwer Academic Publishers.

* The ideas in this paper were developed over a number of years. During part of this time my research was supported by the National Science Foundation, grant number GS-2574; more recently it was supported by the John Simon Guggenheim Memorial Foundation.

[1] The argument in the opposite direction—from the indicative conditional to the material conditional—is uncontroversially valid.

conditional in this way—pradoxes that must be explained away by anyone who wants to defend the thesis that the direct argument is valid. Yet anyone who denies the validity of that argument must explain how an invalid argument can be as compelling as this one seems to be.

There are thus two strategies that one may adopt to respond to this puzzle: defend the material conditional analysis and explain away the paradoxes of material implication, or reject the material conditional analysis and explain away the force of the direct argument.[2] H. P. Grice, in his William James lectures,[3] pursued the first of these strategies, using principles of conversation to explain facts about the use of conditionals that seem to conflict with the truth-functional analysis of the ordinary indicative conditional. I will follow the second strategy, defending an alternative semantic analysis of conditionals according to which the conditional entails, but is not entailed by, the corresponding material conditional. I will argue that, although the premiss of the direct argument does not *semantically entail* its conclusion, the inference is nevertheless a *reasonable inference*. My main task will be to define and explain a concept of reasonable inference which diverges from semantic entailment, and which justifies this claim.

Grice's strategy and mine have this in common: both locate the source of the problem in the mistaken attempt to explain the facts about assertion and inference solely in terms of the semantic content, or truth conditions, of the propositions asserted and

[2] This does not exhaust the options. Three other possible strategies might be mentioned. (1) Defend the direct argument, not by accepting the truth-functional analysis of the conditional, but by rejecting the truth-functional analysis of the disjunction. (2) Give a three-valued interpretation of the indicative conditional, assigning the neutral value when the antecedent is false. (3) Interpret the indicative conditional as a conditional assertion rather than the assertion of a conditional proposition. Alternative (1) might disarm this particular puzzle, but it seems *ad hoc* and would not help with other persuasive arguments for the material conditional analysis. Alternative (2) would conflict with some basic and otherwise plausible pragmatic generalizations such as that one should not make an assertion unless one has good reason to think that it is true. Alternative (3) seems to me the most promising and plausible alternative to the account I will develop, but to make it precise, I think one needs much of the framework of a pragmatic theory that I shall use in my account.

[3] Photo-copies have been widely circulated; part of it has been published in: D. Davidson and G. Harman (eds.), *The Logic of Grammar* (Encino, Calif., 1975): 64–75.

inferred. Both attempt to explain the facts partly in terms of the semantic analysis of the relevant notions, but partly in terms of pragmatic principles governing discourse. Both recognize that since assertion aims at more than truth, and inference at more than preserving truth, it is a mistake to reason too quickly from facts about assertion and inference to conclusions about semantic content and semantic entailment.

My plan will be this: first, I will try to explain, in general terms, the concept of reasonable inference and to show intuitively how there can be reasonable inferences which are not entailments. Second, I will describe a formal framework in which semantic concepts like content and entailment as well as pragmatic concepts like assertion and inference can be made precise. Third, within this framework, I will sketch the specific semantic analysis of conditionals, and state and defend some principles relating conditional sentences to the contexts in which they are used. Fourth, I will show that, according to these analyses, the direct argument is a reasonable inference. Finally, I will look at another puzzling argument involving reasoning with conditionals—an argument for fatalism—from the point of view of this framework.

1

Reasonable inference, as I shall define it, is a pragmatic relation: it relates speech acts rather than the propositions which are the contents of speech acts. Thus it contrasts with entailment which is a purely semantic relation. Here are rough informal definitions of the two notions: first, reasonable inference: an inference from a sequence of assertions or suppositions (the premisses) to an assertion or hypothetical assertion (the conclusion) is *reasonable* just in case, in every context in which the premisses could appropriately be asserted or supposed, it is impossible for anyone to accept the premisses without committing himself to the conclusion; second, entailment: a set of propositions (the premisses) *entails* a proposition (the conclusion) just in case it is impossible for the premisses to be true without the conclusion being true as well. The two relations are obviously different since they relate different things, but one might expect them to be equivalent in the sense that an inference would be reasonable if and only if the set of propositions expressed in the premisses entailed the proposition expressed in the conclusion. If this equivalence held, then the pragmatic concept of inference would of course have no interest. I shall argue that, and try to show why, the equivalence does not hold. Before discussing the specific framework in which this will be shown, let me try to explain in general terms how it is possible for an inference to be reasonable, in the sense defined, even when the premisses do not entail the conclusion.

The basic idea is this: many sentences are context-dependent; that is, their semantic content depends not just on the meanings of the words in them, but also on the situations in which they are uttered. Examples are familiar: quantified sentences are interpreted in terms of a domain of discourse, and the domain of discourse depends on the context; the referents of first- and second-person pronouns depend on who is speaking, and to whom; the content of a tensed sentence depends on when it is uttered. Thus context constrains content in systematic ways. But also, the fact that a certain sentence is uttered, and a certain proposition expressed, may in turn constrain or alter the context. There are two ways this may happen: first, since particular utterances are appropriate only in certain contexts, one can infer something about a context from the fact that a particular utterance is made (together with the assumption that the utterance is appropriate); second, the expression of a proposition alters the context, at the very least by changing it into a context in which that proposition has just been expressed. At any given time in a conversation, the context will depend in part on what utterances have been made, and what propositions expressed, previously in the conversation. There is thus a two-way interaction between contexts of utterance and the contents of utterances. If there are general rules governing this interaction, these rules may give rise to systematic relations between propositions expressed at different points in a conversation, relations which are mediated by the context. Such relations may become lost if one ignores the context and considers propositions in abstraction from their place in a discourse. It is because entailment relates propositions independently of their being asserted, supposed, or accepted, while reasonable inference concerns propositions which are expressed and accepted that the two relations may diverge.

These general remarks are not an attempt to show that the notions of entailment and reasonable inference do in fact diverge, but only an attempt to point to the source of the divergence that will be shown. To show the divergence, I must say what contexts are, or how they are to be represented formally. I must say, for some specific construction (here, conditionals) how semantic content is a function of context. And I must state and defend some rules which relate contexts to the propositions expressed in them.

2

The framework I will use begins with, and takes for granted, the concept of a possible world. While model theory based on possible worlds is generally agreed to be a powerful and mathematically elegant tool, its intuitive content and explanatory power are disputed. It is argued that a theory committed to the existence of such implausible entities as possible worlds must be false. Or at least the theory cannot do any philosophical work unless it can provide some kind of substantive answer to the question, what is a possible world? Possible worlds are certainly in need of philosophical explanation and defence, but for the present I will make just a brief remark which will perhaps indicate how I understand this basic notion.[4]

It is a common and essential feature of such activities as enquiring, deliberating, exchanging information, predicting the future, giving advice, debating, negotiating, explaining, and justifying behaviour, that the participants in the activities seek to distinguish, in one way or another, among alternative situations that may arise, or might have arisen. Possible-worlds theory, as an explanatory theory of rational activity, begins with the notion of an alternative way that things may be or might have been (which is all that a possible world is) not because it takes this notion to be unproblematic, but because it takes it to be fundamental to the

---

[4] See David Lewis, *Counterfactuals* (Cambridge, Mass., 1973): 84–91 for a defence of realism about possible worlds.

different activities that a theory of rationality seeks to characterize and relate to each other. The notion will get its content, not from any direct answer to the question, what is a possible world? or from any reduction of that notion to something more basic or familiar, but from its role in the explanations of such a theory. Thus it may be that the best philosophical defence that one can give for possible worlds is to use them in the development of substantive theory.

Taking possible worlds for granted, we can define a *proposition* as a function from possible worlds into truth values.[5] Since there are two truth values, this means that a proposition is any way of dividing a set of possible worlds into two parts—those for which the function yields the value true, and those for which it yields the value false. The motivation for this representation of propositions is that, as mentioned above, it is an essential part of various rational activities to distinguish among alternative possible situations, and it is by expressing and adopting attitudes toward propositions that such distinctions are made.

How should a context be defined? This depends on what elements of the situations in which discourse takes place are relevant to determining what propositions are expressed by context-dependent sentences and to explaining the effects of various kinds of speech acts. The most important element of a context, I suggest, is the common knowledge, or presumed common knowledge and common assumption of the participants in the discourse.[6] A speaker inevitably takes certain information for granted when he speaks as the common ground of the participants in the conversation. It is this information which he can use as a resource for the communication of further information, and against which he will expect his speech acts to be understood. The presumed common ground in the sense intended—the *presuppositions* of the speaker—need not be the beliefs which are really common to the speaker and his audience; in fact, they need

[5] See M. J. Cresswell, *Logics and Languages* (London, 1973): 23–4, and Stalnaker, 'Pragmatics,' in G. Harman and D. Davidson (eds.), *Semantics of Natural Languages* (Dordrecht, 1972): 381–2 for brief discussions of the intuitive motivation of this definition of proposition.

[6] For a fuller discussion and defence of this concept, see Stalnaker, 'Presuppositions', *Journal of Philosophical Logic*, 2 (1973): 447–57.

not be beliefs at all. The presuppositions will include whatever the speaker finds it convenient to take for granted, or to pretend to take for granted, to facilitate his communication. What is essential is not that the propositions presupposed in this sense be believed by the speaker, but rather that the speaker believe that the presuppositions are common to himself and his audience. This is essential since they provide the context in which the speaker intends his statements to be received.

In the possible-worlds framework, we can represent this background information by a set of possible worlds—the possible worlds not ruled out by the presupposed background information. I will call this set of possible worlds the *context set*.[7] Possible worlds within the set are situations among which the speaker intends his speech acts to distinguish. I will sometimes talk of propositions being *compatible with* or *entailed by* a context. This means, in the first case, that the proposition is true in some of the worlds in the context set, and in the second case that the proposition is true in all of the worlds in the context set. Intuitively, it means, in the first case, that it is at least an open question in the context whether or not the proposition is true, and in the second case, that the proposition is presupposed, or accepted, in the context.

Propositions, then, are ways of distinguishing among any set of possible worlds, while context sets are the sets of possible worlds among which a speaker means to distinguish when he expresses a proposition.

3

The semantic analysis of conditionals that I will summarize here is developed and defended more fully elsewhere.[8] The analysis was constructed primarily to account for counterfactual conditionals—

[7] Elsewhere, I have called this set the *presupposition* set, but this terminology proved misleading since it suggested a set of presuppositions—propositions presupposed—rather than a set of possible worlds. The terminology adopted here was suggested by Lauri Karttunen.

[8] Stalnaker, 'A Theory of Conditionals', in N. Rescher (ed.), *Studies in Logical Theory* (Blackwell: Oxford, 1968): 98–112, Essay II in this volume, and Stalnaker and R. H. Thomason, 'A Semantic Analysis of Conditional Logic', *Theoria*, 36 (1970): 23–42. See also Lewis, *Counterfactuals*. The formal differences between Lewis's theory and mine are irrelevant to the present time.

conditionals whose antecedents are assumed by the speaker to be false—but the analysis was intended to fit conditional sentences generally, without regard to the attitudes taken by the speaker to antecedent or consequent or his purpose in uttering them, and without regard to the grammatical mood in which the conditional is expressed.

The idea of the analysis is this: a conditional statement, *if A, then B*, is an assertion that the consequent is true, not necessarily in the world as it is, but in the world as it would be if the antecedent were true. To express this idea formally in a semantic rule for the conditional, we need a function which takes a proposition (the antecedent) and a possible world (the world as it is) into a possible world (the world as it would be if the antecedent were true). Intuitively, the *value* of the function should be that world in which the antecedent is true which is most similar, in relevant respects, to the actual world (the world which is one of the *arguments* of the function). In terms of such a function—call it '*f*'—the semantic rule for the conditional may be stated as follows: a conditional *if A, then B*, is true in a possible world i just in case B is true in possible world $f(A,i)$.[9]

It may seem that little has been accomplished by this analysis, since it just exchanges the problem of analysing the conditional for the problem of analysing a semantic function which is equally problematic, if not more so. In one sense this is correct: the analysis is not intended as a reduction of the conditional to something more familiar or less problematic, and it should not satisfy one who comes to the problem of analysing conditionals with the epistemological scruples of a Hume or a Goodman. The aim of the analysis is to give a perspicuous representation of the formal structure of conditionals—to give the *form* of their truth conditions. Even if nothing substantive is said about how antecedents select counterfactual possible worlds, the analysis still has non-trivial, and in some cases surprising, consequences for the logic of conditionals.

---

[9] If A is the impossible proposition—the one true in *no* possible world—then there will be no possible world which can be the value of the function, $f(A,i)$, and so the function is left undefined for this case. To take care of this special case, the theory stipulates that all conditionals with impossible antecedents are true.

But what more can be said about this selection function? If it is to be based on *similarity* in some respect or other, then it must have certain formal properties. It must be a function that determines a coherent ordering of the possible worlds that are selected. And, since whatever the respects of similarity are that are relevant, it will always be true that something is more similar to itself than to anything else, the selection function must be one that selects the actual world whenever possible, which means whenever the antecedent is true in the actual world. Can anything more substantive be said about the relevant respects of similarity on which the selection is based? Not, I think, in the *semantic* theory of conditionals. Relevant respects of similarity are determined by the context, and the semantics abstracts away from the context by taking it as an unexplained given. But we can, I think, say something in a pragmatic theory of conditional statements about how the context constrains the truth conditions for conditionals, at least for indicative conditionals.

I cannot *define* the selection function in terms of the context set, but the following constraint imposed by the context on the selection function seems plausible: if the conditional is being evaluated at a world in the context set, then the world selected must, if possible, be within the context set as well (where C is the context set, if $i \in C$, then $f(A,i) \in C$). In other words, all worlds within the context set are closer to each other than any worlds outside it. The idea is that when a speaker says 'If A', then everything he is presupposing to hold in the actual situation is presupposed to hold in the hypothetical situation in which A is true. Suppose it is an open question whether the butler did it or not, but it is established and accepted that whoever did it, he or she did it with an ice-pick. Then it may be taken as accepted and established that if the butler did it, he did it with an ice-pick.

The motivation of the principle is this: normally a speaker is concerned only with possible worlds within the context set, since this set is defined as the set of possible worlds among which the speaker wishes to distinguish. So it is at least a normal expectation that the selection function should turn first to these worlds before considering *counterfactual* worlds—those presupposed to be non-actual. Conditional statements can be directly relevant to their primary uses—deliberation, contingency planning, making hedged predictions—only if they conform to this principle.

Nevertheless, this principle is only a defeasible presumption and not a universal generalization. For some special purposes a speaker may want to make use of a selection function which reaches outside of the context set, which is to say he may want to suspend temporarily some of the presuppositions made in that context. He may do so provided that he indicates in some way that his selection function is an exception to the presumption. Semantic determinants like domains and selection functions are a function of the speaker's intentions; that is why we must allow for exceptions to such pragmatic generalizations. But they are a function of the speaker's intention *to communicate* something, and that is why it is essential that it be conveyed to the audience that an exception is being made.

I take it that the subjunctive mood in English and some other languages is a conventional device for indicating that presuppositions are being suspended, which means in the case of subjunctive *conditional* statements, that the selection function is one that may reach outside of the context set. Given this conventional device, I would expect that the pragmatic principle stated above should hold without exception for indicative conditionals.

In what kinds of cases would a speaker want to use a selection function that might reach outside of the context set? The most obvious case would be one where the antecedent of the conditional statement was counterfactual, or incompatible with the presuppositions of the context. In that case one is forced to go outside the context set, since there are no possible worlds in it which are eligible to be selected. But there are non-counterfactual cases as well.[10] Consider the argument, 'The murderer used an ice-pick. But if the butler had done it, he wouldn't have used an ice-pick. So the murderer must have been someone else.'[11] The subjunctive conditional premiss in this *modus tollens* argument

---

[10] I was slow to see this despite the existence of clear examples in the literature. Comments by John Watling in a discussion of an earlier version of this essay helped me to see the point.

[11] This is Watling's example.

cannot be counterfactual since if it were the speaker would be blatantly begging the question by presupposing, in giving his argument, that his conclusion was true. But that premiss does not conform to the constraint on selection functions, since the consequent denies the first premiss of the argument, which presumably is accepted when the second premiss is given.

Notice that if the argument is restated with the conditional premiss in the indicative mood, it is anomalous.

My second example of a subjunctive non-counterfactual conditional which violates the constraint is adapted from an example given by Alan Anderson many years ago.[12] 'If the butler had done it, we would have found just the clues which we in fact found.' Here a conditional is presented as evidence for the truth of its antecedent. The conditional cannot be counterfactual, since it would be self-defeating to presuppose false what one is trying to show true. And it cannot conform to the constraint on selection functions since if it did, it would be trivially true, and so no evidence for the truth of the antecedent. Notice, again that when recast into the indicative mood, the conditional seems trivial, and does not look like evidence for anything.

The generalization that all indicative conditionals conform to the pragmatic constraint on selection functions has the following consequence about appropriateness-conditions for indicative conditionals: *It is appropriate to make an indicative conditional statement or supposition only in a context which is compatible with the antecedent.* In effect, this says that *counterfactual* conditionals must be expressed in the subjunctive. This follows since indicative conditionals are those which must conform to the constraint, while counterfactuals are, by definition, those which cannot.

I need just one more assumption in order to show that the direct argument is a reasonable inference—an assumption about conditions of appropriateness for making assertions. The generalization that I will state is a quite specific one concerning disjunctive statements. I am sure it is derivable from more general conversational principles of the kind that Grice has discussed, but since I am not sure exactly what form such general principles

[12] 'A Note on Subjunctive and Counterfactual Conditionals', *Analysis,* 12 (1951): 35–8.

should take, I will confine myself here to a generalization which has narrow application, but which can be clearly stated and easily defended. The generalization is this: *a disjunctive statement is appropriately made only in a context which allows either disjunct to be true without the other*. That is, one may say *A or B* only in a situation in which both *A and not-B* and *B and not-A* are open possibilities. The point is that each disjunct must be making some contribution to determining what is said. If the context did not satisfy this condition, then the assertion of the disjunction would be equivalent to the assertion of one of the disjuncts alone. So the disjunctive assertion would be pointless, hence misleading, and therefore inappropriate.[13]

4

All of the ingredients of the solution to the puzzle are now assembled and ready to put together. It may seem that this is a rather elaborate apparatus for such a simple puzzle, but each of the elements—propositions and contexts, the semantic analysis of conditionals, the pragmatic constraint on conditions, and the generalization about appropriateness—is independently motivated. It is not that this apparatus has been assembled just to solve the little puzzle; it is rather that the puzzle is being used to illustrate, in a small way, the explanatory capacity of the apparatus.

[13] As with the pragmatic constraint on selection functions, there may be exceptions to this generalization. One exception is a statement of the form *A or B or both*. (I assume that the meaning of 'or' is given by the truth table for inclusive disjunction.) But statements which conflict with the principle must satisfy two conditions if they are to be appropriate. First, the statement must wear on its face that it is an exception so that it cannot be misleading. Second, there must be some explanation available of the purpose of violating the generalization, so that it will not be pointless. In the case of the statement *A or B or both*, it is clear from the logical relation between the last disjunct and the others that it must be an exception, so it satisfies the first condition. The explanation of the point of adding the redundant third disjunct is this: the disjunctive statement, *A or B*, requires that *A and not-B* and *B and not-A* be compatible with the context, but leaves open whether *A and B* is compatible with the context. The addition of the third disjunct, while adding nothing to the *assertive content* of the statement, does change the appropriateness-conditions of the statement, and thus serves to indicate something about the context, or about the presuppositions of the speaker.

The argument we began with has the form *A or B*, *therefore*, *if not-A, then B*. This inference form is a reasonable inference form just in case every context in which a premiss of that form could appropriately be asserted or explicitly supposed, and in which it is accepted, is a context which entails the proposition expressed by the corresponding conclusion. Now suppose the premiss, *A or B*, is assertable and accepted. By the constraint on the appropriateness of disjunctive statements, it follows that the context is compatible with the conjunction of *not-A* with *B*. Hence the antecedent of the conditional conclusion, *not-A*, is compatible with the context. Now it follows from the pragmatic constraint on selection functions that if a proposition *P* is *compatible* with the context, and another proposition *Q* is *accepted* in it, or *entailed* by it, then the conditional, *if P, then Q*, is entailed by it as well. So, since *not-A* is compatible with the context, and the premiss *A or B* is accepted, the conditional, *if not-A, then A or B*, must be accepted as well. But this conditional proposition entails the conclusion of the argument, *if not-A, then B*. So the inference is a reasonable one.

Since the argument works the other way as well, it follows that the indicative conditional and the material conditional are equivalent in the following sense: in any context where either might appropriately be asserted, the one is accepted, or entailed by the context, if and only if the other is accepted, or entailed by the context. This equivalence explains the plausibility of the truth-functional analysis of indicative conditionals, but it does not justify that analysis since the two propositions coincide only in their assertion and acceptance conditions, and not in their truth conditions. The difference between the truth conditions of the two propositions will show itself if one looks at acts and attitudes other than assertion and acceptance. To take the simplest case, it may be reasonable to deny a conditional, even when not denying the corresponding material conditional. For example, I know *I* didn't do it, so I know that it is false that if the butler didn't do it, I did. But since I don't know whether the butler did it or not, I am in no position to deny the material conditional, which is equivalent to the disjunction, either the butler did it or I did. I may even think that that disjunction is very probably true.

There are two other familiar inference forms involving conditionals which are judged to be reasonable, although invalid, by this analysis: contraposition and the hypothetical syllogism. It was one of the surprising consequences of the *semantic* analysis sketched above that these inferences are, in general, invalid. Nevertheless, these consequences count in favour of the semantic analysis rather than against it since there are clear counter-examples to both inference forms. But all the counter-examples involve subjunctive conditionals which are counterfactual conditionals whose antecedents are presupposed to be false. Now we can explain why there are no purely indicative counter-examples, and also why the arguments have the appearance of validity which they have. Both argument forms can be shown to be reasonable inferences, given that all conditionals involved are indicative, and given the assumption that indicative conditionals always conform to the pragmatic constraint on selection functions.[14]

5

I want to conclude by looking at a notorious argument involving indicative conditionals. The argument for fatalism is, I will argue, unreasonable as well as invalid. But it gains its appearance of force from the fact that it is an artful sequence of steps, each one of which has the form of a reasonable or of a valid inference. The trick of the argument, according to the diagnosis I will give, is that it exploits the changing context in an illegitimate way. Subordinate conclusions, legitimately drawn within their own subordinate contexts, are illegitimately detached from those contexts and combined outside of them. To make clear what I mean, let me sketch the argument. The specific form it takes, and the example used to present it, are taken from Michael Dummett's discussion of fatalism in his paper, 'Bringing about the Past'.[15] The setting of the example is wartime Britain during an air raid. I reason as follows: 'Either I will be killed in this raid or I will not be killed.

---

[14] Strictly, the inference to the contrapositive is reasonably only relative to the further assumption that the indicative *conclusion* is not inappropriate.

[15] *Philosophical Review*, 73 (1964): 338–59.

Suppose that I will. Then even if I take precautions I will be killed, so any precautions I take will be ineffective. But suppose I am not going to be killed. Then I won't be killed even if I neglect all precautions; so, on this assumption, no precautions are necessary to avoid being killed. Either way, any precautions I take will be either ineffective or unnecessary, and so pointless.'

To give an abstract representation of the argument, I will let K mean 'I will be killed', P mean 'I take precautions', Q mean 'precautions are ineffective', and R mean 'precautions are unnecessary'. The argument, reduced to essentials, is this:

1. *K or not-K*
2. | *K*
3.   ⌐ *If P, K*
4. | *Q*
5. |_ *not-K*
6.   ⌐ *if not-P,not-K*
7. | *R*
8. *Q or R*

Now I take it that the main problem posed by this argument is not to say what is wrong with it, but rather to explain its illusion of force. That is, it is not enough to say that step *x* is invalid and leave it as that, even if that claim is correct. One must explain why anyone should have thought that it was valid. Judged by this criterion, Dummett's analysis of the argument does not solve the problem, even though, I think, what he says about the argument is roughly correct. Dummett argues that any sense of the conditional which will validate the inference from 2 to 3 (and 5 to 6) must be too weak to validate the inference from 3 to 4 (and 6 to 7). Hence, however the conditional is analysed, the argument as a whole cannot be valid. Dummett's argument to this conclusion is convincing, but it would be a full solution to the problem only if he supplemented it by showing that there *are* in our language distinct senses of the conditional that validate each of those steps. This I do not think he can do, since I do not think the force of the argument rests on an equivocation between two senses of the conditional.

According to the semantic and pragmatic analyses sketched

above, there is *one* sense of the conditional according to which the inference from 2 to 3 is a *reasonable inference*,[16] and which is also strong enough to justify the inference from 3 to 4. The fallacy, according to the diagnosis, is thus in neither of the steps that Dummett questions. Both of the sub-arguments are good arguments in the sense that anyone who was in a position to accept the premiss, while it remained an open question whether or not the antecedent of the conditional was true, would be in a position to accept the conclusion. That is, if I were in a position to accept that I were going to be killed even though I hadn't yet decided whether or not to take precautions, then I would surely be reasonable to conclude that taking precautions would be pointless. Likewise if I knew or had reason to accept that I would not be killed.

The problem with the argument is in the final step, an inference which seems to be an instance of an unproblematically valid form—constructive dilemma which has nothing essential to do with conditionals. The argument form that justifies step 8 is this: *A or B*; *C* follows from *A*; *D* follows from *B*; therefore, *C or D*. It is correct that the conclusion follows *validly* from the premiss provided that the sub-arguments are *valid*. But it is not correct that the conclusion is a *reasonable inference* from the premiss, provided that the sub-arguments are *reasonable inferences*. In the fatalism argument, the sub-arguments are reasonable, but not valid, and this is why the argument fails. So it is a confusion of validity with reasonable inference on which the force of the argument rests.

6

One final remark: my specific motivation for developing this account of indicative conditionals is of course to solve a puzzle, and to defend a particular semantic analysis of conditionals. But I have a broader motivation which is perhaps more important. That

---

[16] As with contraposition, the inference from 2 to 3 is reasonable only relative to the futher assumption that the conclusion of the inference is appropriate, which means in this case, only relative to the assumption that *P*, the antecedent of the conditional, is compatible with the context. This assumption is obviously satisfied since the setting of the argument is a deliberation about whether or not to make *P* true.

is to defend, by example, the claim that the concepts of pragmatics (the study of linguistic contexts) can be made as mathematically precise as any of the concepts of syntax and formal semantics; to show that one can recognize and incorporate into abstract theory the extreme context-dependence which is obviously present in natural language without any sacrifice of standards of rigour.[17] I am anxious to put this claim across because it is my impression that semantic theorists have tended to ignore or abstract away from context-dependence at the cost of some distortion of the phenomena, and that this practice is motivated not by ignorance or misperception of the phenomenon of context-dependence, but rather by the belief that the phenomenon is not appropriately treated in a formal theory. I hope that the analysis of indicative conditionals that I have given, even if not correct in its details, will help to show that this belief is not true.

APPENDIX

Entailment and reasonable inference relate propositions and speech acts, respectively, but in both cases, given an appropriate language, one can define corresponding logical notions—notions of entailment and reasonable inference which relate formulas, or sentences independently of their specific interpretations.

Let **L** be a language which contains sentences. A *semantic interpretation* of the language will consist of a set of possible worlds and a function which assigns *propositions* (functions from possible worlds into truth-values) to the sentences, relative to *contexts*. The formal semantics for the language will define the class of legitimate interpretations by saying, in the usual way, how the interpretation of complex expressions relates to the interpretation of their parts. A *context* is an n-tuple, the first term of which is a *context set* (a set

---

[17] I recognize, of course, that the definitions and generalizations presented here are nothing like a rigorous formal theory. But some parts of the apparatus (in particular, the semantics for conditionals) have been more carefully developed elsewhere, and I believe it is a relatively routine matter to state most of the definitions and generalizations which are new in precise model theoretic terms. Just to show how it might go, I will give in an appendix a very abstract definition of a logical concept of reasonable inference.

of possible worlds). The other terms are whatever else, if anything, is necessary to determine the propositions expressed by the sentences.

Notation: I will use P, P_1, P_2, etc. as meta-variables for sentences, ϕ, ϕ_1, ϕ_2, etc. as meta-variables for propositions (for convenience, I will identify a proposition with the set of possible worlds for which it takes the value true); k, k_1, k_2, etc. will be variables ranging over contexts. $S(k)$ will denote the context set of the context k. $\parallel P \parallel_k$ will denote the proposition expressed by P in context k under the interpretation in question. (Reference to the interpretation is suppressed in the notation.)

Entailment. One may define several notions of entailment. The basic notion is a language-independent relation between propositions: ϕ_1 entails ϕ_2 if and only if ϕ_2. includes ϕ_1. The *logical* concept of entailment, entailment-in-**L**, is a relation between *sentences* of **L**: P_1 entails P_2 if and only if for all interpretations and all contexts k, $\parallel P_1 \parallel_k$ entails $\parallel P_2 \parallel_k$. Logical entailment is entailment in virtue of the logical structure of the sentences. Similarly, the logical concept of reasonable inference will identify the inferences which are reasonable in virtue of the logical structure of the sentences.

Pragmatic interpretations. To define the logical notion of reasonable inference, we need to expand the concept of an interpretation. A *pragmatic interpretation* of **L** will consist of a semantic interpretation, an *appropriateness relation*, and a *change function*. The appropriateness relation A is a two-place relation whose arguments are a sentence of **L** and a context. A(P, k) says that the assertive utterance of P in context k is appropriate. The change function g is a two-place function taking a sentence of **L** and a context into a context. Intuitively, g(P, k) denotes the context that results from the assertive utterance of P in context k.

Since **L** is unspecific here, I leave these notions almost completely unconstrained, but it is easy to see how the generalizations about disjunctive and conditional statements would be stated as postulates which give some substance to these notions as applied to a language containing these kinds of statements. Just as the semantics for a specific language will include semantic rules specifying the elements of the context and placing constraints on the allowable semantic interpretations, so the pragmatic theory for a specific language will include rules constraining the two distinctively pragmatic elements of a pragmatic interpretation, as well as the relations among the elements of the context.

I will give here just two constraints which will apply to any language intended to model a practice of assertion.

1. $A(P, k)$ only if $\|P\|_k \cap S(k) \neq 0$.

One cannot appropriately assert a proposition in a context incompatible with it.

2. $S(g(P, k)) = S(k) \cap \|P\|_k$.

Any assertion changes the context by becoming an additional presupposition of subsequent conversation. (In a more careful formulation the second of these would be qualified, since assertions can be rejected or contradicted. But in the absence of rejection, I think it is reasonable to impose this constraint.)

Both the appropriateness relation and the change function can be generalized to apply to finite sequences of sentences in the following way: Let σ be a finite sequence of sentences of **L**, P_1, P_2, . . . P_n. Let k_1, k_2, . . . k_n be a sequence of contexts defined in terms of σ and a context k as follows: $k_1 = k$; $k_{i+1} = g(k_i, P_i)$. Then $A(\sigma, k)$ if and only if, for all i from l to n, $A(P_i, k_i)$. $g(\sigma, k) =_{df} k_n$.

Reasonable inference. The inference from a sequence of sentences of **L**, σ, to a sentence of **L**, P is *reasonable-in-***L** if and only if for all interpretations and all contexts k such that $A(\sigma, k)$, $S(g(\sigma, k))$ entails $\| P \|_{g(\sigma, k)}$.

Note that there is no language-independent concept of reasonable inference analogous to the language-independent notion of entailment. The reason is that, while we have in the theory a notion of proposition that can be characterized independently of any language in which propositions are expressed, we have no corresponding non-linguistic concept of statement, or assertion. One could perhaps be defined, but it would not be a simple matter to do so, since the identity conditions for assertion types will be finer than those for propositions. The reason for this is that different sentences may have different appropriateness-conditions even when they express the same proposition.

VIII

LOGIC AND CONVERSATION

H. P. GRICE

IT is a commonplace of philosophical logic that there are, or appear to be, divergences in meaning between, on the one hand, at least some of what I shall call the FORMAL devices—$\sim$, $\wedge$, $\vee$, $\supset$, (x) $\exists$ (x) $\int x$ (when these are given a standard two-valued interpretation)—and, on the other, what are taken to be their analogues or counterparts in natural language—such expressions as *not*, *and*, *or*, *if*, *all*, *some* (or *at least one*), *the*. Some logicians may at some time have wanted to claim that there are in fact no such divergences; but such claims, if made at all, have been somewhat rashly made, and those suspected of making them have been subjected to some pretty rough handling.

Those who concede that such divergences exist adhere, in the main, to one or the other of two rival groups, which for the purposes of this essay I shall call the formalist and the informalist groups. An outline of a not uncharacteristic formalist position may be given as follows: In so far as logicians are concerned with the formulation of very general patterns of valid inference, the formal devices possess a decisive advantage over their natural counterparts. For it will be possible to construct in terms of the formal devices a system of very general formulas, a considerable number of which can be regarded as, or are closely related to, patterns of inferences the expression of which involves some or all of the devices: Such a system may consist of a certain set of simple formulas that must be acceptable if the devices have the meaning that has been assigned to them, and an indefinite number of further formulas, many of them less obviously acceptable, each of which can be shown to be acceptable if the members of the original set are acceptable. We have, thus, a way of handling dubiously acceptable patterns of inference, and if, as is sometimes possible, we can apply a decision procedure, we have an even better way. Furthermore, from a philosophical point of view, the possession by the natural counterparts of those elements in their meaning, which they do not share with the corresponding formal devices, is to be regarded as an imperfection of natural languages; the elements in question are undesirable excrescences. For the presence of these elements has the result that the concepts within which they appear cannot be precisely/clearly defined, and that at least some statements involving them cannot, in some circumstances, be assigned a definite truth value, and the indefiniteness of these concepts is not only objectionable in itself but leaves open the way to metaphysics—we cannot be certain that none of these natural language expressions is metaphysically 'loaded'. For these reasons, the expressions, as used in natural speech, cannot be regarded as finally acceptable, and may turn out to be, finally, not fully intelligible. The proper course is to conceive and begin to construct an ideal language, incorporating the formal devices, the sentences of which will be clear, determinate in truth value, and certifiably free from metaphysical implications; the foundations of science will now be philosophically secure, since the statements of the scientist will be expressible (though not necessarily actually expressed) within this ideal language. (I do not wish to suggest that all formalists would accept the whole of this outline, but I think that all would accept at least some part of it.)

To this, an informalist might reply in the following vein. The philosophical demand for an ideal language rests on certain assumptions that should not be conceded; these are, that the primary yardstick by which to judge the adequacy of a language is its ability to serve the needs of science, that an expression cannot be guaranteed as fully intelligible unless an explication or analysis of its meaning has been provided, and that every explication or analysis nust take the form of a precise definition that is the expression/assertion of a logical equivalence. Language serves many important purposes besides those of scientific enquiry; we can know perfectly well what an expression means (and so *a fortiori* that it is intelligible) without knowing its analysis, and the provision of an analysis may (and usually does) consist in the specification, as generalized as possible, of the conditions that count for or against the applicability of the expression being analysed. Moreover, while it is no doubt true that the formal devices are especially amenable to systematic treatment by the logician, it remains the case that there are very many inferences and arguments, expressed in natural language and not in terms of these devices, that are nevertheless recognizably valid. So there must be a place for an unsimplified, and so more or less unsystematic, logic of the natural counterparts of these devices; this logic may be aided and guided by the simplified logic of the formal devices but cannot be supplanted by it; indeed, not only do the two logics differ, but sometimes they come into conflict; rules that hold for a formal device may not hold for its natural counterpart.

Now, on the general question of the place in philosophy of the reformation of natural language, I shall, in this essay, have nothing to say. I shall confine myself to the dispute in its relation to the alleged divergences mentioned at the outset. I have, moreover, no intention of entering the fray on behalf of either contestant. I wish, rather, to maintain that the common assumption of the contestants that the divergences do in fact exist is (broadly speaking) a common mistake, and that the mistake arises from an inadequate attention to the nature and importance of the conditions governing conversation. I shall, therefore, proceed at once to enquire into the general conditions that, in one way or another, apply to conversation as such, irrespective of its subject-matter.

IMPLICATURE

Suppose that A and B are talking about a mutual friend, C, who is now working in a bank. A asks B how C is getting on in his job, and B replies, *Oh quite well, I think*; *he likes his colleagues, and he hasn't been to prison yet*. At this point, A might well enquire what B was implying, what he was suggesting, or even what he meant by saying that C had not yet been to prison. The answer might be any one of such things as that C is the sort of person likely to yield to the temptation provided by his occupation, that C's colleagues are really very unpleasant and treacherous people, and so forth. It might, of course, be quite unnecessary for A to make such an enquiry of B, the answer to it being, in the context, clear in advance. I think it is clear that whatever B implied, suggested, meant, etc., in this example, is distinct from what B said, which was simply that C had not been to prison yet. I wish to introduce, as terms of art, the verb *implicate* and the related nouns *implicature* (cf. *implying*) and *implicatum* (cf. *what is implied*). The point of this manœuvre is to avoid having, on each occasion, to choose between this or that member of the family of verbs for which *implicate* is to do general duty. I shall, for the time being at least, have to assume to a considerable extent an intuitive understanding of the meaning of *say* in such contexts, and an ability to recognize particular verbs as members of the family with which *implicate* is associated. I can, however, make one or two remarks that may help to clarify the more problematic of these assumptions, namely that connected with the meaning of the word *say*.

In the sense in which I am using the word *say*, I intend what someone has said to be closely related to the conventional meaning of the words (the sentence) he has uttered. Suppose someone to have uttered the sentence *He is in the grip of a vice.* Given a knowledge of the English language, but no knowledge of the circumstances of the utterance, one would know something about what the speaker had said, on the assumption that he was speaking standard English, and speaking literally. One would know that he had said, about some particular male person or animal x, that at the time of the utterance (whatever that was), either (1) x was unable to rid himself of a certain kind of bad character trait or (2) some part of x's person was caught in a certain kind of tool or instrument (approximate account, of course). But for a full identification of what the speaker had said, one would need to know (a) the identity of x, (b) the time of utterance, and (c) the meaning, on the particular occasion of utterance, of the phrase *in the grip of a vice* [a decision between (1) and (2)]. This brief indication of my use of *say* leaves it open whether a man who says (today) *Harold Wilson is a great man* and another who says (also today) *The British Prime Minister is a great man* would, if each knew that the two singular terms had the same reference, have said the same thing. But whatever decision is made about this question, the apparatus that I am about to provide will be capable of accounting for any implicatures that might depend on the presence of one rather than another of these singular terms in the sentence uttered. Such implicatures would merely be related to different maxims.

In some cases the conventional meaning of the words used will determine what is implicated, besides helping to determine what is said. If I say (smugly), *He is an Englishman; he is, therefore, brave*, I have certainly committed myself, by virtue of the meaning of my words, to its being the case that his being brave is a consequence of (follows from) his being an Englishman. But while I have said that he is an Englishman, and said that he is brave, I do not want to say that I have SAID (in the favoured sense) that it follows from his being an Englishman that he is brave, though I have certainly indicated, and so implicated, that this is so. I do not want to say that my utterance of this sentence would be, STRICTLY SPEAKING, false should the consequence in question fail to hold. So SOME implicatures are conventional, unlike the one with which I introduced this discussion of implicature.

I wish to represent a certain subclass of non-conventional implicatures, which I shall call CONVERSATIONAL implicatures, as being essentially connected with certain general features of discourse; so my next step is to try to say what these features are.

The following may provide a first approximation to a general principle. Our talk exchanges do not normally consist of a succession of disconnected remarks, and would not be rational if they did. They are characteristically, to some degree at least, co-operative efforts; and each participant recognizes in them, to some extent, a common purpose or set of purposes, or at least a mutually accepted direction. This purpose or direction may be fixed from the start (e.g. by an initial proposal of a question for discussion), or it may evolve during the exchange; it may be fairly definite, or it may be so indefinite as to leave very considerable latitude to the partipants (as in a casual conversation). But at each stage, SOME possible conversational moves would be excluded as conversationally unsuitable. We might then formulate a rough general principle which participants will be expected (*ceteris paribus*) to observe, namely: Make your conversational contribution such as is required, at the stage at which it occurs, by the accepted purpose or direction of the talk exchange in which you are engaged. One might label this the CO-OPERATIVE PRINCIPLE.

On the assumption that some such general principle as this is acceptable, one may perhaps distinguish four categories under one or another of which will fall certain more specific maxims and sub-maxims, the following of which will, in general, yield results in accordance with the Co-operative Principle. Echoing Kant, I call these categories Quantity, Quality, Relation, and Manner. The category of QUANTITY relates to the quantity of information to be provided, and under it fall the following maxims:

1. Make your contribution as informative as is required (for the current purposes of the exchange).
2. Do not make your contribution more informative than is required.

(The second maxim is disputable; it might be said that to be over-informative is not a transgression of the CP but merely a waste of time. However, it might be answered that such over-informativeness may be confusing in that it is liable to raise side-issues; and there may also be an indirect effect, in that the hearers may be misled as a result of thinking that there is some particular POINT in the provision of the excess of information. However this may be, there is perhaps a different reason for doubt about the admission of this second maxim, namely that its effect will be secured by a later maxim, which concerns relevance.)

Under the category of QUALITY falls a super-maxim — 'Try to make your contribution one that is true' — and two more specific maxims:

1. Do not say what you believe to be false.
2. Do not say that for which you lack adequate evidence.

Under the category of RELATION I place a single maxim, namely 'Be relevant'. Though the maxim itself is terse, its formulation conceals a number of problems that exercise me a good deal: questions about what different kinds and focuses of relevance there may be, how these shift in the course of a talk exchange, how to allow for the fact that subjects of conversation are legitimately changed, and so on. I find the treatment of such questions exceedingly difficult, and I hope to revert to them in a later work.

Finally, under the category of MANNER, which I understand as relating not (like the previous categories) to what is said but, rather, to HOW what is said is to be said, I include the super-maxim—'Be perspicuous'—and various maxims such as:

1. Avoid obscurity of expression.
2. Avoid ambiguity.
3. Be brief (avoid unnecessary prolixity).
4. Be orderly.

And one might need others.

It is obvious that the observance of some of these maxims is a matter of less urgency than is the observance of others; a man who has expressed himself with undue prolixity would, in general, be open to milder comment than would a man who has said something he believes to be false. Indeed, it might be felt that the importance of at least the first maxim of Quality is such that it should not be included in a scheme of the kind I am constructing; other maxims come into operation only on the assumption that this maxim of Quality is satisfied. While this may be correct, so far as the generation of implicatures is concerned it seems to play a role not totally different from the other maxims, and it will be convenient, for the present at least, to treat it as a member of the list of maxims.

There are, of course, all sorts of other maxims (aesthetic, social, or moral in character), such as 'Be polite', that are also normally observed by participants in talk exchanges, and these may also generate non-conventional implicatures. The conversational maxims, however, and the conversational implicatures connected with them, are specially connected (I hope) with the particular purposes that talk (and so, talk exchange) is adapted to serve and is primarily employed to serve. I have stated my maxims as if this purpose were a maximally effective exchange of information; this specification is, of course, too narrow, and the scheme needs to be generalized to allow for such general purposes as influencing or directing the actions of others.

As one of my avowed aims is to see talking as a special case or variety of purposive, indeed rational, behaviour, it may be worth noting that the specific expectations or presumptions connected with at least some of the foregoing maxims have their analogues in the sphere of transactions that are not talk exchanges. I list briefly one such analogue for each conversational category.

1. QUANTITY. If you are assisting me to mend a car, I expect your contribution to be neither more nor less than is required; if, for example, at a particular stage I need four screws, I expect you to hand me four, rather than two or six.

2. QUALITY. I expect your contributions to be genuine and not spurious. If I need sugar as an ingredient in the cake you are assisting me to make, I do not expect you to hand me salt; if I need a spoon, I do not expect a trick spoon made of rubber.

3. RELATION. I expect a partner's contribution to be appropriate to immediate needs at each stage of the transaction; if I am mixing ingredients for a cake, I do not expect to be handed a good book, or even an oven cloth (though this might be an appropriate contribution at a later stage).

4. MANNER. I expect a partner to make it clear what contribution he is making, and to execute his performance with reasonable dispatch.

These analogies are relevant to what I regard as a fundamental question about the CP and its attendant maxims, namely what the basis is for the assumption which we seem to make, and on which (I hope) it will appear that a great range of implicatures depend, that talkers will in general (*ceteris paribus* and in the absence of indications to the contrary) proceed in the manner that these principles prescribe. A dull but, no doubt at a certain level, adequate answer is that it is just a well-recognized empirical fact that people DO behave in these ways; they have learned to do so in childhood and not lost the habit of doing so; and, indeed, it would involve a good deal of effort to make a radical departure from the habit. It is much easier, for example, to tell the truth than to invent lies.

I am, however, enough of a rationalist to want to find a basis that underlies these facts, undeniable though they may be; I would like to be able to think of the standard type of conversational practice not merely as something that all or most do IN FACT follow but as something that it is REASONABLE for us to follow, that we SHOULD NOT abandon. For a time, I was attracted by the idea that observance of the CP and the maxims, in a talk exchange, could be thought of as a quasi-contractual matter, with parallels outside the realm of discourse. If you pass by when I am struggling with my stranded car, I no doubt have some degree of expectation that you will offer help, but once you join me in tinkering under the hood, my expectations become stronger and take more specific forms (in the absence of indications that you are merely an incompetent meddler); and talk exchanges seemed to me to exhibit, characteristically, certain features that jointly distinguish co-operative transactions:

1. The participants have some common immediate aim, like getting a car mended; their ultimate aims may, of course, be independent and even in conflict—each may want to get the car mended in order to drive off, leaving the other stranded. In characteristic talk exchanges, there is a common aim even if, as in an over-the-wall chat, it is a second-order one, namely that each party should, for the time being, identify himself with the transitory conversational interests of the other.

2. The contributions of the participants should be dovetailed, mutually dependent.

3. There is some sort of understanding (which may be explicit but which is often tacit) that, other things being equal, the transaction should continue in appropriate style unless both parties are agreeable that it should terminate. You do not just shove off or start doing something else.

But while some such quasi-contractual basis as this may apply to some cases, there are too many types of exchange, like quarrelling and letter-writing, that it fails to fit comfortably. In any case, one feels that the talker who is irrelevant or obscure has primarily let down not his audience but himself. So I would like to be able to show that observance of the CP and maxims is reasonable (rational) along the following lines: that anyone who cares about the goals that are central to conversation/communication (e.g. giving and receiving information, influencing and being influenced by others) must be expected to have an interest, given suitable circumstances, in participation in talk exchanges that will be profitable only on the assumption that they are conducted in general accordance with the CP and the maxims. Whether any such conclusion can be reached, I am uncertain; in any case, I am fairly sure that I cannot reach it until I am a good deal clearer about the nature of relevance and of the circumstances in which it is required.

It is now time to show the connection between the CP and maxims, on the one hand, and conversational implicature on the other.

A participant in a talk exchange may fail to fulfil a maxim in various ways, which include the following:

1. He may quietly and unostentatiously VIOLATE a maxim; if so, in some cases he will be liable to mislead.

2. He may OPT OUT from the operation both of the maxim and of the CP; he may say, indicate, or allow it to become plain that he is unwilling to co-operate in the way the maxim requires. He may say, for example, *I cannot say more*; *my lips are sealed*.

3. He may be faced by a CLASH: He may be unable, for example, to fulfil the first maxim of Quantity (Be as informative as is required) without violating the second maxim of Quality (Have adequate evidence for what you say).

4. He may FLOUT a maxim; that is, he may BLATANTLY fail to fulfil it. On the assumption that the speaker is able to fulfil the maxim and to do so without violating another maxim (because of a clash), is not opting out, and is not, in view of the blatancy of his performance, trying to mislead, the hearer is faced with a minor problem: How can his saying what he did say be reconciled with the supposition that he is observing the overall CP? This situation is one that characteristically gives rise to a conversational implicature; and when a conversational implicature is generated in this way, I shall say that a maxim is being EXPLOITED.

I am now in a position to characterize the notion of conversational implicature. A man who, by (in, when) saying (or making as if to say) that p has implicated that q, may be said to have conversationally implicated that q, PROVIDED THAT (1) he is to be presumed to be observing the conversational maxims, or at least the co-operative principle; (2) the supposition that he is aware that, or thinks that, q is required in order to make his saying or making as if to say p (or doing so in THOSE terms) consistent with this presumption; and (3) the speaker thinks (and would expect the hearer to think that the speaker thinks) that it is within the competence of the hearer to work out, or grasp intuitively, that the supposition mentioned in (2) IS required. Apply this to my initial example, to B's remark that C has not yet been to prison. In a suitable setting A might reason as follows: '(1) B has apparently violated the maxim "Be relevant" and so may be regarded as having flouted one of the maxims conjoining perspicuity, yet I have no reason to suppose that he is opting out from the operation of the CP; (2) given the circumstances, I can regard his irrelevance as only apparent if, and only if, I suppose him to think that C is potentially dishonest; (3) B knows that I am capable of working out step (2). So B implicates that C is potentially dishonest.'

The presence of a conversational implicature must be capable of being worked out; for even if it can in fact be intuitively grasped, unless the intuition is replaceable by an argument, the implicature (if present at all) will not count as a CONVERSATIONAL implicature; it will be a CONVENTIONAL implicature. To work out that a particular conversational implicature is present, the hearer will rely on the following data: (1) the conventional meaning of the words used, together with the identity of any references that may be involved; (2) the CP and its maxims; (3) the context, linguistic or otherwise, of the utterance; (4) other items of background knowledge; and (5) the fact (or supposed fact) that all relevant items falling under the previous headings are available to both participants and both participants know or assume this to be the case. A general pattern for the working out of a conversational implicature might be given as follows: 'He has said that p; there is no reason to suppose that he is not observing the maxims, or at least the CP; he could not be doing this unless he thought that q; he knows (and knows that I know that he knows) that I can see that the supposition that he thinks that q IS required; he has done nothing to stop me thinking that q; he intends me to think, or is at least willing to allow me to think, that q; and so he has implicated that q.'

EXAMPLES

I shall now offer a number of examples, which I shall divide into three groups.

GROUP A: *Examples in which no maxim is violated, or at least in which it is not clear that any maxim is violated*

A is standing by an obviously immobilized car and is approached by B; the following exchange takes place:

(1) A: *I am out of petrol.*

B: *There is a garage round the corner.* (Gloss: B would be infringing the maxim 'Be relevant' unless he thinks, or thinks it possible, that the garage is open, and has petrol to sell; so he implicates that the garage is, or at least may be open, etc.)

In this example, unlike the case of the remark *He hasn't been to prison yet*, the unstated connection between B's remark and A's remark is so obvious that, even if one interprets the supermaxim of Manner, 'Be perspicuous', as applying not only to the expression of what is said but also to the connection of what is said with adjacent remarks, there seems to be no case for regarding that supermaxim as infringed in this example. The next example is perhaps a little less clear in this respect:

(2) A: *Smith doesn't seem to have a girl-friend these days.*

B: *He has been paying a lot of visits to New York lately.*

B implicates that Smith has, or may have, a girl-friend in New York. (A gloss is unnecessary in view of that given for the previous example.)

In both examples, the speaker implicates that which he must be assumed to believe in order to preserve the assumption that he is observing the maxim of relation.

GROUP B: *An example in which a maxim is violated, but its violation is to be explained by the supposition of a clash with another maxim*

A is planning with B an itinerary for a holiday in France. Both know that A wants to see his friend C, if to do so would not involve too great a prolongation of his journey:

(3) A: *Where does C live?*

B: *Somewhere in the South of France.* (Gloss: There is no reason to suppose that B is opting out; his answer is, as he well knows, less informative than is required to meet A's needs. This infringement of the first maxim of Quantity can be explained only by the supposition that B is aware that to be more informative would be to say something that infringed the maxim of Quality. 'Don't say what you lack adequate evidence for', so B implicates that he does not know in which town C lives.)

GROUP C: *Examples that involve exploitation, that is, a procedure by which a maxim is flouted for the purpose of getting in a conversational implicature by means of something of the nature of a figure of speech*

In these examples, though some maxim is violated at the level of what is said, the hearer is entitled to assume that that maxim, or at least the overall Co-operative Principle, is observed at the level of what is implicated.

(1a) *A flouting of the first maxim of Quantity*

A is writing a testimonial about a pupil who is a candidate for a philosophy job, and his letter reads as follows: 'Dear Sir, Mr X's command of English is excellent, and his attendance at tutorials has been regular. Yours, etc.' (Gloss: A cannot be opting out, since if he wished to be uncooperative, why write at all? He cannot be unable, through ignorance, to say more, since the man is his pupil; moreover, he knows that more information than this is wanted. He must, therefore, be wishing to impart information that he is reluctant to write down. This supposition is tenable only on the assumption that he thinks Mr X is no good at philosophy. This, then, is what he is implicating.)

Extreme examples of a flouting of the first maxim of Quantity are provided by utterances of patent tautologies like *Women are women* and *War is war.* I would wish to maintain that at the level of what is said, in my favoured sense, such remarks are totally non-informative and so, at that level, cannot but infringe the first maxim of Quantity in any conversational context. They are, of course, informative at the level of what is implicated, and the hearer's identification of their informative content at this level is dependent on his ability to explain the speaker's selection of this PARTICULAR patent tautology.

(3*b*) *An infringement of the second maxim of Quantity, 'Do not give more information than is required', on the assumption that the existence of such a maxim should be admitted*

A wants to know whether *p*, and B volunteers not only the information that *p*, but information to the effect that it is certain that *p*, and that the evidence for its being the case that *p* is so-and-so and such-and-such.

B's volubility may be undesigned, and if it is so regarded by A it may raise in A's mind a doubt as to whether B is as certain as he says he is ('Methinks the lady doth protest too much'). But if it is thought of as designed, it would be an oblique way of conveying that it is to some degree controversial whether or not *p*. It is, however, arguable that such an implicature could be explained by reference to the maxim of Relation without invoking an alleged second maxim of Quantity.

(2*a*) *Examples in which the first maxim of Quality is flouted*

1. *Irony.* X, with whom A has been on close terms until now, has betrayed a secret of A's to a business rival. A and his audience both know this. A says '*X is a fine friend*'. (Gloss: It is perfectly obvious to A and his audience that what A has said or has made as if to say is something he does not believe, and the audience knows that A knows that this is obvious to the audience. So, unless A's utterance is entirely pointless, A must be trying to get across some other proposition than the one he purports to be putting forward. This must be some obviously related proposition; the most obviously related proposition is the contradictory of the one he purports to be putting forward.)

2. *Metaphor.* Examples like *You are the cream in my coffee* characteristically involve categorial falsity, so the contradictory of what the speaker has made as if to say will, strictly speaking, be a truism; so it cannot be THAT such a speaker is trying to get across. The most likely supposition is that the speaker is

attributing to his audience some feature or features in respect of which the audience resembles (more or less fancifully) the mentioned substance.

It is possible to combine metaphor and irony by imposing on the hearer two stages of interpretation. I say *You are the cream in my coffee*, intending the hearer to reach first the metaphor interpretant 'You are my pride and joy' and then the irony interpretant 'You are my bane.'

3. *Meiosis.* Of a man known to have broken up all the furniture, one says *He was a little intoxicated*.

4. *Hyperbole.* Every nice girls loves a sailor.

(2*b*) Examples in which the second maxim of Quality, 'Do not say that for which you lack adequate evidence', is flouted are perhaps not easy to find, but the following seems to be a specimen. I say of X's wife, *She is probably deceiving him this evening*. In a suitable context, or with a suitable gesture or tone of voice, it may be clear that I have no adequate reason for supposing this to be the case. My partner, to preserve the assumption that the conversational game is still being played, assumes that I am getting at some related proposition for the acceptance of which I DO have a reasonable basis. The related proposition might well be that she is given to deceiving her husband, or possibly that she is the sort of person who would not stop short of such conduct.

(3) *Examples in which an implicature is achieved by real, as distinct from apparent, violation of the maxim of Relation* are perhaps rare, but the following seems to be a good candidate. At a genteel tea-party, A says *Mrs X is an old bag*. There is a moment of appalled silence, and then B says *The weather has been quite delightful this summer, hasn't it?* B has blatantly refused to make what HE says relevant to A's preceding remark. He thereby implicates that A's remark should not be discussed and, perhaps more specifically, that A has committed a social gaffe.

4. *Examples in which various maxims falling under the supermaxim 'Be perspicuous' are flouted*

1. *Ambiguity.* We must remember that we are concerned only with ambiguity that is deliberate, and that the speaker intends or expects to be recognized by his hearer. The problem the hearer

has to solve is why a speaker should, when still playing the conversational game, go out of his way to choose an ambiguous utterance. There are two types of case:

(*a*) Examples in which there is no difference, or no striking difference, between two interpretations of an utterance with respect to straightforwardness; neither interpretation is notably more sophisticated, less standard, more recondite, or more far-fetched than the other. We might consider Blake's lines: 'Never seek to tell thy love, Loved that never told can be.' To avoid the complications introduced by the presence of the imperative mood, I shall consider the related sentence, *I sought to tell my love, love that never told can be*. There may be a double ambiguity here. *My love* may refer to either a state of emotion or an object of emotion, and *love that never told can be* may mean either 'Love that cannot be told' or 'love that if told cannot continue to exist'. Partly because of the sophistication of the poet and partly because of internal evidence (that the ambiguity is kept up), there seems to be no alternative to supposing that the ambiguities are deliberate and that the poet is conveying both what he would be saying if one interpretation were intended rather than the other, and vice versa; though no doubt the poet is not explicitly SAYING any one of these things but only conveying or suggesting them (cf. 'Since she [nature] pricked thee out of women's pleasure, mine be thy love, and thy love's use their treasure').

(*b*) Examples in which one interpretation is notably less straightforward than another. Take the complex example of the British General who captured the town of Sind and sent back the message *Peccavi*. The ambiguity involved ('I have Sind'/'I have sinned') is phonemic, not morphemic; and the expression actually used is unambiguous, but since it is in a language foreign to speaker and hearer, translation is called for, and the ambiguity resides in the standard translation into native English.

Whether or not the straightforward interpretant ('I have sinned') is being conveyed, it seems that the non-straightforward must be. There might be stylistic reasons for conveying by a sentence merely its non-straightforward interpretant, but it would be pointless, and perhaps also stylistically objectionable, to go to the trouble of finding an expression that non-straightforwardly conveys that *p*, thus imposing on an audience the effort involved in finding this interpretant, if this interpretant were otiose so far as communication was concerned. Whether the straightforward interpretant is also being conveyed seems to depend on whether such a supposition would conflict with other conversational requirements, for example, would it be relevant, would it be something the speaker could be supposed to accept, and so on. If such requirements are not satisfied, then the straightforward interpretant is not being conveyed. If they are, it is. If the author of *Peccavi* could naturally be supposed to think that he had committed some kind of transgression, for example, had disobeyed his orders in capturing Sind, and if reference to such a transgression would be relevant to the presumed interests of the audience, then he would have been conveying both interpretants; otherwise he would be conveying only the non-straightforward one.

2. *Obscurity.* How do I exploit, for the purposes of communication, a deliberate and overt violation of the requirement that I should avoid obscurity? Obviously, if the Co-operative Principle is to operate, I must intend my partner to understand what I am saying despite the obscurity I import into my utterance. Suppose that A and B are having a conversation in the presence of a third party, for example, a child, then A might be deliberately obscure, though not too obscure, in the hope that B would understand and the third party not. Furthermore, if A expects B to see that A is being deliberately obscure, it seems reasonable to suppose that, in making his conversational contribution in this way, A is implicating that the contents of his communication should not be imparted to the third party.

3. *Failure to be brief or succinct.* Compare the remarks:

(a) *Miss X sang 'Home sweet home.'*
(b) *Miss X produced a series of sounds that corresponded closely with the score of 'Home sweet home'.*

Suppose that a reviewer has chosen to utter (*b*) rather than (*a*). (Gloss: Why has he selected that rigmarole in place of the concise and nearly synonymous *sang*? Presumably, to indicate some striking difference between Miss X's performance and those to which the word *singing* is usually applied. The most obvious supposition is that Miss X's performance suffered from some hideous defect. The reviewer knows that this supposition is what is likely to spring to mind, so that is what he is implicating.)

I have so far considered only cases of what I might call particularized conversational implicature—that is to say, cases in which an implicature is carried by saying that *p* on a particular occasion in virtue of special features of the context, cases in which there is no room for the idea that an implicature of this sort is NORMALLY carried by saying that *p*. But there are cases of generalized conversational implicature. Sometimes one can say that the use of a certain form of words in an utterance would normally (in the ABSENCE of special circumstances) carry such-and-such an implicature or type of implicature. Non-controversial examples are perhaps hard to find, since it is all too easy to treat a generalized conversational implicature as if it were a conventional implicature. I offer an example that I hope may be fairly non-controversial.

Anyone who uses a sentence of the form *X is meeting a woman this evening* would normally implicate that the person to be met was someone other than X's wife, mother, sister, or perhaps even close platonic friend. Similarly, if I were to say *X went into a house yesterday and found a tortoise inside the front door*, my hearer would normally be surprised if some time later I revealed that the house was X's own. I could produce similar linguistic phenomena involving the expressions *a gardener*, *a car*, *a college*, and so on. Sometimes, however, there would normally be no such implicature ('I have been sitting in a car all morning'), and sometimes a reverse implicature ('I broke a finger yesterday'). I am inclined to think that one would not lend a sympathetic ear to a philosopher who suggested that there are three senses of the form of expression *an X*: one in which it means roughly 'something that satisfies the conditions defining the word *X*', another in which it means approximately 'an X (in the first sense) that is only remotely related in a certain way to some person indicated by the context', and yet another in which it means 'an X (in the first sense) that is closely related in a certain way to some person indicated by the context'. Would we not much prefer an account on the following lines (which, of course, may be incorrect in detail)?: When someone, by using the form of expression *an X*, implicates that the X does not belong to or is not otherwise closely connected with some identifiable person, the implicature is present because the speaker has failed to be specific in a way in which he might have been expected to be specific, with the consequence that it is likely to be assumed that he is not in a position to be specific. This is a familiar implicature situation and is classifiable as a failure, for one reason or another, to fulfil the first maxim of Quantity. The only difficult question is why it should, in certain cases, be presumed, independently of information about particular contexts of utterance, that specification of the closeness or remoteness of the connection between a particular person or object and a further person who is mentioned or indicated by the utterance should be likely to be of interest. The answer must lie in the following region: Transactions between a person and other persons or things closely connected with him are liable to be very different as regards their concomitants and results from the same sort of transactions involving only remotely connected persons or things; the concomitants and results, for instance, of my finding a hole in MY roof are likely to be very different from the concomitants and results of my finding a hole in someone else's roof. Information, like money, is often given without the giver's knowing to just what use the recipient will want to put it. If someone to whom a transaction is mentioned gives it further consideration, he is likely to find himself wanting the answers to further questions that the speaker may not be able to identify in advance; if the appropriate specification will be likely to enable the hearer to answer a considerable variety of such questions for himself, then there is a presumption that the speaker should include it in his remark; if not, then there is no such presumption.

Finally, we can now show that, conversational implicature being what it is, it must possess certain features:

1. Since, to assume the presence of a conversational implicature, we have to assume that at least the Co-operative Principle is being

observed, and since it is possible to opt out of the observation of this principle, it follows that a generalized conversational implicature can be cancelled in a particular case. It may be explicitly cancelled, by the addition of a clause that states or implies that the speaker has opted out, or it may be contextually cancelled, if the form of utterance that usually carries it is used in a context that makes it clear that the speaker is opting out.

2. In so far as the calculation that a particular conversational implicature is present requires, besides contextual and background information, only a knowledge of what has been said (or of the conventional commitment of the utterance), and in so far as the manner of expression plays no role in the calculation, it will not be possible to find another way of saying the same thing, which simply lacks the implicature in question, except where some special feature of the substituted version is itself relevant to the determination of an implicature (in virtue of one of the maxims of Manner). If we call this feature NON-DETACHABILITY, one may expect a generalized conversational implicature that is carried by a familiar, non-special locution to have a high degree of non-detachability.

3. To speak approximately, since the calculation of the presence of a conversational implicature presupposes an initial knowledge of the conventional force of the expression the utterance of which carries the implicature, a conversational implicatum will be a condition that is not included in the original specification of the expression's conventional force. Though it may not be impossible for what starts life, so to speak, as a conversational implicature to become conventionalized, to suppose that this is so in a given case would require special justification. So, initially at least, conversational implicata are not part of the meaning of the expressions to the employment of which they attach.

4. Since the truth of a conversational implicatum is not required by the truth of what is said (what is said may be true—what is implicated may be false), the implicature is not carried by what is said, but only by the saying of what is said, or by 'putting it that way'.

5. Since, to calculate a conversational implicature is to calculate what has to be supposed in order to preserve the supposition that

the Co-operative Principle is being observed, and since there may be various possible specific explanations, a list of which may be open, the conversational implicatum in such cases will be a disjunction of such specific explanations; and if the list of these is open, the implicatum will have just the kind of indeterminacy that many actual implicata do in fact seem to possess.

IX

DO CONDITIONALS HAVE TRUTH-CONDITIONS?*

DOROTHY EDGINGTON

1. INTRODUCTION

IN the first part of this paper (Sects. 2 and 4) I rule out the possibility of truth-conditions for the indicative conditional 'If A, B' which are a truth-function of A and B. In the second part (Sect. 6) I rule out the possibility that such a conditional has truth-conditions which are *not* a truth-function of A and B; I rule out accounts which appeal, for example, to a stronger-than-truth-functional 'connection' between antecedent and consequent, which may or may not be framed in terms of a relation between possible worlds, in stating what has to be the case for 'If A, B' to be true. I conclude, therefore, that the mistake philosophers have made, in trying to understand the conditional, is to assume that its function is to make a statement about how the world is (or how other possible worlds are related to it), true or false, as the case may be. Along the way (Sects. 3 and 5) I develop a positive account of what it is to believe, or to be more or less confident, that if A, B, in terms of which an adequate logic of conditionals can be developed. The argument against truth-conditions is independent of this positive account of the conditional, as I show that any truth-conditional account has counterintuitive con-

Dorothy Edgington, 'Do Conditionals Have Truth-Conditions?', first published in *Critica* XVIII, 52 (1986): 3–30. Used by permission of *Critica, Revista Hispanoamericana de Filosofia.*

* Earlier versions of this essay were read to the Oxford Philosophical Society in 1984 and the Conference on the Philosophy of Logic and Language in Leicester, 1985. It formed part of the material of a lecture course on Conditionals given in the Instituto de Investigacions Filosóficas, Universidad Nacional Autónoma de México in the summer of 1985. I am grateful to these audiences and many other people for useful comments, and especially to Raúl Orayen for his enthusiasm and constructive criticism.

sequences, as well as clashing with my positive thesis. But the positive account prevents the essay from merely having created a paradox, or a vacuum.

The essay is inspired by Ernest Adams's book, *The Logic of Conditionals*.[1] My positive thesis is a less technical variant of his. He proves the negative result too, but hardly perspicuously. My aim, in trying to extract an intuitively compelling argument from a somewhat baffling piece of algebra, is not only to make this way of thinking about conditionals more widely, and more deeply, appreciated. It is also, by weakening the assumptions, to provide a stronger proof of the negative result. I hope to render the positive thesis more plausible, too, by presenting it less technically.

It should not need emphasis that in the conditional we have an indispensable form of thought, which plays a large part in both theoretical reasoning about what is the case and practical reasoning about what to do. Its basic role may be described thus: we are not omniscient; we do not know as much as it would be useful for us to know. We are constantly faced with a range of epistemic possibilities—things that, as far as we know, may be true, when the question whether they are true is relevant to our concerns. As part of such practical or theoretical reasoning, it is often necessary to *suppose* (or assume) that some epistemic possibility is true, and to consider what else would be the case, or would be likely to be the case, given this supposition. The

[1] Ernest Adams, *The Logic of Conditionals* (Dordrecht, 1975). Some historical background: Robert Stalnaker was, I believe, the first to suggest that insight into the semantics of conditionals might be gained from the probability theorist's notion of a conditional probability, $P(B/A)$ (the probability of B given A). See his 'Probability and Conditionals', *Philosophy of Science* (1970), repr. in W. L. Harper, R. Stalnaker, and G. Pearce (eds.), *Ifs* (Dordrecht, 1981). Judgements about how probable it is that if A, B, seem to coincide with judgements about the probability of B given A. Stalnaker suggested that we should define the conditional as that proposition whose probability is so measured. David Lewis was the first to prove that there is no such proposition. See his 'Probabilities of Conditionals and Conditional Probabilities', *Philosophical Review* (1976), repr. in Harper, Stalnaker, and Pearce (eds.), *Ifs*. (Essay IV in this volume.) As a result, Stalnaker and Lewis rejected the equation of the probability of a conditional with a conditional probability, the former defending a non-truth-functional account, the latter the truth-functional account of indicative conditional propositions. Adams, instead retains the equation, and denies that the conditional is, strictly speaking a proposition. In this essay, I support Adams. I am also indebted, in the proof of Sect. 6, to I. F. Carlstrom and C. S. Hill's review of Adams in *Philosophy of Science* (1978).

conditional expresses the outcome of such thought processes. It is worth remembering that any type of speech act can be performed with the scope of a supposition. There are conditional questions, commands, etc., as well as conditional assertions.

> If he phones, what shall I say?
> If I'm late, don't stay up.
> If you're determined to do it, you ought to do it today.

To assert or believe that if A, B is to assert (believe) B within the scope of the supposition, or assumption, that A.[2] This is bland enough, it would seem, to be not worth denying. Now, from a truth-conditional perspective, this double illocutionary force—an assumption, and an assertion within its scope—is eliminable—is reducible to, or equivalent to, a plain assertion. If conditionals have truth-conditions, to assert 'If A, B' is to assert that its truth-conditions obtain. One way of presenting the conclusion of this essay, then, is that the double illocutionary force is *in*eliminable; there is no proposition such that asserting *it* to be the case is equivalent to asserting that B is the case given the *supposition* that A is the case. For any proposed truth-condition, I shall show that there are epistemic situations in which there is a divergence between assent to the proposition with that truth-condition and assent to the conditional.

The main argument of the essay concerns indicative conditionals. The thesis extends to subjunctive or counterfactual conditionals, but I shall not have space to argue that here.[3] The distinction, from the present perspective, is not between two types of conditional connection, but between two types of supposition, or better, two kinds of context in which a supposition is made. One can suppose that A, taking oneself to know that not-A; and one can suppose that A, not taking oneself to know that not-A. Typically, the subjunctive or counterfactual conditional is the result of the first kind of supposition, the open or indicative

[2] I take this formulation from J. L. Mackie, *Truth, Probability and Paradox* (Oxford, 1973), ch. 4. Mackie had the right idea, but did not have adequate arguments for his rejection of truth-conditions.

[3] See Adams, *Logic of Conditionals*, ch. 4. More support for a unified theory of indicative and counterfactual conditionals is found in Brian Ellis, 'A Unified Theory of Conditionals', *Journal of Philosophical Logic* (1978), and 'Two Theories of Indicative Conditionals', *Australasian Journal of Philosophy* (1984).

conditional the result of the second kind. An apparent difficulty which actually clarifies the point: I take myself to know that the carpet I am now looking at is not red. I may say 'If it had been red, it would have matched the curtains.' But I may also say 'If it *is* red—well, I have gone colour-blind or am suffering some sort of delusion'. In the subjunctive, I am taking it for granted that I am right in thinking it is not red. In the indicative, I am supposing that I am wrong. I am considering it to be an epistemic possibility that it is red, despite appearances. The importance of this for present purposes is that the positive account of indicative conditionals to follow assumes that the antecedent is always treated as epistemically possible by the speaker. When that condition is not satisfied, the conditional will be treated as a subjunctive, in the extension of the thesis. It will not matter if this distinction between two kinds of supposing does not match perfectly the grammatical distinction. It is enough if any conditional thought can be explained in one of the two envisaged ways.

One further remark about the methodology of this essay: while it is no part of my purpose to deny that some conditionals are certain, on a priori or other grounds, the argument hinges upon the undeniable fact that many conditionals, like other propositions, are assented to or dissented from with a degree of confidence less than certainty. We are frequently uncertain whether if A, B, and our efforts to reduce our uncertainty often terminate, at best, in the judgement that it is probable (or improbable) that if A, B. Of course, the truth-conditions theorist does not have to deny these undeniable facts. For him, to judge it more or less probable that if A, B is to judge it more or less probable that its truth-conditions obtain. But this pinpoints his mistake. I show that uncertainty about a conditional is not uncertainty about the obtaining of any truth-conditions. If a conditional had truth-conditions, it would be. Therefore, a conditional does not have truth-conditions. That is the structure of the argument to follow.

2. THE TRUTH-FUNCTIONAL ACCOUNT

There are sixteen possible truth-functions of A and B. Only one is a candidate for giving the truth-conditions of 'If A, B'. Indeed, the following two assumptions are sufficient to prove that *if* 'If A, B' is truth-functional, it has the standard truth-function (that is, it is equivalent to '~(A & ~B)' and to '~A v B'). (1) 'If P & Q then P' is true, whatever the truth-values of P and of Q; (2) Sentences of the form 'If A, B' are sometimes false, i.e. are not all tautologies. So we may safely speak of *the* truth-functional account.

It is important to recognize that there are powerful arguments in favour of the truth-functional account. Here are two. First, take any two propositions, B and C. Information that at least one of them is true seems sufficient for the conclusion that if C is not true, B is true. The converse inference is uncontroversial.[4] Let C be ~A, and we appear to have vindicated the equivalence between '~A v B' and 'If A, B'. Second, information that A and C are not both true seems to license the inference that if A is true, C is not. Again, the converse implication is uncontroversial. Let C be ~B, and we appear to have vindicated the equivalence between '~(A & ~B)' and 'If A, B'. (I shall show later that my positive account will preserve the force of these arguments, while no account in terms of non-truth-functional truth-conditions can.)

But alas, there are well known difficulties for the truth-functional account: ~A entails ~(A & ~B), for any B. B entails ~(A & ~B), for any A. So, according to this account,

> The Labour Party will not win the next election

entails

> If the Labour Party wins the next election, the National Health Service will be dismantled by the next government.

Anyone who accepts the former and rejects the latter is (on this account) inconsistent.

Similarly,

> The Conservative Party will win the next election

entails

> If a horrendous scandal emerges during the campaign

---

[4] Suppose that if C is not true, B is true. Then, either C is true or (it isn't, in which case) B is true.

involving the Prime Minister and most of the Cabinet, the Conservative Party will win the next election.

Again, anyone who accepts the former and rejects the latter has, on this account, inconsistent beliefs.

H. P. Grice argued[5] that the truth-functional account can withstand these objections, provided that we are careful to distinguish the false from the misleading but true. There are many ways in which one can speak the truth yet mislead. One way is to say something weaker than some other relevant thing one is in a position to say. Consider disjunctions. I am asked where John is. I firmly believe he is in the bar, and I know that he never goes near libraries. Inclined to be unhelpful but not wishing to lie, I say

He is either in the bar or in the library.

I could go on: or at the opera or at the church or . . .)

My hearer naturally concludes that this is the most precise information I am in a position to give, and also concludes from the truth (let us assume) that I told him

If he's not in the bar he is in the library.

The conditional, like the disjunction, according to Grice, is true provided that he's in the bar, but misleadingly asserted on these grounds.

I shall now show that this defence of the truth-functional account fails. Grice drew our attention to the existence of propositions which a person *has grounds to believe true* but which it would be unreasonable, in normal contexts, to assert. A contrast is invoked between what one may reasonably *believe* and what one may reasonably *say*, given one's grounds. I do not dispute that it is important to recognize this phenomenon. It does, I think, correctly explain the behaviour of disjunctions. Being sure that John is in the bar, I cannot consistently *disbelieve* the proposition 'He is either in the bar or in the library'; indeed, if I have any epistemic attitude to that proposition, it should be one of belief, however inappropriate it is for me to assert it.

[5] H. P. Grice, 'Logic and Conversation', in D. Davidson and G. Harman (eds.), *The Logic of Grammar* (Encino, Calif., 1975).

A good enough test of whether the Gricean story fits the facts about disjunctions is this: I am asked to respond, 'Yes', 'No', or 'No opinion', to the disjunction. Being sure of one disjunct, I should surely answer 'Yes'.

Here there is a striking contrast between disjunctions and conditionals. Imagine an opinion poll shortly before an election. Again, the subject is asked to respond 'Yes' if he thinks a proposition true, 'No' if he thinks it false, 'No opinion' otherwise. The subject is honest and prides himself on his consistency. Here are some of this responses:

1. The Labour Party will win (L) . . . .   No
2. The Labour Party won't win (~L) . . . .   Yes
3. Either the Labour Party won't win or __ (~L ∨ __)   Yes
   (Fill in the blank as you will: If he accepts that (2) is true, he must, if rational, accept that at least one of two propositions, of which (2) is one, is true.)
4. If the Labour Party wins, the National Health Service will be dismantled by the next government (If L, N) . . . .   No

Now, on the truth-functional account, this person has blatantly inconsistent beliefs. His saying 'Yes' to (2) and 'No' to (4) is on a par with someone's saying 'Yes' to 'It's red and square' and 'No' to 'It's red'. The parallel is exact, for, on the truth-functional account, to deny (4) is equivalent to accepting L & ~ N; he cannot consistently accept this yet deny L. But it is surely quite clear that our subject, in accepting (2) and rejecting (4), is not contradicting himself.

In the case of disjunctions, the predicted Gricean contrast between what it is reasonable to believe and what it is reasonable to say, given one's grounds, is discernible. In the case of conditionals, it is not. (I do not mean that the distinction does not apply to conditionals, but that it fails as a defence of the truth-functional account.) The purpose of the opinion poll is simply to elicit someone's opinions, irrespective of whether they would constitute appropriate remarks in an ordinary conversational interchange. We can stipulate that the subject is honest and serious. We must either accuse him of gross inconsistency, or accept that the conditional is not truth-functional.

This case against the truth-functional account cannot be made in terms of beliefs of which one is *certain*. Someone who is 100 per cent certain that the Labour Party won't win has (on my account of the matter) no obvious use for an *indicative* conditional beginning 'If they win'. But someone who is, say, 90 per cent certain that they won't win can have beliefs about what will be the case if they do. The truth-functional account has the immensely implausible consequence that such a person, if rational, is at least 90 per cent certain of any conditional with that antecedent.

The principle I am appealing to is this:

> If A entails B, it is irrational to be more confident of A than of B.

For instance, it is irrational to be more confident that a thing is red than that it is coloured. If the entailment is one-way, any way of rendering A true renders B true, but not conversely. B may be true when A is not. B has more chance of being true than A.[6]

Given that some entailments are exceedingly complex, the principle, in its full generality, no doubt has the consequence that no one is fully rational. But here we are dealing with a simple, decidable, truth-functional entailment of the most basic kind. If the truth-functional account were correct, it would be a straightforward matter to get the subject to recognize that he has inconsistent beliefs.

3. WHAT IT IS TO JUDGE THAT IF A, B

The critique of the truth-functional account has yet to be completed, but it is useful here to introduce, by way of contrast, my positive account of the consistent judgements our subject *is* making when he accepts (2) and rejects (4). Figure 1 is a diagrammatic representation of how likely he considers the various possibilities, L, ~L, N, ~N, L & N, L & ~N, etc., to be, vertical height representing probability. In considering whether if L, N, the subject assumes L; that is, he ignores the ~L-possibilities, the lower part of the diagram. Considering just those

---

[6] The principle is provable in probability theory: writing '$\leftrightarrow$' for logical eqivalent, $B \leftrightarrow (A \& B) \vee (\sim A \& B)$. So $P(B) = P(A \& B) + P(\sim A \& B)$. If A entails B, $A \leftrightarrow A \& B$. So $P(B) = P(A) + P(\sim A \& B) \geq P(A)$.

possibilities above the wide line, he asks how likely it is that N. Answer: very unlikely. On the other hand, he is committed to believing L ⊃ N, that is ~L v N, to be slightly more probable than ~L, that is, very likely.

FIG. 1

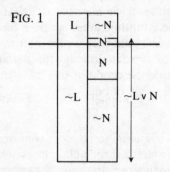

To judge it probable that A ⊃ B is to judge it improbable that A & ~B. To judge it probable that if A, B is not only to judge it improbable that A & ~B, but to judge this to be less probable than A & B. 'Is B likely given A?' is the question 'Is A & B nearly as likely as A?' (see Figure 2).

FIG. 2

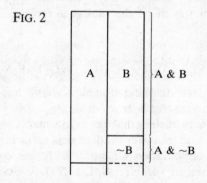

That A & ~B be small, which is necessary and sufficient for the conditional to be probable on the truth-functional account, is necessary but not sufficient on this account. If A & ~B is large, greater than ½, say, there isn't room for A & B to be larger still.

However, A & ~B can be small and A & B smaller still, as in the original example. In such a case, the material implication is probable but the conditional is not.

A simple example of the contrast between the two accounts: How likely is it that if this (fair) die lands an even number, it will land six? On my approach, we assume that the die lands an even number; given that assumption, there are three equal possibilities, one of which is six. So the answer is ⅓. On the truth-functional approach, the answer is ⅔: If the die lands not-even or six, that is, if it lands, 1, 3, 5, or 6, the conditional is true. So the conditional has four chances out of six of being true.

4. THE CASE AGAINST TRUTH FUNCTIONALITY CONTINUED

Let us continue our questionnaire to consider the second paradox of material implication:

5. The Conservative Party will win (C) . . . .   Yes
6. Either ____ or the Conservative Party will win
   (_ v C) (Fill in the blank as you like.) . . . .   Yes
7. If a horrendous scandal emerges involving the Prime
   Minister and most of the Cabinet, the Conservative
   Party will win (If S, C) . . . .   No

Such answers are not inconsistent. I grant that someone who is 100 per cent certain that the Conservatives will win will accept any conditional with an antecedent which he takes as an epistemic possibility and C as consequent. But that is not enough to prove the validity of the inference from C to 'If S, C'. Suppose our subject is 90 per cent certain that the Conservatives will win. He allows that they may not win, and that if certain, in his view unlikely, things happen, they will not win. So it is consistent to have a high degree of confidence that C and a low degree of confidence that if S, C. On the truth-functional account, this is, again, logically on a par with being very confident that it's red and square but very unconfident that it's square. On the other hand, his high degree of confidence in (5) does constrain him to at least that degree of confidence in (6) (see Figure 3).

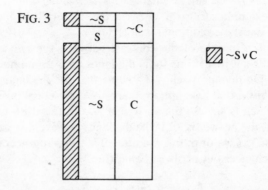

FIG. 3

~SvC

I said that the Gricean defence depends on a contrast between when a conditional is fit to be believed and when it is fit to be asserted. I have shown that the conditions under which a conditional is believed do not fit the truth-functional account. So this defence fails. Frank Jackson defends the truth-functional account differently.[7] His thesis is that for a conditional to be assertable, it must not only be believed that its truth-conditions are satisfied, but the belief must be *robust* or *resilient* with respect to the antecedent. This means that one would not abandon belief in the conditional if one were to discover the antecedent to be true. This ensures that an assertable conditional is fit for *modus ponens*. This condition is not satisfied if one believes A ⊃ B solely on the grounds that ~A. If one discovered that A, one would abandon one's belief that A ⊃ B, rather than conclude that B. I think this defence is open to the same objections as Grice's. There is simply no evidence that one *believes* a conditional whenever one believes the corresponding material implication, and then is prepared to *assert* it only if some further condition is satisfied.

I have been assuming that if a sentence is correctly assigned certain truth-conditions, a competent speaker believes that sentence if and only if he believes these conditions are fulfilled; and, provided that he is honest and has no wish to hide his opinion, will say so if asked 'Do you believe that A?' It may be

---

[7] Frank Jackson, 'On Assertion and Indicative Conditionals', *Philosophical Review* (1979) (Essay VI in this volume), and 'Conditionals and Possibilia', *Proceedings of the Aristotelian Society* (1980–1).

objected that the distinction between its truth-conditions and other aspects of a sentence's use is more a theorist's, less a practitioner's distinction than I have allowed. If this is so, then we must ask, what theoretical purpose is served by the assignment of these truth-conditions? To explain the validity of inferences? But it does this very badly. I have shown this for the two simplest types of example, but these generate indefinitely many other counterintuitive 'valid' inferences. Here is a new 'proof' of the existence of God:[8] 'If God does not exist, then it is not the case that if I pray my prayers will be answered (by Him). I do not pray. (So it *is* the case that if I pray . . .) So God exists'. The extent to which the truth-functional account succeeds in capturing the validity of inferences is explained by the fact that the material implication is essentially weaker than the indicative conditional (see above) and so is the extent to which it fails.

Another suggestion is that the truth-functional account explains the behaviour of embedded conditions: it explains the contribution of the truth-conditions of 'If A, B' to those of '(If A, B) or (if C, D)', for example. But, unsurprisingly, the truth-functional account yields counterintuitive results for sentences containing conditionals as constituents. For example, it tells us that the following is a tautology:

(If A, B) or (if not-A, B).

So anyone who rejects the first conditional must, on pain of contradiction, accept the second. So if I reject the conditional 'If the Conservatives lose, Thatcher will resign', I am committed to accepting 'If the Conservatives win, Thatcher will resign'![9]

We have not been able to find any theoretical purpose well served by these truth-conditions. There does not appear to be any indirect evidence in its favour to mitigate against the direct evidence against it—the fact that belief in a conditional and belief in a material implication do not coincide.

[8] I owe this example to W. D. Hart.

[9] Lewis, in 'Probabilities of Conditionals and Conditional Probabilities', gives as his reason for rejecting the no-truth-conditions view that it cannot explain embedded conditionals (*Ifs*, 136). He goes on to defend the truth-functional account, attempting to explain away some of its paradoxical features. But he does not address the problem that the truth-functional account gives absurd results for embedded conditionals.

5. THE POSITIVE ACCOUNT CONTINUED

I outlined my positive account of belief in a conditional in Sect. 3. In considering how likely it is that if A, B, one assumes A, that is, ignores the possibility that ~A. Relative to that assumption, one considers how likely it is that B (see Figure 2). This yields the following criterion:

> X believes that (judges it likely that) if A, B, to the extent that he judges that A & B is nearly as likely as A
>
> or, roughly equivalently, to the extent that he judges A & B to be more likely than A & ~B.

If we were to make the idealizing assumption that a person's subjective probability judgements are precise enough to be assigned numbers between one and zero inclusive, we could be more precise and say that the measure of X's degree of confidence in the conditional 'If A, B' is the ratio

$$\frac{P_x (A \& B)}{P_x (A)}$$

This ratio is known in probability theory as *the conditional probability of B given A*. Our positive thesis could be stated, then

> A person's degree of confidence in a conditional, if A, B, is the conditional probability he assigns to B given A.

However, my argument does not depend upon the idealizing assumption of precise numerical values. Also, even if we grant numerical values, the ratio must not be taken as a reductive definition of the conditional probability, as though one first had to ascertain how probable it is that A and that A & B, and then divide the second by the first. Typically, one does not have to decide how likely it is that A in order to judge that B is likely given A. I may have given no thought to the matter of how likely it is that the Labour Party will win yet be confident that if they win public spending will increase; this latter confidence entails confidence that, however likely it is that they win, it is nearly as likely that (they win and public spending increases). The nonreducibility is particularly obvious when, as part of some practical reasoning, one considers conditionals of the form 'If I do x, such-and-such will happen.' It would be absurd to hold that I have to know how likely it is that I will do x before I can assess such a conditional.

Let us consider some special cases. If I am certain of a conditional, for example that if he is a bachelor, he is unmarried, then, however likely it is that he is a bachelor, it is equally likely that he is a bachelor and unmarried. The ratio is 1. A conditional in which I have the lowest possible degree of confidence, for example, that if he's a bachelor, he's married, I assign probability 0 to the conjunction of antecedent and consequent, and hence to the ratio. If I think it is 50 : 50 that if you toss this coin, it will land heads, then, whatever the probability that you toss it, the probability that (you toss it and it lands heads) is half as much: the ratio is 1 : 2.

This measure has the advantage of allowing the probability of the conditional to be independent of the probability of the antecedent. On the truth-functional account, the probability that if you toss the coin it lands heads depends crucially on how probable it is that you toss it. Suppose it is much less likely now that you toss the coin than it was a minute ago. The probability of the material implication, which is equivalent to:

Either you won't toss it, or (you will and it will land heads)

has greatly increased. But the probability of the consequent on the assumption that the antecedent is true has remained the same.

Non-truth-functional accounts of the truth-conditions of conditionals demand some sort of 'strong connection' between antecedent and consequent for the conditional to be true. Such a connection is clearly lacking in

If you toss this (fair) coin, it will land heads.

On such accounts, the conditional is then certainly false. It should have probability 0. But surely, if someone is told 'the probability is 0 that if you toss it it will land heads', he will think it is a double-tailed or otherwise peculiar coin. Keeping the structure but changing the content of the example—a dog either bites or cowers when strangers approach, apparently at random, and with about equal frequency of each. Could one in good faith tell a stranger that the probability is zero (i.e. it is certainly false) that if he approaches, the dog will bite?

I think I have said enough to render plausible the claim that the measure of acceptability of a conditional 'If A, B' is the conditional probability of B given A. Without idealizing, the basic thesis that to assess how probable it is that if A, B, one assumes A, and considers how probable it is that B, under that assumption; and that that thought process is equivalent to considering whether A & B is nearly as likely as A. More evidence for the thesis comes from considering which inference-patterns involving conditionals are valid. There is not space to present this evidence fully,[10] but I shall end this section by saying something about the inference from 'A v B' to 'If not-A, B'. As I said at the beginning of Sect. 2, if this inference were valid, the truth-functional account would be correct. And the inference appears very plausible. We shall see how to explain these facts.

FIG. 4

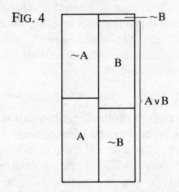

If I am agnostic about A, and agnostic about B, but confident that A or B, I must believe that if not-A, B. (See Figure 4. If in almost all possibilities, either A or B is true; and A and B are each true in approximately half the possibility-space; then in almost all not-A possibilities, B is true.) This is the normal situation in which a belief that A or B will play an active role in my mind, as a

_____
[10] See Adams, *Logic of Conditionals*, ch. 1.

premiss or as anything else, for example, someone has told me that A or B, or I have eliminated all but these two possibilities.

On the other hand, if my belief that A or B derives solely from my belief that A, the inference is not justified. For example, I wake up and look at the clock. It says eight o'clock. It is fairly reliable but by no means infallible. I am 90 per cent confident that it is eight o'clock (within whatever degree of precision with which we make such statements). So, were I to consider the matter, I must be at least 90 per cent confident that it is either eight o'clock or eleven o'clock. But this gives me no grounds for confidence that if it is not eight, it is eleven (see Figure 5).

FIG. 5

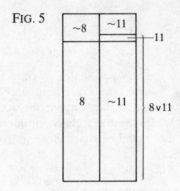

As it is rare and rather pointless to consider disjunctions in circumstances such as these, it is not surprising that we mistake 'A or B; therefore, if not-A, B' for a valid argument.

6. THE CASE AGAINST NON-TRUTH-FUNCTIONAL TRUTH CONDITIONS

If a conditional has truth-conditions, the probability of a conditional is the probability that those conditions obtain. Suppose that a conditional has truth-conditions which are not a truth-function of its antecedent and consequent. This means that the number of logically possible combinations of truth-values of A, B, 'If A, B' is between five and eight. That is, at least one and at most all four possible combinations of truth-values for A and B split(s) into two possibilities: 'If A, B' true; 'If A, B' false. At most three of the following eight combinations of truth-value can be ruled out a priori:

	A	B	If A, B
1a	T	T	T
1b	T	T	F
2a	T	F	T
2b	T	F	F
3a	F	T	T
3b	F	T	F
4a	F	F	T
4b	F	F	F

What follows is a 'tetralemma'. I shall now show that wherever truth-functionality is assumed to fail, there are consequences incompatible with the positive thesis about the acceptance of a conditional; and that where there is a clash, intuition continues to favour the positive thesis rather than the non-truth-functional truth-conditions thesis.

First, suppose

Assumption 1: A conditional has truth-conditions which are not truth functional when A and B are both true.

Thus 1a and 1b are two distinct possibilities. On this assumption, 'If A, B' would be like 'A before B' and 'A because B'. For example, the truth of 'John went to Paris' and of 'Mary went to Paris' leaves open the question whether 'John went to Paris *before* Mary went to Paris' is true; its truth depends on more than the truth-values of its constituents.

Consequence of Assumption 1:

C_1: Someone may be sure that A is true and sure that B is true, yet not have enough information to decide whether 'If A, B' is true; one may consistently be agnostic about the conditional while being sure that its components are true (as for 'A before B').

This consequence is central to my argument. I pause to clarify and defend it. It does not *quite* follow *merely* from the assumption of non-truth-functionality. There are exceptions to claims of the same form. But the exceptions are special cases, which do not cast doubt on the case of conditionals.

First exception: take the operator 'It is self-evident that . . .'. 'It is self-evident that A' is not a truth-function of A when A is true. But it does not follow that one may be sure that A yet agnostic about whether it is self-evident that A. For there is no room for uncertainty about propositions of this last form. However, such an operator clearly contrasts with the operators. 'If', 'before', 'because', which, in general, make contingent a posteriori claims, about which there is plenty of room for uncertainty. Of course there are self-evident conditionals, such as 'If he's a bachelor, he's unmarried'; but they owe their self-evidence to the particular contents of the constituent propositions. They are not self-evident just because of the meaning of 'if'.

It could be objected that my argument, resting on C_1, will not have shown that those conditionals which *are* self-evident don't have truth-conditions. But this would be to claim that 'if' is ambiguous: that it has a different meaning in 'If he's a bachelor he's unmarried' and 'If John is in Paris, so is Mary.' I see no grounds for an ambiguity. My positive thesis has the consequence that self-evident conditionals are certain—the consequent is certain on the supposition that the antecedent is true; and that conditionals about which one may be uncertain cannot be understood in terms of truth-conditions. It offers a unified account of indicative conditionals which is incompatible with a unified account in terms of truth conditions. Unified accounts are prima-facie preferable to accounts which postulate ambiguities. In the absence of a strong case for ambiguity, then, my argument still applies to all conditionals.

A second counter-example to the general claim about non-truth-functionality I owe to Raúl Orayen: Interpret 'A*B' as 'I am sure that A and sure that B'. This is not a truth-function of A and B when A and B are both true. But it does not follow that I can be sure that A and sure that B yet agnostic about A*B. It could be replied that, as we do not have incorrigible access to our own beliefs, it *is* possible to be sure that A, sure that B, yet unsure about whether one is sure, i.e. unsure about A*B.[11] But in any case, any putative truth conditions of 'If A, B' will surely be unlike those of 'A*B' in being independent of the state of mind of any one individual. The hypothesis under consideration, Assumption 1, is that the truth of A and of B is insufficient to determine the truth of 'If A, B'. One doesn't have to be an extreme realist about truth to insist that whatever else is necessary is *in general* nothing to do with one individual's epistemic state. I say 'in general' because, as before, there will be special cases—conditionals which are *about* the state of mind of some one individual; and *perhaps* to some of these, the individual concerned has incorrigible access. But, to repeat, we are in the business of interpreting 'If' for all conditionals. The contribution it makes to the (alleged) truth conditions of sentences in which it occurs makes no reference to my state of mind—though in special cases, the A or the B in 'If A, B' may do so.

C_1 still stands, then. Now C_1 is incompatible with our positive account. Being certain that A and that B, a person must think A & B is just as likely as A. He is certain that B on the assumption that A is true.

C_1 also conflicts with common sense. Admittedly, the conditional 'If A, B' is not of much interest to someone who is sure that both A and B are true. But he can hardly doubt or deny that if A, B, in this epistemic state. Establishing that the antecedent and consequent are true is surely one incontrovertible way of verifying a conditional. If you deny that if A, B, and I know that A and B are both true, I am surely in a position to correct you.

Assumption 1 must, then, be rejected. Truth-functionality cannot fail when A and B are both true. 'A & B' is sufficient for 'If, A, B'. Putative possibility 1b does not exist. We proceed to the second stage of the argument.

> Assumption 2: A conditional has truth-conditions which are not truth-functional when A is true and B is false.

Consequence of Assumption 2:

C_2: Someone may be sure that A is true and sure that B is false

---

[11] I owe this point to Raymundo Morado.

yet not have enough information to settle whether 'If A, B' is true, and hence be agnostic about the latter.

As with C_1, this is incompatible with our positive account, and also with common sense. Such a person knows enough to reject the claim that B is true on the assumption that A. 'A & ~B' is sufficient to refute 'If A, B'. Assumption 2 is false. Putative possibility 2a does not exist.

We have shown, then, that if a conditional has truth conditions, they are truth-functional for the two cases in which A is true. We shall now consider the cases in which A is false.

> Assumption 3: A conditional has truth-conditions which are not truth-functional when A is false and B is true.

Now suppose someone is sure that B but is uncertain whether A. On our positive account, he knows enough to be sure that if A, B: If B is certain, A & B is just as probable as A. This also accords with common sense. But according to Assumption 3, there are three possibilities—three ways the world may be—compatible with his knowledge:

A	B	If A, B
T	T	T
F	T	T
F	T	F

(I rely on the fact that we have established truth-functionality for the top line.)

A may be false, and if it is, some further condition has to be satisfied for 'If A, B' to be true, and he may not know whether it is satisfied. According to Stalnaker,[12] for instance, the further condition is that B be true in the closest possible world to the actual world in which A is true. And he might not know enough about the actual world to know whether this is so.

An example might help. I complain to John that he has not

---

[12] Stalnaker, 'A Theory of Conditionals', in *Studies in Logiocal Theory*, *American Philosophical Quarterly*, Monograph 2 (Oxford, 1968), repr. in E. Sosa (ed.), *Causation and Conditionals* (Oxford, 1975) and in *Ifs*. (Essay II in this volume.)

replied to my letter. He says he did—he posted the reply some weeks ago. I am not sure whether to believe him. Let A be 'He posted the reply' and B be 'I didn't receive it.' Our positive account has it that B is certain on the assumption that A, and so does common sense. But by Assumption 3, I should reason like this: 'I didn't receive the letter. Suppose he posted it: then the conditional is true. But suppose he didn't post it: this, together with the fact that I didn't receive it, is not sufficient for the conditional. It depends (say) on whether in the closest possible world in which he *did* post it, I still didn't receive it. And I can't be sure of that'.

Assumption 3, then, is incompatible with our positive account, and once more, intuition vindicates our account. Assumption 3 must be rejected. Putative possibility 3b does not exist.

Finally, Assumption 4: Truth-functionality fails when 'A' and 'B' are both false.

Now consider someone who is sure that A and B have the same truth-value, but is uncertain which. For example he knows that John and Mary spent yesterday evening together, but doesn't know whether they went to the party. According to our positive account and according to common sense, he knows enough to be sure that if John went to the party (J), Mary did (M). (J & M is as likely as J; M is certain on the assumption that J.) But according to Assumption 4, he has to consider three possibilities compatible with his knowledge:

J	M	If J, M
T	T	T
F	F	T
F	F	F

J and M may both be false, and if they are, some further condition has to be satisfied for 'If J, M' to be true. Perhaps the further question, if John and Mary didn't go, is whether Mary would have gone if John had, and he can't be certain of that. Our positive account and Assumption 4 diverge, and intuition, once more, favours our account. Assumption 4 must be rejected. Putative possibility 4b does not exist.

We have reached the end of our proof. That the conditional has non-truth-functional truth-conditions entails that at least one of Assumptions 1 to 4 is true. But whichever we take, we can find conditionals whose acceptability (or unacceptability), both intuitively and in terms of our positve account, conflicts with that assumption.

Given truth-conditions, we have a paradox. It is no accident that, given truth-conditions, there is philosophical disagreement about whether or not they are truth-functional. For there are acceptable conditionals whose acceptability cannot be accommodated by any non-truth-functional account. I have used some of these in the above proof. And there are unacceptable conditionals whose unacceptability cannot be accommodated by the truth-functional account. I used these earlier in the case against truth-functionality. But our positive account resolves this paradox. The mistake is to think of conditionals as part of fact-stating discourse.

Perhaps we can get closer to the heart of the paradox with the following case. I am wondering whether A and whether B. Someone comes along who knows their truth-values, but feels unable to tell me all he knows. He says 'The most I am able to tell you is this: ~(A & ~B).' This is enough for me to conclude that if A, B. Now, ~ (A & ~B) *does not entail* 'If A,B'. That is the truth-functional account, with all its difficulties. But *belief that ~(A ~B) in the absence of belief that* ~A *is sufficient for belief that if A, B* (see Figure 6). No non-truth-functional truth-conditions can accommodate that fact.

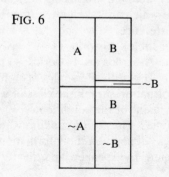

FIG. 6

A further comment is needed in view of the conflict between the last sentence and the thesis of Robert Stalnaker's 'Indicative Conditionals', reprinted in this volume. Stalnaker aims to show that the inference from 'A or B' to 'if ~A, B' is reasonable in circumstances in which the former is assertable, though invalid given his non-truth-functional truth conditions. (Clearly, the same should go for the inference from ~(A & ~B) . . . 'If A, B'.)

A variant of my argument in the penultimate paragraph, applied to Stalnaker-conditionals, is as follows. Initially lacking all relevant information, I am agnostic between these four exclusive and exhaustive possibilities: (1) A & B; (2) A & ~B; (3) ~A and the nearest A-world (the world the selection function selects for A) is a B-world; (4) ~A and the nearest A-world is a ~B-world. If either (1) or (3) obtains, 'If A, B' is true; if either (2) or (4) obtains, 'If A, B' is false. I now learn, on good authority, that (2) is false. On Stalnaker's account this is not enough for certainty that if A, B, because the possibility (4) remains. (The falsity of (2) does not entail the falsity of (4); if it did, (4) would entail (2), but (4) is incompatible with (2).) Intuitively, though, and according to my account of the acceptability of conditionals, learning that (2) is false, while remaining agnostic about A, is sufficient for certainty that if A, B. So much the worse for Stalnaker-conditionals.

Here is how Stalnaker avoids this conclusion. His thesis is set in terms of the pragmatics of communication, but has a crucial semantic component: the truth conditions of an indicative conditional depend on a 'context set', namely the set of possible worlds not ruled out by the speaker (and hearer). He claims, in effect, that the only possible worlds in play for an indicative conditional are those which are taken as epistemic possibilities on a given occasion of utterance. Now, once (2) A & ~B is ruled out, *no* epistemically possible A-world is a ~B-world; i.e. *all* epistemically possible A-worlds are B-worlds; so the nearest such A-world must be a B-world. Possibility (4) has disappeared because my new information shrank the class of worlds which are relevant to the assessment of the conditional.

But what conditional? The 'truth conditions' of a conditional sentence, on this view, depend on the information of the speaker (or taken for granted by speaker and hearer). Change the information, and a different proposition is expressed. I have not discovered to be true what I was previously wondering about, become certain of what I was previously uncertain; rather, there was one proposition I was wondering about, and another, with different 'truth conditions', of which I am certain.

This gets *acceptance* right by making 'truth' and 'truth condition' radically information-dependent. If one party is certain that if A, B and another is not (but regards A as possible), they *cannot* be disagreeing about the obtaining of the same truth conditions. They *must* be equivocating. For the former's context set must rule out A & ~B, and the latter's must not. The set of possible worlds in play is different in the two cases. Contrary to appearance, it is rather that one asserts that P, and the other doubts that Q. (At least, I cannot see how Stalnaker avoids this consequence; and if he does, I cannot see how he avoids my argument.)

Further, if a context set is sufficiently bigoted or bizarre, any old (non-contradictory) conditional can come out 'true': 'If we dance, it will rain tomorrow', for instance. We dance, and the drought continues unabated. Given what we now know, we would not have uttered those words. But the context is different—in its own context, what was said was 'true'.

My argument against truth conditions assumes, *contra* Stalnaker, that the same proposition, with the same truth conditions, can be accepted in one state of information, not accepted in another. In Sect. 7, when I claim that my argument is neutral as to the nature of truth, this qualification should be borne in mind. I did not quite ignore the possibility of radical information dependence of truth, but brushed it aside as unworthy of serious consideration, early in Sect. 6, in the discussion following Assumption 1.

Whether this is really a qualification or concession depends on whether 'Stalnaker-truth' is really truth. So information-relative a concept seems to me to lack central features of the concept of truth: its role as the ideal upshot of epistemic enquiry—as what epistemic endeavours strive for, as what will serve us well if attained—requires more of a gap between truth and what speakers take for granted. I leave that to the reader to judge.

7. SOME CONCLUDING OBSERVATIONS

The argument makes no assumptions about what truth consists in—beyond the fact that one may take various epistemic attitudes to the question whether a given proposition has that property. Whatever 'true' means, to judge it likely that it applies to B on the assumption that it applies to A is not equivalent to judging it likely that it applies to something else. The linguistic or mental act of *supposing* is ineliminable from conditionals, and they cannot be reduced to straight assertions or beliefs.

Another way of putting the conclusion is this. One can be certain or uncertain about a proposition, A. Uncertainty about A ($\sim$A, A $\vee$ B, etc.) has a structure which is not only compatible with the proposition's having one or other truth-value, but requires that it does. One can be certain or uncertain about whether if A, B. Uncertainty about a conditional has a structure which does not require that the conditonal has one or other truth-value; moreover, it is incompatible with this.

There are several reasons why this argument is important. This is the most general one: a hard argument against (or for) the applicability of the concept of truth to a given area of discourse is a rare thing. It is just possible that this one may shed light on controversies about the applicability of the concept in other areas. Given certain key features of the epistemology of discourse of the kind in question, we can ask, does this epistemology fit with even a minimal metaphysics of truth?

Another reason why the consequences of the argument are far-reaching is that it has become increasingly fashionable to 'analyse' other important philosophical concepts in terms of conditionals, for example, causation, natural laws, dispositional properties, and more recently, knowledge. The standard account of statements of the form 'All A's are B' is also a striking example. There is much that needs to be re-examined in the light of this thesis.

Perhaps most importantly, the criterion for the validity of deductive arguments needs to be restated in the light of this thesis. The standard criterion is that valid arguments preserve truth. But such arguments contain conditionals, and according to the thesis I have defended, conditionals are not suitable candidates for truth.

Now, our interest in the validity of arguments is epistemological. A valid argument is one such that it is irrational to accept the premisses and reject the conclusion. Construing acceptance as high subjective probability, and acceptance of a conditional in terms of high conditional probability, Adams has shown how to give a precise criterion of validity along these lines, which coincides with the standard one for arguments without conditionals.[13] It explains why certain patterns of inference involving conditionals are valid; and it isolates the unusual conditions under which others, which appear valid, fail. I discussed one such example at the end of Sect. 5.

Finally, this argument should not be construed as part of a general attack on truth-conditional semantics. It depends on a contrast between the roles of the constituent sentences of a conditional and the conditional itself. It does not require, but fits well with a truth-conditional account of our understanding of the former.

Indeed, this anti-realist argument about conditionals is more puzzling for a general anti-realist than for a philosopher with strong realist tendencies. For the latter, let us say, a declarative sentence identifies a possible state of affairs. It is true if and only if the state of affairs identified obtains. For him, the argument shows that there are no conditional states of affairs. For an anti-realist who construes truth along the lines of what is ideally rationally acceptable, it is much more puzzling that the notion cannot be applied to conditionals. But, as I said before, the argument itself makes no assumptions about the nature of truth.

---

[13] See Adams, *Logic of Conditionals*, ch. 2. It is worth remarking that the existence of logical consequences of moral judgements, rules, laws, etc., also suggests that the classical account of validity is limited in scope.

X

INTERPRETATIONS OF 'IF'-SENTENCES*

V. H. DUDMAN

THIS essay is about how the English language generates 'if'-sentences, and the messages it thereby encodes. These messages are the *interpretations of 'if'-sentences* of my title, and we can discover their *structures*, I shall show, by considering how they are encoded into their 'if'-sentences. By seeing the message articulated in the sentence, we perceive how the message is slotted together out of its informational fragments, so that our semantic speculations can be grounded in structural fact.

And, after all, every semantic theory relies upon *some* structural apprehensions about its target messages. To propose that something is 'true when its consequent is true or its antecedent false', for example, or 'true just when its consequent is true in the nearest antecedent world', is *ipso facto* to propose a form in which there occur factors meet to count as consequent and antecedent. But the only structure a message *has*, I submit, is the one I have been speaking of, the one imposed by language as the price of encodement as a sentence. And this structure is discoverable by routine grammatical investigation, as I shall illustrate below. Moreover, the success of the semantic theory is going to depend on getting this structure right, on recognizing the right factors and putting them together right. Therefore *grammar is a necessary preliminary to semantics*.

Overwhelmingly, however, the grammatical preliminaries are

V. H. Dudman, 'Interpretations of "If"-Sentences', © 1991 V. H. Dudman. Used by permission of the author.

* This essay was greatly improved by suggestions of D. H. Mellor.

dispensed with, and semantic theories arise which are demonstrably untenable on structural grounds. It will emerge, indeed, that every known semantics for 'if', and every logical notation for it, is in just this unhappy position: grammatically untenable. Everywhere, the same ternary analysis is adopted, into 'antecedent', 'consequent', and operator. And this ternary analysis is seriously and demonstrably mistaken. Interpretations of 'if'-sentences are of more than one kind, but no kind has the fêted ternary structure. For the semantics of 'if', nothing less is required than a new beginning.

My *message m* is simultaneously the item from which the sentence S is generated in the mind of the speaker, and the item conveyed to the hearer's mind when S is successfully broadcast. It is crucial to appreciate the direction of the relationship: the language generates *S from m*. S does not determine *m*. English is forever arriving at the same sentence from different messages via different encoding programmes. The point is that two different programmes, each for encoding its own kind of message, can and regularly do overlap in their output sentences. Examples will multiply below. It means that semantic proposals are misapplied to sentences. Their objects are the originating messages.[1]

If ordinary people are allowed to have any, it would be no surprise to find their metaphysical apprehensions enshrined in their forms of speech. Suppose they felt, for example, that there were facts about the past and present but none about the future. Their language might well evolve just two basically different kinds of atomic encoding programme, one for encoding claims of past and present fact and the other for encoding (say) personal reactions of the speaker to imagined future developments. And thus it would have become impossible to state a future fact in that language, exactly in accordance with the immanent metaphysics. Now, in the tale with which I seek to divert the reader below, all this and more counts for sober truth as applied to English. If there are future facts, English lacks the means of formulating them. I

---

[1] Thus, at greater length my 'Conditional Interpretations of "If"-sentences', *Australian Journal of Linguistics*, 4 (1984): 143–204; 'Towards a Theory of Predication for English', *Australian Journal of Linguistics*, 5 (1985); 143–96; and 'Antecedents and Consequents', *Theoria*, 52 (1986): 168–99.

foreshow this particular submission partly by way of advertisement, but also to emphasize again, to a reader entitled to a quite different perspective, that my concern is simply with the English language and the things that can be said in it.

Communication proceeds as a succession of personal earnests on the part of the speaker. She[2] broadcasts a sequence of *separate sentences*. (Her full stops, there to mark the separations, are of course silent.) And each separate sentence is *asserted*: it comes with the speaker's own imprimatur. The speaker is not just transmitting its then interpretation to the hearer. She is *affirming* it to him. So after we have expounded the substance of this or that interpretation of an 'if'-sentence, there remains the question what affirming it amounts to.

The conditional idea has long fascinated speculative minds. One result is that there are hundreds of philosophers in the world today who care how 'if' works in English. To those with a broader interest in the English language, this attention can only be welcome. From their point of view it is however a strangely narrow enthusiasm, as if a chemist were to focus just on one kind of molecule without paying much mind to either molecules in general or atoms at all. The fact is that locutions involving 'if' are comparatively recondite, and exact treatment of them is not to be expected without prior treatment of more fundamental idioms. Still, respectful of the reader's particular predilection, I shall strive here to minify these necessary preliminaries, confining them to Sects. 2 to 4.

1. THE FOUR CATEGORIES

English generates what we casually call 'if'-sentences by just four basically different encoding programmes, and as a result interpretations of 'if'-sentences divide into four grammatical *categories*. This section will introduce the four without getting technical.

We recognize the handiwork of the first encoding programme when we appreciate that each sentence (A) has an interpretation

---

[2] My *s*peaker is *s*he and my *h*earer is *h*e.

under which both 'the door was locked' and 'Grannie leapt in through the window' are understood as if standing alone:

(A) Because/as/since/due to the fact that/if/provided that/ whether or not/unless/while/despite the fact that/ (al)- though the door was locked, Grannie leapt in through the window.

When this encoding programme selects 'if', the originating message belongs to our *first* category. As an essential feature, first-category messages are *compound*, compounded out of prior messages.

The second encoding programme is for encoding habitual messages, present, past, or past past:

After/before/(as soon) as/immediately/once/when(ever)/ where(ver) if/provided that/whether or not/unless the door is [was, had been] locked, Grannie leaps [leapt, had leapt] in through the window.

When this encoding programme selects 'if', the originating message belongs to our *second* category.

The third programme encodes the vast echelons of messages, including future interpretations of (B), (C), and (D), present interpretations of (E) and (F), and past interpretations of (D) and (F):

(B) If/provided that/whether or not/unless the door is locked Grannie will/can/may/shall/must/should/ought to/ needn't/ daren't leap in through the window

(C) If/provided that/whether or not/unless the door was locked Grannie would/could/might leap in through the window

(D) If/provided that/whether or not/unless the door had been locked Grannie would/could/might have leapt in through the window

(E) If/provided that/whether or not/unless she was alive Grannie would/could/might be in prison

(F) If/provided that/whether or not/unless she had been alive Grannie would/could/might have been in prison.

(We say (D) about the future when we have been saying (B) or (C) about the future and then learn of Grannie's assassination.) Plainly there is a pattern unifying the messages thus encoded. Actually it is that time-about is always later than time-registered-by-form. But these matters are best postponed until we turn technical: suffice it for the moment to perceive the influence of a single encoding programme. It will be observed that this programme always bestows a secondary auxiliary—'will', 'can', etc.—upon the sentences it generates. When this encoding programme selects 'if', the originating message belongs to our *third* category.

I call third-category messages *conditional*, thus attempting to march off with a prized term. I have no conscience about this. For one thing, rival proprietors of 'conditional' have rarely said what they meant by it. For another, they have nevertheless said enough to indicate that for them a conditional is a *sentence*. Wicked waste.

The fourth encoding programme is grammatically egregious, but the messages it encodes, such as the natural interpretation of

> If Tom was fat his sister was immense

are without logical interest. I mention the *fourth* category here only for completeness.[3]

And now it is time to get technical. When next we encounter 'if', we shall be armed with a working analysis of simpler idioms.

2. SOME TECHNIQUES

The elemental English sentence divides into a subject and a predicate. Some sentences have lesser sentences for constituents and are not subject–predicate sentences. These are called

[3] Received logical thought about 'if'-sentences rejects my four categories. It favours a dichotomous taxonomy which draws a line smack dab through my third category so as to separate two 'moods'. There is one mood for past-tense conditionals and another for everything else, although it is unclear how much else is recognized and especially whether habitual interpretations are. But certainly present-tense conditionals like the future interpretations of (B) are classified with compound interpretations instead of with other conditionals. How to respond? Polite incredulity gives way to gathering outrage when investigation reveals that the sole authority for this improbable taxonomy resides with a hallowed pair of antique terms of art. Take away 'indicative' and 'subjunctive' and the whole idea collapses.

compound sentences. But otherwise English sentences are *simple* in the sense that they basically comprise a subject and a predicate.

And every predicate contains a *fulcrum*, either a finite form of a verb ('*fell*', is falling', 'had fallen') or a second auxiliary ('*might* fall', '*must* have fallen'). In the latter case, it is always followed by the base of a verb ('might *fall*', 'must *have* fallen'). Following F. R. Palmer,[4] we can assign sentences to the 'primary pattern' or the 'secondary pattern', according as their predicates contain a finite form of a verb or a secondary auxiliary followed by the base of a verb.

We can now define messages as *compound* or *simple*, and, if the latter, *primary* or *secondary*, according to the stamps of the sentences required to encode them.

Now, the fulcrum of a simple sentence always registers temporal relation to the point O of speech. There is one batch of fulcrums that always register presentness, i.e. identity with O, and the rest always register pastness with respect to O. As regards verbs, the 'V-s' and the 'general' form (as in 'I/you/we/they agree') both register presentness while the 'V-ed' form registers pastness. As for *secondary auxiliaries*, they are inflectional forms of *modals* and segregate as in Table 1:

TABLE 1

Modal	Secondary auxiliary	
	Present	*Past*
WILL	will	would
CAN	can	could
MAY	may	might
SHALL	shall	should$_2$
MUST	must	
SHOULD	should$_1$	
OUGHT	ought	
NEED	need	
DARE	dare	

[4] F. R. Palmer, *A Linguistic Study of the English Verb* (London: Longman, 1965); revised 1974 as *The English Verb*.

The result is that every simple message has a piece of temporal intelligence, presentness or pastness, as an informational factor. Not only that; sometimes pastness can be particularized as *past*pastness: pastness with respect to an already past point. This facility, when available, is afforded by phase modification. *Phase modification* involves replacing an inflectional form of a verb by the same inflectional form of HAVE followed by the '*V*-en' form of the verb: 'fell' by 'had fallen', 'might fall' by 'might have fallen', and so on.

In sum every simple message has a *tense t*. First, the speaker has to choose between registering presentness or pastness at the fulcrum, and if she chooses pastness, there is *sometimes* the option of registering pastpastness by phase modifying.

And that, in a nutshell, is my theory of tense for English. It was convenient to give it in advance, for it will play a crucial role in what follows, where every example is meant to confirm it.

As well as a tense, every simple message has a time *y* that it is intuitively about, and the question arises of the relationship between *t* and *y*. For some messages, we shall find, *t* is *y*. For others, *y* and *t* are separate points. For me, this difference marks the absolutely fundamental division among simple messages. *Propositions* have *t* and *y* identical. For *judgements* they are different.

It is time now to descend to detailed analysis of basic simple messages. Naturally I begin with primary ones.

3. PRIMARY MESSAGES

The primary-pattern sentence

(G) Grannie leapt in through the window

is ambiguous between an interpretation m_1 deponing a single past leap, and an interpretation m_2 deponing a past habit of leaping. Comparing them we discover the same tense, the same Grannie, and the same concept of leaping in through windows. The difference is that the tense of m_1 is the time of Grannie's leap, while the tense of m_2 is the time of Grannie's tendency to leap, or whatever it is. Let us nail all this down.

Whether generated from m_1 or m_2, (G) comprises a *subject* 'Grannie' and a *predicate* 'leapt in through the window'. The predicate is obtained by imposing a formal choice upon the *verb phrase* 'LEAP in through the window'. The subject is chosen in order to identify Grannie as the *notional subject s* of the message, whether m_1 or m_2. The form is chosen to locate t. And the verb-phrase is chosen to specify a *root condition r*, in this case that of leaping in through the window. Root conditions are conceptual affairs, and doubly unsaturated: satisfiable *by* a notional subject *at* a time.

So m_1 and m_2 have the same r, the same s, and the same t. The difference is that m_1 alleges the satisfaction of r by s at t, whereas m_2 alleges the currency at t of something like a *propensity* on the part of s to satisfy r. I respond by recognizing a *predication condition H(r)* ingredient in m_2. What m_2 depones is the satisfaction of $H(r)$ by s at t. Predication conditions are conceptual elaborations out of root conditions.

Let me explain more thoroughly. My argument is that basic habitual messages always seem to make tolerable sense when expounded using 'propensity'. And this is enough to establish the formal difference: in m_1 s satisfies r, while in m_2 it satisfies some elaboration $H(r)$ of (r). (The presenting problem for any semantic theory of habituals is to explain how $H(r)$ is elaborated out of r, conceptually. I should expect a solution to be rich in metaphysical implications, because of the connection with natural laws.)

Actually, it is an expository convenience to recognize a predication condition even in m_1's case. This time I write '$I(r)$', and speak of *direct* predication, as distinct from the *habitual* predication of m_2. English has other modes of predication, at least two, and I am oversimplifying here by ignoring them.[5] I shall write '$P(r)$' to represent predication conditions generally.

Both m_1 and m_2 are claims of fact about their tenses. Each depones actual, historical satisfaction of its $P(r)$ by its s at a time y; and in each case $t = y$. On the basis of this gravely inadequate

---

[5] There is *futurate* predication, as in 'The conference begins [began, according to our original plan] next Monday', and what I call *rounded predication*, which produces past messages with no present analogues. See my 'Towards a Theory of Predication for English', sects. 9, 14, and 15.

treatment, I propose quite generally that primary messages are *propositions*, messages which are true or false at *O* because they are claims of historical fact about times no later than *O*, namely their tenses. And by *affirming* a primary message the speaker personally attests to its truth at *O*.[6]

4. SECONDARY MESSAGES

To the grammarian—by way of preamble—it is a fundamental methodological presumption that extra words in the sentence are there to encode extra factors in the message. True, the exception is defeasible. 'If I should die before I wake . . . encodes nothing that 'If I die before I wake . . .' doesn't. But in general more words mean more ideas. There is no other quarter-sensible way a code might work.

Reflections in this vein quickly discover that secondary messages are at least one idea richer than primary ones. When a secondary-pattern sentence is generated, something conditions the choice of modal, and there is nothing in a primary message to do any comparable thing.

To the grammarian—still preambling—every recognition of brute irreducible diversity is naturally an admission of defeat. Accordingly, it is another fundamental methodological presumption of code-breaking that every word and lexeme is univocal until shown otherwise. This applies with especial force to the modals. Secondary messages are wonderfully diverse, which might prompt the novice to endow individual modals with whole arrays of meanings. But to the code-breaker, what all this versatility betrays is considerable underlying *control*: it must be a tight, tidy system which presides over all this flexibility. An elegant system, not given to the unnecessary perplexity that sheer

---

[6] Some things people want to say to each other are so abstract that location in time is quite inapplicable, e.g. arithmetical things. The facts here are exceedingly simple. English signals presentness in '7 is odd' no less than in 'Grannie is odd'; but the signalled presentness is *not* a factor of the encoded arithmetical message, which is far too abstract to have anything to do with time. The signalled presentness is simply *ignored* as inappropriate. So these high abstractions are exceptional to my claim that every simple message has a tense, and indeed to my general conclusions connecting factual content with tense. The natural interpretation of '7 is odd' is a proposition right enough. But it is a claim of *non-historical* fact.

arbitrary ambiguity engenders. The overwhelming presumption, then, is that each modal has a single, invariant informational trigger, a unique meaning.

I concede that this presumption fails for MAY. 'He may go' is ambiguous between a 'perhaps' interpretation and a permissive one, both intuitively about the future; and this equivocation can only be sheeted home to the modal. I also concede that there are awkward uses of 'should' in subordinate clauses. But I see nothing in any other quarter to challenge the presumption, and accordingly I am on the look-out for nine or so simple, native conceptions to serve as the English *modalities*, the meanings of the individual modals: two for MAY, one for each other modal, and the *same* one for SHOULD and OUGHT. Where to start looking I have no idea: the presenting problem is to find some unifying perspective from which to view the selection process for a modal. It would take a real philosopher (it seems to me) to devise a modal system that fitted English. Of course it would take a lot of patient sifting through the teeming evidence, too. For me, meanwhile, the modalities remain unknown constants.

The difference between the patterns is that the secondary has the capacity for all the informational ingredients encodable in the primary, plus at least a modality M. And so, at last, to the grammar of secondary messages.

English generates secondary-pattern sentences by three different encoding programmes. Two of them employ the restricted version of my tense code, with no past past: only the fulcrum registers tense. However, the third encoding programme uses the full battery, just as in the primary pattern.

Encoded in three basic ways, secondary messages divide into three grammatical *categories*. And in each category we discover a different relationship between y and t.

Some secondary messages have t and y identical:

> Grannie will (often)/can (sometimes)/may (occasionally) leap in through the window
> Grannie would (often)/could (sometimes)/might (occasionally) leap in through the window.

I call them *proper* messages. In outermost structure, proper messages are indiscernible from primary ones. In substance too: these latest examples are habitual, entirely. And propositions, as inspection will confirm. In a proper message, t is once again the time of a predication condition's satisfaction by s, with M playing a comparatively minor role, helping to elaborate that predication condition out of a prior one. In the other secondary messages, the ones where t and y are different points, M plays a more prominent role.

The characteristic trait of a *practical* message is that y is located by phase. When $y < O$ the sentence is phase-modified and when $y = O$ it is not. Meanwhile, t is located by the fulcrum, quite independently:

> Grannie must/can't/may/will/needn't/daren't/could/might/ would be [have been] hiding in the cellar.

Innocently described, these messages are *judgements* concerning Grannie's hiding in the cellar. And what conditions the choice of modal is the kind of judgement, each modal enunciating a different *verdict* concerning that common subject-matter.

The defining trait of a *projective* message is that y is later than t. It is thus with future interpretation of (H), (I), and (J), present interpretations of (K) and (L), and past interpretations of (J) and (L):

(H) Grannie will/can/may/shall/must/should/ought to/needn't/ daren't leap in through the window

(I) (Given half a chance) Grannie would/could/might leap in through the window

(J) Grannie would/could/might have leapt in through the window

(K) (But for Sir Jasper's meddling) Grannie would/could/might be in prison

(L) (But for Sir Jasper's meddling) Grannie would/could/might have been in prison.

Once again the technical term 'judgement' seems apt in an innocent sense. For instance the various future interpretations of (H), (I), and (J) are all untendentiously judgements about Grannie's leaping in through the window at a time later than the tense, with the *verdict* determing the choice of modal.

Comparing our two categories of judgement, I discern a fundamental difference. A practical message is a verdict about $P(r)$'s *actual*, *historical* satisfaction by s, whereas a projective one is about $P(r)$'s satisfaction by s in a situation which can only be *imagined*.

Since practical messages play only a small part in the story of 'if', I shall not pursue them here. But I commend them to logicians' attention.

The presenting problem of the projective category is to explain why $t < y$. My attempt invokes a particular kind of *thinking*. Every animal is able, as a condition of survival, to *anticipate*, to foresee outcomes of things actually going on around it. The animal does this (not, save the mark, by drawing conclusions from premises, but) by envisioning the unfolding of a causally continuous sequence of events; by following in its mind's eye a train of developments which starts from current perceived realities and proceeds steadily futurewards in ways experience has taught it to expect. In short, the animal anticipates by conducting a *fantasy*.

No less a condition of the animal's survival is its ability to act upon its imaginative productions. Pointless the magpie's foreseeing a mid-air collision unless that foresight prompts it to evasive action. And in fact we animals are found to observe a strict rule in these matters: first anticipate, then react.

Now, in my design, the thinking that issues in projective message is exactly isosmorphic. There is a *fantasy* followed by a *verdict*, the latter arrived at by contemplating the contents of the former, and expressed by the choice of modal.

The fantasy is always set against a background of historical fact. Thus the magpie anticipates a future collision by fixing upon some complex in its present actual circumstances: the imagined subsequent course of events is imagined as developing out of this complex. Indeed, a fantasy always has a beginning in historical time: there is always a point b, present, past, or past past, and the fantasy develops out of actual historical *realities* of this point b. I call b the *basis* of the judgement,[7] and teach that for a projective message, $t = b$.

And the message itself, the projective *judgement*, is obtained by inspecting the contents of a fantasy which starts at b and then

[7] I used to say its *point of view*.

venturing a verdict concerning s's satisfying $P(r)$ at a time y within the fantasy. Therefore $t < y$.

Why do we say (J) instead of (H) upon learning that Grannie has been assassinated? In my submission, because in the former case the fantasy sets out from how things actually are now, whereas in the latter it sets out from how things actually were at a point, necessarily past past, before she was shot—as it must do, if she is to leap through the window in it alive. Given how things are now, we are likelier to reserve the present form for ventures such as

Grannie won't/can't be with us tonight.

There, then, is preliminary confirmation that $t = b$ for projective messages. I shall offer more later.

The need for a fantasy is particularly apparent when y is future, because there is no other rational way of reaching expectations about the future than by trying to envisage outcomes of actual historical realities, present at latest.

A natural corollary of the fantasy theory of projectives is that these messages are neither true nor false, And this is splendid, for neither they are. For a message to be true or false, a certain absoluteness is required of it, and projective messages lack this absoluteness. Take the future interpretation m_3 of

(M) Grannie will leap in through the window.

The observational fact is that its proponent remains uncommitted to the natural interpretation m_4 of

If Grannie is gunned down in the street she will leap in through the window.

Indeed the proponent of m_3 freely admits not only that Grannie will *not* leap in through the window if she is gunned down, but also that no one, not even Grannie, is utterly safe from being gunned down. Therefore the proponent of m_3 cannot seriously mean that Grannie's leap is going to ensue *without fail*. And so generally: whatever one predicts, there will always be *some* catastrophe (a) which (in the absence of further catastrophe) can be relied upon to upset the prediction, and yet (b) whose non-occurrence one is in no position to predict. Therefore the prediction cannot be meant to hold *come what may*. A prediction like m_3 can be intended to hold only 'in the normal course of events', and when m_3 fails to commit its proponents to m_4, it is because getting gunned down does not count as part of m_3's normal course of events. But of course the trouble with the normal course of events is that, because of the endless contingency of events, it is *never specifiable*. And this is what rules truth out of court for projectives.

I do not deny that the proponent of m_3 is alleging something quite definite. But there is no call to reckon on m_3 true or false to account for *that*. The noun phrase 'Grannie' and the verb phrase 'LEAP in through the window' are selected for (M) to encode exactly the same definite informational fragments as they encode in 'Grannie leapt in through the window last night', and *ex hypothesi* WILL is selected to encode some highly specific conception. On these grounds alone the encoded informational content is going to be definite. It is a further, separate question whether this definite message is of a nature to be either true or false. And here the onus is surely upon the exponent of truth values. Judgements are about real Grannies leaping through real windows, certainly, but a judgement incorporates a verdict, and there is nothing in the world that the verdict corresponds to. The verdict is just a *reaction* of the speaker. We English-speakers react very similarly to our environments, and it is hardly surprising to find us wanting to communicate the reactions we share, and perfecting encoding programmes which permit the direct expression of a selection of them. Verdicts are no less objective than other informational factors. Objective, I mean, in Frege's sense: the same for us all. It is just that they do not conduce to truth and falsity. That is how the back-room thinking can be as free-wheeling as it is. Why, we have seen fantasies ignoring the possibility of Grannie's being shot down, notwithstanding what a difference that would make.

In another sense, though, judgements are subjective. The verdict is the *speaker's* reaction: a judgement always has to be somebody's. By contrast, propositions are autonomous. Of course it takes a person to affirm a proposition, just as it takes a person to affirm a judgement; but the proposition is true or false at O

regardless of who affirms it, whereas there can be no judgement without a judge. This is no play on words. Pen a page or two of story in purely reportive mode; then affirm a practical or projective message and observe how the relationship of author to reader instantly changes. This subjectivity makes for a difficulty later when we find judgements being hypothesized.

Tradition accords English a 'future tense', with 'will' as its marker. The notion is that the role of 'will' is to locate y directly in the future *by locating t in the future*, it being simply presumed that here again $t = y$. Thus (M) merely says about the future what 'Grannie leapt in through the window' says about the past, and m_3 is reckoned a proposition of future fact.

Actually, as we have amply seen, having 'will' in a sentence is neither sufficient nor necessary for locating y in the future. The real connection is between futurity and a particular style of encoding programme, and is this: $y > O$ only for a *projective* message. 'Will' is no different from any other present-form secondary auxiliary: when $y > O$, it is simply because $b = O$ for some projective m.

So $y > O$ only for a judgement. As foreshadowed English encodes propositions about the past and present, but none about the future.

But supposing Einstein, say, to believe in future facts, mightn't he allege one by venturing (M)? Certainly: by private dispensation. The easiest way of working it would undoubtedly be to declare WILL ambiguous between *another* meaning which took care of all the other cases—the cases where 'will' uncontentiously acts just like 'can', 'may', 'must', 'should'$_1$, 'ought', 'need', and 'dare'—and this special future meaning. They are interesting questions whether WILL in this sense has a second form 'would' and if so what *it* registers, for with 'will' locating y directly in the future, what might 'would' do that is remotely describable as corresponding? The basic trouble is that the Einstein dispensation presses into its service an idiom designed for something structurally quite different. Better to devise a new finite form of the verb.

Speculating in the introduction about the influence of primeval metaphysics, I envisaged a dichotomy of simple messages into propositions about the past and present and judgements about the future, although not at that stage in those terms. Scrutiny of English and its productions discovers that this picture is basically correct. But incomplete: there turn out to be judgements I failed to anticipate. For one thing, it emerges that the same judgements we make about the future can in fact be made about any time, provided that they are based on facts of an earlier time. Moreover, there transpires to be another kind of judgement altogether, about how things have actually turned out, rather than about imagined developments.

No doubt the metaphysics enshrined in English is a metaphysics of the swamp, awaiting illumination and even revision by great minds. None the less it remains a legitimate object of investigation in its own right. We can ask, for instance, how *do* past and future differ in primeval metaphysics? At all events, we need some plausible explanation why English never locates *t* later than *O*.

This is the moment to summarize *simple messages*. They divide into prImary, prOper, prActical, and projEctive, the last three all secondary. For **I** and **O**, $t = y$, while for **A** and **E** they are different points. Both **A** and **E**, but neither **I** nor **O**, include a *verdict* among their informational factors. Otherwise all four share the same informational factors (save that **A** enjoys the additional advantage of locating *y*).

All these theses are *grammatical*. I am encouraged by them to advance the semantic theses that **I** and **O** are propositions while **A** and **E** are judgements.[8]

5. THE THIRD CATEGORY

The category of projective messages has a celebrated subset, whose members include all the examples I gave in Sect. 1 with (B) to (F). These include conditionals. A *conditional* is a projective interpretation of a sentence with a conditional clause embedded in its predicate. *Conditional clauses* are easily recognized. Each begins with 'if', and registers a tense *t'* which is earlier than the time *x* it intuitively adverts to.

[8] It seems to me that the natural interpretation of 'One must/should$_1$/need/dare not insult El Cid' is an **O**, with *t* and *y* identically *O*. Yet many would scruple to assign a truth value to it. And if that stops it from counting as a 'proposition' then my semantic diagnosis needs complicating. But not the prior grammatical dichotomy.

The crucial perception has already emerged. Conditionals are *simple* messages, not compound: they are encoded in subject–predicate sentences, with the conditional clause a constituent of the predicate. Under its future conditional interpretation m_5,

(N) If the door is locked, Grannie will leap in through the window.

has exactly the same outermost structure as (M) under m_3. Each divides into a subject 'Grannie' and a predicate comprising everything else: modal, syntactical form, verb phrase . . ., and, in the case of (N), an entire subordinate clause whose first word is 'if'.

A clause is always internal to some simple sentence, embedded in either the subject or the predicate. So clauses must encode components of simple messages—*complications* of simple messages, let us say officially. Complications are of many kinds, but I ignore all others to focus on those encoded as subordinate clauses of condition.

These complications evidently have four basic factors: scrutinize (N) in the light of m_5. The subject of the clause is selected in order to identify the notional subject s' of the complication. The verb-phrase of the clause is selected to specify a root condition r', the latter integral to a predication condition $P'(r')$. The syntactical form of the clause's predicate is selected to register the tense t' of the complication, in accordance with the canons of my theory of tense. And 'if' is evidently selected to announce a particular kind of operation. The complication is always intuitively about the satisfaction of $P'(r')$ by s' at a time x which is later than t'. How this conception serves to complicate the overall projective message depends on the operation, concerning which a word shortly.

Concerning the relation of t' to t I must be brief. The forms of both predicates, containing and contained, are chosen to locate the same point b, basis of the overall message. Occasionally this point is located as past past in one place and merely past in the other:

If she was alive today Grannie would/could/might have been in prison

If she had been alive today Grannie would/could/might be in prison.

There is no inconsistency in this, since the past past *is* past. But let me acknowledge that t and t' need not be identical if past.[9]

The relation between x and y in a conditional is usually very exact, but it varies enormously from case to case. Moreover, this temporal relationship, so clear and definite, is encoded nowhere in the sentence. We are looking at *unsignalled information*, information which, although ingredient in the message, plays no part in triggering the sentence which is broadcast to convey it. As to whether the time-order really is ingredient in the message, I need only point to the absurdity that results when 'beforehand' is appended to (B), (C), or (D). Messages are an amalgam of signalled and unsignalled information, the latter communicated by the hearer's reading it in in his efforts to make sense of the former. How he reads the time-order into conditionals I have sought to explain elsewhere.[10]

Since 'if' is a very frequent word, it is unsurprising to find it announcing a very simple operation. It effects the gratuitous introduction, at some time x later than b, of $P'(r')$'s satisfaction by s' into the sustaining fantasy of the embracing projective message. (By its *gratuitous* introduction I mean that $P'(r')$'s imagined satisfaction comes *not* as a development eventuating out of the chosen realities of b but independently, as something which intrudes upon that otherwise simpler development.) The fantasy sustaining m_3 sets out from realities of O and unfolds futurewards in expected ways. The fantasy sustaining m_5 does that too, but it also includes, gratuitously, the door's being locked. Accordingly, the situation at y has two strands in its causal antecedents: it results from the intrusion of $P'(r')$'s satisfaction at x upon the situation developing from b. And then in either case the message as a whole is a judgement concerning Grannie's leaping in through the window at y, and it is arrived at in the usual way: by inspecting the contents of the fantasy and expressing a verdict. The result of thus elaborating the sustaining fantasy is to confine the judgement: in

[9] I used to recognize a *change-over point* c, and teach that $t' = c$.
[10] See my 'Conditional Interpretations of If-sentences', sects. 41–6.

effect, where (M) says 'will', (N) says 'will-if-the-door-is-locked'. And the more elaborate the fantasy the more circumscribed the judgement.

First thoughts are rarely best about conditionals. Let me describe two automatic reactions that have to be revised upon reflection.

Intuition discovers a compelling difference between m_3 and, for example, the past-y conditional interpretation m_6 of

> If the door had been locked Grannie would have leapt in through the window.

Whereas the proponent of m_3 is apparently leaving it open whether the door is to be locked, the proponent of m_6 seems at first blush to be conceding or confiding that it wasn't. The determining factor turns out to be the location of x. It is exactly when x is past or present that the fantasy is felt to diverge from fact. But then, when x is future there *is* no fact. One thing about having x in the past or present is that then there is a t such that $t = x$ and hence a *proposition* deponing historical satisfaction of $P'(r')$ by s'. According to the presentiment I am describing, to affirm a conditional whose $x \leqslant O$ is *ipso facto* to concede the falsity of this 'allied' proposition.

Now, notwithstanding its inital attraction, this presentiment is mistaken, for it forgets clear counter-examples. It is certainly true that *sometimes*, indeed mostly, the intention with which the conditional is transmitted involves setting aside the acknowledged falsity of the allied proposition, the object indeed being to speculate how history might have turned out from antecedents different from the actual in this very regard. *Sometimes*, then, non-future conditionals are uttered with what might be called 'counterfactuals' intent. But not always. As philosophers now know, conditionals with non-future x are also ventured in disproofs and reconstructions, where presumption of the allied proposition's falsity would make nonsense of the enterprise ('She didn't leap in through the window, and she would have if the door had been locked; so the door can't have been locked'; 'Suppose the door was actually locked. If the door had been locked she would have leapt in through the window, and that would explain why we found the window shattered.' And anyway, it makes perfect sense to say 'Whether or not the door actually *was* locked, if it *had* been locked . . .'. I need hardly add that the message is the same whether ventured 'counterfactually' or not, so that counterfactuality can have *nothing to do* with the semantics of these conditionals.

What now of conditionals with x in the future? Whilst believing Grannie to be alive, we perhaps affirm the future interpretation m_7 of

> If Grannie leaps in through the window tonight we will be ready for her.

Upon learning of her assassination, we switch to a future conditional interpretation m_8 of

> If Grannie had leapt in through the window tonight we would have been ready for her,

although we also say things like the natural interpretation m_9 of

> If Grannie leaps in through the window tonight it will be a miracle/as a ghost/in a box.

Casual comparison suggests that the proponent of m_7 leaves it open whether Grannie is to leap in through the window, while the proponent of m_8 concedes that this is no longer possible. But really m_8 is chosen to have a *live* Grannie leaping in through the window, and it is because *this* has ceased to be possible that b is in the past past. When $b = O$ as in m_9 we still have Grannie leaping in through the window at x, but this time a Grannie who is dead at O. Once more, then, first thoughts are absolutely wrong: whether or not $P'(r')$ is to be satisfied has *nothing to do* with the real determinants.

In further confirmation that $t = b$ for projective messages, compare the future interpretations of (O) and (P):

> (O) If war is declared tomorrow I will enlist.
> (P) If war was declared tomorrow I would enlist.

Intuition discovers some slight difference between them, but it is hard to nail down. (The former locution is 'more definite', one often hears.) Jespersen feels that the formal difference 'denotes a slight difference only in degree of probability'[11]—probability, he means, of war's being declared tomorrow, so far as regards (O) and (P), with (P)'s degree the lesser. But this sounds thin: who wants to signal slight differences among the probabilities of future contingencies? And anyway, it makes perfect sense to say 'If war is declared tomorrow—which I admit is a million-to-one-shot—I will enlist.' It is true that it is (P) one expects to hear in times of international harmony and confidence, and (O) that one expects when war is imminent. But this accords perfectly with my theory. By locating *b* at the point of speech, (O) validates even the most recent communiqué; and therefore, at a time of mounting international tension and mobilizing armies, the speaker who selects (O) confides a resolve informed by the latest-known developments. On the other hand, the effect of the past forms in (P) is to waive up-to-the-minute news; and therefore, at times when the contingency of hostilities is remote, the speaker who prefers (P) to (O) is spared the need to entertain so rapid a deterioration in diplomatic relations, that is, so *sudden* a war. Sometimes an imminent war is averted at the eleventh hour, whereupon the relieved speaker says

If war had been declared tomorrow I would have enlisted.

As the reader has doubtless seen already, the effect is to locate *b* as past with respect to the thankfully past eleventh hour.

When a conditional has *b* in the past there are historical facts later than *b*. Moreover, these facts are sometimes taken over into the sustaining fantasy, as we shall see. We should therefore expect a big logical difference between past-tense conditionals and present-tense ones, the latter having no facts later than *b* to borrow. But exact scrutiny discovers no difference at all in the inferential powers of past-tense and present-tense conditionals. There is a puzzle here, which I hope to resolve when I explain the basis upon which facts later than *b* are borrowed.

Being projective, conditionals are already beyond the true-or-false pale. But their plight becomes especially evident when we focus on their *if*-conditions. The fantasy sustaining a conditional is

[11] O. Jespersen, *A Modern English Grammar on Historical Principles,* pt. 5 (London, 1940): 377.

one in which s' is imagined to satisfy $P'(r')$ at x. Now, a condition cannot *just* be satisfied, in no circumstances at all. Any satisfaction will be circumstantial satisfaction. Moreover, the outcome when the condition is satisfied is going to depend critically and minutely on these circumstances. However, there patently lacks the means of sufficiently specifying them. So the situation at y is underdetermined, and the conditional could never aspire to truth.[12] The obvious inference is that the conditional locution is meant for something other than reporting truths.

Sustaining each conditional, there is a purely imaginative enactment in which, quite without regard for how the details might be managed, some unspecified things are kept developing in expected ways from prior realities while another thing intrudes independently. Always, the situation at y, target of the verdict, is outcome of the *if*-condition's satisfaction at x *in circumstances which have matured out of realities of a prior time b*. We agree that any outcome when something happens depends also upon attendant circumstances. And attendant circumstances, when one thinks about it, have to be things that are, were, or had been going to eventuate anyway. But what does that come to? In my design, it means that these 'reigning' circumstances (let us call them) are direct casual descendants of realities of a prior time b. They belong to the first of the two strands I distinguished above in the causal ancestry of the situation at y. Debating whether Grannie would have leapt in through the window if the door had been locked, we happily seize the fact that Grannie was hopping-mad as she approached the door at x and import it into our fantasy. We feel justified in this because whether she was enraged as she approached the door can have nothing to do with whether the door was locked. If she was enraged as she approached the door, this must have been *a direct result of prior realities*.

When $b = O$ there are no facts for a fantasy to borrow. Imagining a condition satisfied at some future x means imagining it satisfied in circumstances which are going to obtain whether it is satisfied or not: direct causal descendants of present realities. In short, when facts later than b are imported into the fantasy sustaining a past-tense conditional, their status there is exactly that

[12] 'Conditional Interpretations', sects. 36–40.

of *any* attendant circumstances in the fantasy sustaining a present-tense conditional: that of direct outcomes of realities of b. This is my resolution of the puzzle about the indifference of conditionals' inferential powers to their tenses.

The same conditional can be sustained by different fantasies, in which different realities of b mature into different reigning circumstances at x. Tiring of Grannie, I instance the conditional interpretation of m_{10} of

> If Her Majesty was here she would be revolted.

When it is affirmed in reproof of a present orgy, b is a time whose historical realities include deposits of fact from which both the orgy in progress now at x and Her Majesty's actual moral character at x are to eventuate just as they really have. This is convenient, given that the motive for affirming the conditional is to censure the orgy by referring it to Her Majesty's enduring moral standards. But when m_{10} is affirmed to illustrate fastidiousness in Her Majesty ('If she was here, even at this harmless gathering . . .'), the reigning circumstances at x are her fastidiousness, naturally, and our present harmless gathering. And when m_{10} is affirmed to illustrate tergiversation in Her Majesty ('Time was when Her Majesty would have been charmed by our little diversions, but now . . .'), the reigning circumstances are her increased intolerance and our little diversions. Yet again, m_{10} can be affirmed to illustrate virulent irreverence in mine host Sir Jasper ('Whenever a dignitary is coming to visit, Sir Jasper deliberately arranges something deeply and pointedly offensive—quite unlike this evening's innocent entertainment'). Here the realities of b include Her Majesty's moral character and eminence, together with Jasper's proclivity for offending the eminent. Each of these actual traits is imagined to survive from b until x, as such traits are wont to do.[13]

One way of countering a conditional is by challenging one of the

---

[13] If a fantasy will sustain a conditional when it is affirmed with counterfactual intent, it will also sustain it for affirmation without it, e.g. there is no need for counterfactual intent when we imagine Her Majesty at our orgy ('Her Majesty cannot be here, for no one here is revolted'; 'That revolted lady over there may be Her Majesty'). Same reigning circumstances, different intent.

reigning circumstances of its affirmation. This is done by affirming another conditional:

> If Her Majesty was here, the orgy would be in remission.

This affirmation naturally relies on a sustaining fantasy of its own, with different reigning circumstances.

As we have seen, a conditional can be affirmed with different motives. But always affirmation consists in the personal outlay of a verdict.

Formally, the basic conditional is just a projective message with a built-in complication. Formally, the basic projective message incorporates s, $P(r)$, v, and t, whatever the significance of those four cyphers. Formally, in sum, the basic conditional comprises five immediate informational factors, none remotely describable as 'antecedent', 'consequent', or 'operator'. These structural facts are simple deliverances of English grammar, confirmable by a routine exercise in code-breaking. Nowhere is the need more urgent for a break with the past than in the semantics of conditionals. For it is plainly impossible to devise an adequate semantics for the third category while working with so mistaken a set of informational factors and so distorted a structure as that proposed by the received ternary analysis.

6. THE SECOND CATEGORY

A habitual message is often embellished with a *frequency*:

> Grannie frequently/always/often/usually/sometimes/occasion-ally/seldom/never/etc. leaps in through the window.

Or with a modality: compare the proper messages we encountered in Sect. 4. And there is another common elaboration. It is achieved by embedding a subordinate clause in the predicate:

> If the door is locked Grannie leaps in through the window.

The effect is of course to modify what the habit is a habit *of*. Instead of a propensity simply to leap in through the window, Grannie now has a propensity to *leap in through the window if the door is locked*. In place of $H(r)$, we now have H of some condition

involving not only r but also an s', a $P'(r')$, and an operator. In
effect, the subordinate clause does the job of 'ϕ' in $H(\phi(r))$, whose
satisfaction at t by s is the substance of the message. Unlike the
third category, the second always has t' and t identical, and both
identical with y, the time of the propensity's currency. I need
hardly add that I reckon the second category to the class of
propositions. To affirm one is personally to attest to its truth at O.

7. THE FIRST CATEGORY

Two houses standing side by side are nothing like a house, and a
compound message is nothing like a simple one. A simple message
has a notional subject of its own, a tense of its own, and a
predication condition, perhaps a verdict; but a compound message
has none of these things. As we move at last to the first category
we must expect to encounter a new set of issues.

The most notable, unerringly raised by Frege, is that of
affirmation. The basic rule of discourse, that each separate
sentence is asserted, leaves it unsettled what happens when the
separate sentence is compound—what happens, as regards
assertion, to the prior sentences. We shall keep an eye on this side
of things as we proceed. There is also the question what
affirmation amounts to for the compound message itself. It varies,
we shall find.

As regards grammar, the crucial observation is that the simplest
compound sentences divide into *two* immediate constituents.
Under its first-category interpretation m_{11},

(Q) If the door was locked Grannie leapt in through the window

divides into an *independent sentence* 'Grannie leapt in through the
window', and what I call a *subsidiary string* 'if the door was
locked', whose immediate constituents, in turn, are the
conjunction 'if' and the *dependent sentence* 'the door was locked'.
Contrary to the overwhelming implication of the term,
'conjunctions' do not join. English has no 'binary connectives'. 'If'
occurs here prefixed to *one* sentence, not joining two. The
clinching evidence is that m_{11} is found encoded in the following
stylistic variants of (Q):

Grannie leapt in through the window if the door was locked
Grannie, if the door was locked, leapt in through the window.

That is, the subsidiary string can precede, follow, or even interrupt the independent sentence. However (reflection will confirm) the independent sentence can never interrupt the dependent. Again the ternary analysis comes a cropper.

The encoding programme for the first category is plainly as follows, and I call it *Recipe 1*: (*i*) encode the independent message as the independent sentence; (*ii*)(*a*) chose one of (A)'s initial expressions from Sect. 1 and (*b*) generate the dependent sentence from the dependent message, and (*c*) prefix the result of (*a*) to the result of (*b*); (*iii*) amalgamate the result of *(ii)* into the result of (*i*). The intended sense of 'amalgamate into' has already emerged. Our first category is that parochial subset of messages encoded by Recipe 1 for which it selects 'if' at (*ii*)(*a*).

My semantic proposal is that 'if' is chosen by Recipe 1 to accord the dependent message the status of a 'hypothesis', i.e. to announce that it is being *treated as true* (*or*, if a judgement, *as accepted*) *whether or not it really is*. The 'whether or not' explains why affirming a first-category message is never sufficient for affirming its dependent message.

As for the independent message, I submit that it is always *presumptively* affirmed, in the sense that it is affirmed unless there is rational reason otherwise. When the conjunction is 'because' or 'although' there is never rational reason otherwise. But when the conjunction is 'if', there is usually rational reason otherwise. Let us consider some examples.

Many are cast, we find, in a classical mould, with the hypothesized dependent message a *premiss* from which the independent message is *inferred*, usually *deduced*:

(R) If Socrates is a man, Socrates is mortal.

If the latter was surprised and delighted too, he disguised it like a diplomat (P. G. Wodehouse).

Well, if the kid's old man is an actor, he is not working at it. He sticks close to his room all the time (Damon Runyon).

I call these inferential messages *hypotheticals*. Usually hypotheticals rely on further premisses or *grounds*, sometimes stated (as by Runyon), mostly not, but in general readily identifiable (that men are by nature mortal; that the latter remained po-faced). These grounds are of course *commitments* of the speaker, implicitly if not explicitly affirmed. Indeed Wodehouse's manœuvre is just an indirect means of affirming the ground.

Because hypothesizing has nothing to do with affirming, the dependent message of a hypothetical is unaffirmed unless elsewhere, whereupon the independent message is found concluded from an unaffirmed premiss and hence not rationally warranting affirmation unless on some other account. And indeed hypotheticals are paradigm for their unaffirmed independent messages. They also enjoy a well-advertised range of deductive accomplishments, with roles in *modus ponens*, *modus tollens*, hypothetical syllogism, contraposition, *consequentia mirabilis*, and such. This is all because they are condensed arguments, of course. To affirm one is to resort to the argument while withholding commitment from a premiss.

I should add that adopting a proposition as a hypothesis is nothing like adding it to one's 'stock of beliefs'. Nor is there the remotest question of the speaker's *amending* her beliefs to accommodate the proposition. We trust the sponsor of a hypothetical to believe its then ground, perhaps, but that is the nearest belief is involved. The two basic conceptions underlying a hypothetical are those of adopting a hypothesis and drawing a conclusion, neither of which (I submit) has anything to do with believing.[14]

[14] I deprecate the idea of explaining discourse in terms of belief, preferring C. L. Hamblin's notion of individual speakers' *commitments*. To these belief is strictly irrelevant: 'We do not believe everything we say; but our saying it commits us whether we believe it or not' (*Fallacies* (London, 1970): 264). When a speaker affirms a proposition, for example, I construe that as her incurring public commitment to its truth, not as her confiding private belief in its truth. Commitment has desirable properties denied to belief, e.g. it is sheer romancing to suppose that a speaker's current beliefs might be consistent and closed under deduction, but it is a fundamental dialectical requirement that each speaker keep her cumulative *commitments* consistent, and treat entailments of commitments as commitments. As for hypothesizing a message, that for me is just a matter of

Perhaps this is the moment to urge that what is called the Ramsey Test has no application to any semantics for 'if'. Because set up in terms of 'antecedent' and 'consequent', it has no application in the second or third categories. And since it invokes a 'stock' it gets the first category wrong as well. Take our recent Socrates example. It involves just the three propositions that Socrates is a man, that men are mortal, and that Socrates is mortal. As a clear deliverance of intuition, no other message is remotely involved—in confirmation of which, observe that to respond 'Why?' to the proponent of (R) will simply elicit the ground. Not a stock in sight, of beliefs or anything else.

Not all first-category messages are hypotheticals. Sometimes the dependent message is not a premiss of the independent but a presupposition, perhaps, or some scruple of detail concerning the exactness or propriety of the independent message:

(S) If the mayor is married his wife did not accompany him.

(T) The dog, if it was a dog, ran off.

(U) . . . and his smile—if this isn't an absurd statement—had teeth in it (Donald E. Westlake).

The basic intent is plainly to affirm the independent message outright. But some infirmity attends this independent message, and the dependent message is hypothesized to neutralize this infirmity. What gets affirmed overall, when such a message is affirmed, depends very much on the symbiotic relationship. Asserting (T) is pretty much like asserting 'The creature, dog or not, ran off', because the hypothesis is there as insurance against inaccuracy of detail merely. But when the dependent message is a presupposition, the stakes are higher. Take the natural interpretation m_{12} of (S). When its dependent message is false its independent message has a non-existent notional subject in a way simple messages are obviously not meant to. The hypothesis is there, in other words, to neutralize a scruple as to the independent message's very propriety. m_{12} evidently relies on some such ground

according it a certain *status*. Quite unlike the speaker's pretending to herself that she believes it, or anything like that. And if the beliefs of the rational are guided by reasoning, then I do not see how drawing a conclusion might be exponible in terms of belief, either.

as that none of the ladies accompanying the mayor could conceivably have been married to him, and its proponent may justly be taken as committed to something of that sort. But it is because presupposition is such a radical form of dependence that we are driven thus far from the actual words when we enquire what affirming m_{12} amounts to. To say nothing of (U)'s case: where is the independent message this time if the hypothesis fails?

I call these latest examples 'scruple' interpretations. Logically, scruple interpretations behave quite differently from hypotheticals, as is only to be expected. For instance, scruple interpretations are obviously not meant to contrapose.

Sometimes there lacks any connection whatever between dependent and independent message, whereupon the latter, presumptively affirmed, is affirmed outright:

If she wasn't pregnant before she is now.

The examples in this section are meant to illustrate my thesis that first-category messages vary with the *bearing* that the dependent message is meant to have upon the independent. In particular, whether the independent message is affirmed outright depends nicely upon the details of this bearing.[15]

Could compound messages be propositions, true or false at O? Not possibly, in my submission: a message encoded by Recipe 1 is going to be far too subtle to submit to so uncompromising a classification. The prior messages encoded at (i) and (ii)(b) may well be propositions, but to assess what is encoded by the whole recipe as true or false is just asking too much. Dammit, think of the spectrum of options presented by the choice at (i)(a). Surely no one would expect a truth value when Recipe 1 chose

---

[15] I understand Ernest Adams as suggesting that first-category messages might fit on a common scale of *assertability*, the latter an observational trait he undertakes to explain in terms of probabilities (see E. W. Adams, *The Logic of Conditionals* (Dordrecht, 1975)). The explanations I have been attempting in this section are so thoroughly different from his that undoubtedly one of us is fundamentally wrong. My account envisions no common scale. Rather, my explanations tease out the details of conceptual connections, potentially endless in variety. Nor for my part do I observe 'assertability'. Rather, I diagnose that speakers affirm members of the first category just when they think they can achieve some effect by complicating an otherwise outright affirmation with the announcement that a certain message is being hypothesized.

'although'? I cannot see why the case should be different when it chooses 'if'. Truth values are given to only simple messages, I think, and to only half of *them*.

It is a good working rule that if a message is adopted as a hypothesis it is true or false at O. But I hold there are exceptions. In

> If Grannie is older than Sir Jasper if Sir Jasper is younger than the parrot, then Grannie must be at least as old as the parrot,

for example, I see a hypothetical in which the ground is inferred of a hypothetically entertained prior *hypothetical*; but surely we need not treat that prior hypothetical as *true* for the purpose of this exercise?

More seriously, we sometimes encounter *judgements* as hypotheses, a difficulty I mentioned above (Sect. 4). Judgements are tensed verdicts, and a verdict is a personal reaction of a speaker. What happens to this personal element when the judgement is hypothesized? It varies. Sometimes the personal element gets a new owner, namely s'. 'You/he will follow me' has a projective interpretation which can be sponsored as a request, an order, a prediction, or such—of the *speaker*. But in 'if you/she will follow me . . .' it is s'''s personal reaction that is being taken for granted regardless of the facts. That is why intuiton reads 'you/he will follow me' differently in the two cases. Same projective message; different owners. Sometimes, however, there is really no room for the personal dimension. As a price of being hypothesized, the judgement cannot be treated as anyone's:

> If Grannie must have been driving too fast then so must the policeman who caught her

> If Grannie will be dead by sundown then we can start selling her clothes at once.

Such affirmations are typically preceded by someone's affirmation of the hypothesized judgement, and in that case the speaker plainly regards the verdict as belonging to that someone. But in the hypothetical it belongs to no one. I think I discern an answering awkwardness in these messages, and am encouraged by their comparative rarity. I am certainly not moved to treat the hypothesized judgements as candidates for truth.

And that seems a good posture in which to bow out: bent upon deflating truth. I quite see its importance to philosophers. But when we come to the things people actually say using English sentences, it seems to me that truth is by no means an invariant consideration.

NOTES ON THE CONTRIBUTORS

V. H. DUDMAN is a member of the School of History, Philosophy and Politics, Macquarie University

DOROTHY EDGINGTON is a member of the Department of Philosophy, Birkbeck College, University of London

NELSON GOODMAN was formerly a member of the Department of Philosophy, Harvard University

H. P. GRICE was formerly a member of the Department of Philsophy, University of California, Berkeley

FRANK JACKSON (the editor of this volume) is a member of the Department of Philosophy, Monash University

DAVID LEWIS is a member of the Department of Philosophy, Princeton University

ROBERT STALNAKER is a member of the Department of Linguistics and Philosophy, Massachusetts Institute of Technology

SELECTED BIBLIOGRAPHY

BOOKS AND COLLECTIONS

Adams, Ernest, *The Logic of Conditionals* (Dordrecht: Reidel, 1975).

Appiah, Anthony, *Assertion and Conditionals* (Cambridge: CUP, 1985).

Harper, W. L., Stalnaker, R., and Pearce, G. (eds.), *Ifs* (Dordrecht: Reidel, 1981).

Jackson, Frank, *Conditionals* (Oxford: Blackwell, 1987).

Kvart, Igal, *A Theory of Counterfactuals* (Indianapolis: Hackett, 1986).

Lewis, David, *Counterfactuals* (Oxford: Blackwell, 1973).

Mackie, J. L., *Truth, Probability, and Paradox* (Oxford: OUP, 1973).

Pollock, John, *Subjunctive Reasoning* (Dordrecht: Reidel, 1976).

Sanford, David, *If P, then Q* (London: Routledge, 1989). Contains an extensive bibliography.

Sosa, Ernest (ed.), *Causation and Conditionals* (Oxford: OUP, 1975).

Stalnaker, Robert, *Inquiry* (Cambridge, Mass: MIT Press, 1984).

ARTICLES

On the Material (Truth-Functional) Account

Clark, Michael, 'Ifs and Hooks', *Analysis*, 32 (1971): 33–9.

Cohen, L. J., 'Some Remarks on Grice's Views about the Logical Particles of Natural Language', in Y. Bar-Hillel (ed.), *Pragmatics of Natural Languages* (Dordrecht: Reidel, 1971): 50–68.

Grice, H. P., 'Indicative Conditionals', in *Studies in the Way of Words* (Cambridge, Mass.: Harvard University Press, 1989): 58–85.

Jackson, Frank, 'Conditionals and Possibilia', *Proc. of the Aristotelian Society*, 81 (1980/1): 125–37.

Stevenson, C. L., 'If-culties', *Philosophy of Science*, 37 (1970): 27–49.

Strawson, P. F., ' "If" and "⊃" ', in R. E. Grandy and R. Warner (eds.), *Philosophical Grounds of Rationality* (Oxford: Clarendon Press, 1986): 229–42.

The Meta-Linguistic Theory

Chisholm, R. M., 'The Contrary-to-Fact Conditional', *Mind*, 55 (1946): 289–307.

Mackie, J. L., 'Counterfactuals and Causal Laws', in R. J. Butler (ed.), *Analytical Philosophy* (Oxford: Blackwell, 1962): 66–80.

Rescher, Nicholas, 'Belief-Contravening Suppositions', *Philosophical Review*, 70 (1961): 176–96.

On the Possible-Worlds Theory

Bennett, Jonathan, 'Counterfactuals and Possible Worlds', *Canadian Journal of Philosophy*, 4 (1974): 381–402.

Jackson, Frank, 'A Causal Theory of Counterfactuals', *Australasian Journal of Philosophy*, 55 (1977): 3–21.

Lewis, David, 'Counterfactuals and Comparative Possibility', *Journal of Philosophical Logic*, 2 (1973): 418–46.

Slote, M. A., 'Time in Counterfactuals', *Philosophical Review*, 87 (1978): 3–27.

Stalnaker, Robert and Thomason, Richmond, 'A Semantic Analysis of Conditional Logic', *Theoria*, 36 (1970): 23–42.

Tichý, Pavel, 'A New Theory of Subjunctive Conditionals', *Synthese*, 37 (1978): 443–57.

On Conditionals and Conditional Probability

Adams, Ernest, 'The Logic of Conditionals', *Inquiry*, 8 (1965): 166–97.
—— 'Probability and the Logic of Conditionals', in J. Hintikka and P. Suppes (eds.), *Aspects of Inductive Logic* (Amsterdam: North Holland, 1966): 265–316.

Gärdenfors, Peter, 'Belief Revisions and the Ramsey Test for Conditionals', *Philosophical Review*, 95 (1986): 81–93.

Pendelbury, Michael, 'The Projection Strategy and the Truth Conditions of Conditional Statements', *Mind*, 98 (1989): 179–205.

Ramsey, F. P., 'General Propositions and Causality', in *The Foundations of Mathematics* (London: Routledge & Kegan Paul, 1931): 237–55.

Stalnaker, Robert, 'Probability and Conditionals', *Philosophy of Science*, 37 (1970): 64–80.

Van Fraassen, B. C., 'Probabilities of Conditionals', in W. L. Harper and C. A. Hooker (eds.), *Foundations of Probability Theory, Statistical Inference, and Statistical Theories of Science*, i (Dordrecht: Reidel, 1976): 261–300.

On Types of Conditionals

Adams, Ernest, 'Subjunctive and Indicative Conditionals', *Foundations of Language*, 6 (1970): 89–94.

Bennett, Jonathan, 'Farewell to the Phlogiston Theory of Conditionals', *Mind*, 97 (1988): 509–27.

Davis, Wayne, 'Indicative and Subjunctive Conditionals', *Philosophical Review*, 88 (1979): 544–64.

Dudman, V. H., 'Conditional Interpretations of If-sentences', *Australian Journal of Linguistics*, 4 (1984): 143–204.

Ellis, Brian, 'A Unified Theory of Conditionals', *Journal of Philosophical Logic*, 7 (1978): 107–24.

Gibbard, Allan, 'Two Recent Theories of Conditionals', in Harper, Stalnaker, and Pearce (eds.), *Ifs* (Dordrecht: Reidel, 1981): 211–47.

Jackson, Frank, 'Two Theories of Indicative Conditionals', *Australasian Journal of Philosophy*, 62 (1984): 67–76.

INDEX OF NAMES